How to compensate executives

How to compensate executives

James E. Cheeks

 1974

DOW JONES-IRWIN, INC.
Homewood, Illinois   60430

This publication is designed to provide accurate and
authoritative information in regard to the subject matter
covered. It is sold with the understanding that the
publisher is not engaged in rendering legal, accounting, or
other professional service. If legal advice or other expert
assistance is required, the services of a competent
professional person should be sought.

> *From a Declaration of Principles jointly adopted by a Committee
> of the American Bar Association and a Committee of Publishers.*

First printing, February 1974

Printed in the United States of America

Library of Congress Cataloging in Publication Data

Cheeks, James.
    How to compensate executives.

    1. Executives—Salaries, pensions, etc. 2. Non-wage payments. I. Title.
HD4965.2.C45   658.4'07'2   73–90605
ISBN 0–87094–070–8

Preface

EVERY ENTERPRISE has a number of jobs that involve making critical decisions, and it follows that these jobs must be filled with qualified, effective executives if the firm is to survive and grow.

This book presents a guide to planning a compensation program that will insure the continuity of qualified leaders and decision makers necessary for profitable growth. It focuses throughout on the true cost to the company of an executive compensation program and the program's after-tax benefit (or true value) to the executive.

I have written *How to Compensate Executives* as an aid to planning for anyone associated with executive compensation, but it is the chief executive officer who should be most mindful of its contents—not for his own aggrandizement, but because executive retention and continuity is the one responsibility he cannot delegate.

January 1974 J.E.C.

Contents

Contents

chapter 1 Objectives of compensation policy

COMPENSATION planning has three basic goals: to retain, to stimulate, and to attract. First, it must *retain* present company personnel. This is essential. Second, it should *stimulate* useful or profitable effort in the future. Third, it should be able to *attract* necessary additions to the staff.

This book will analyze and demonstrate how to achieve each of these objectives when planning the compensation of executive employees. It should be understood at the outset that planning an executive's pay package has little in common with arranging the employee benefits of the company rank and file. There are many satisfactions in rank-and-file planning, of course, and occasionally even some excitement, as when negotiating a union contract when a strike deadline is close. But executive compensation planning in practice proves more complex and more challenging, requiring special knowledge and special skills.

What makes executive compensation planning so delicate a task is the nature of the executive himself—his knowledge, wants, and temperament—and his relation to the company that employs him. At this point, it seems wise to define the concept of executive, for purposes of compensation planning. In this book, an executive is a particular person whom the company considers important to retain or acquire as an employee, who can be stimulated to further valuable or profitable effort for the company.

In some companies this definition will include individuals who are not usually thought of as executives. In the field of executive compensation planning, whether a person is an executive will not depend on his title, but on the way his company thinks about him, and on the fact that it thinks about him as an individual.

Some companies may have dozens of such executives; the very smallest may have only one or two. The number involved does not affect the need for compensation planning. Obviously, the fewer the executives, the more important they are, and the more important compensation planning for them becomes. Of course, the number of executives will affect what is planned for them, and it will also affect who does the planning. In larger companies, planning is done by personnel officers, an individual executive (such as a vice president or comptroller), a team of executives, or occasionally, a management consulting firm. In small firms, it may be done by the owner of the business, his attorney, or an accountant. Whoever does the initial planning, it is essential that the plan be thoroughly reviewed and fully understood by the company's chief officers.

Noncash rewards in compensation planning

All executives expect to be paid in cash, and preferably lots of cash. But some are willing to forego a certain amount of money now in favor of certain other benefits, now or in the future.

For one prominent executive, a noncash reward of major importance was the opportunity to buy company stock at bargain rates, coupled with a low-interest company loan toward the purchase price. For another, it was the postponement of receipt of a certain amount of salary until a later year, with the postponed amount treated as if invested for his benefit in securities he designated. For still another executive, it was company-paid counseling services, which gave him tax planning advice resulting in a tax saving of over $60,000.

For many thousands of executives, important elements of their compensation package, though not paid to them currently in cash, would include:

1. Coverage under a pension, profit-sharing, stock bonus, or savings or thrift plan.
2. Coverage of their medical bills, and those of their families.
3. Life insurance coverage.
4. Stock options and stock awards.
5. Expense allowances.

There are noncash rewards to fit every need of compensation planning. Most of them will help retain the executive in the company; some will stimulate profitable effort; and many will attract valuable executive recruits.

Executives are shrewd, knowledgeable people, and they will know what rewards your company's competitors are offering. Your company will not be able to match each and every benefit that might be offered by each and every competitor. Your executives realize this, but still expect you to be generous. In fact, liberal noncash rewards can be granted in most cases without undue strain on company finances. This book will examine all important noncash benefits, stressing those which can add significantly to the executive's wealth, comfort and job satisfaction at low cost to the company.

The true cost of executive compensation

There may be nonmonetary considerations in an industry's compensation policy, considerations of prestige, glamour, or image. But by *true cost*, something more practical is meant. As used here, the true cost to a company of compensation it pays its executive is the net *dollar amount* it must give up to obtain the executive's services. To the individual executive, the true value of compensation is the net amount he receives, which is not necessarily what his company parts with. In determining true dollar costs, federal income taxes often play the decisive role.

For instance, suppose a corporation pays an executive a straight cash salary of $50,000 and nothing more. The true cost is not the $50,000 the company pays him, but much less. The typical corporation in the United States pays a federal income tax on profits at a rate of about 48 percent. Thus, with some qualifications, every dollar of cost reduces tax by 48 cents *if* that cost item is deductible for tax purposes. If the company pays $50,000 in compensation, the true cost is only $26,000, since $24,000 (48 percent of $50,000) is absorbed by the federal government where the $50,000 is deductible compensation. To the executive, the true value of the $50,000 is what he has left after his federal taxes are paid. A typical $50,000 a year executive with average personal deductions would expect to keep $38,000 after taxes ($33,000 if such deductions are ignored).

Within limits, the compensation planner could design an all-cash compensation plan. The true dollar cost to the company is only about half (52 percent) of what it pays the executive, assuming the payment qualifies as a tax deduction.[1] The true dollar value to the executive is the dollars received less the tax he must pay on those dollars.

Compensation planning takes on greater importance when the company decides to provide the executive with something more than cash, as most companies do. For example, it might provide him with group life insurance. The company can obtain such insurance coverage at a cost lower than the executive could ar-

---

[1] For how to make the payment deductible, see Chapter 2.

range on his own. This is a net dollar saving even apart from any tax advantage. But just as with cash compensation, the tax deduction makes the true cost to the company only 52 percent of what it pays for the insurance, while the executive has no cost of any kind.[2] The same principle would apply to Blue Cross or Blue Shield or similar coverage paid for by the company.[3]

With other forms of noncash compensation, the planning considerations become complex. Suppose the company decides to reward the executive with a bonus of ten shares of company stock. Here the company may believe it has no dollar cost at all. It is paying its executive something which it may have acquired or created without any expenditure. Yet there may be a substantial, even prohibitive, true cost in such payment.[4] The company could sell that stock in the marketplace, now or in the future. By giving the executive the stock, it is surrendering a valuable profit opportunity of its own, and one which is doubly valuable because there is no federal tax on a company's profit when it sells its own stock.

These brief examples indicate the challenge facing the compensation planner. He must weigh the true cost to the company of any given compensation plan against its true value to the executive, balancing the company's need for economy and financial responsibility against the ambitions and economic desires of valuable executive personnel.

Whatever the compensation package decided on, the executive should be told, periodically and in full detail, what the company is providing for him or paying out for his benefit. This is sometimes necessary for legal or tax reasons, as will be seen in later chapters, but the author recommends it whether necessary or not. Each executive should receive a statement detailing the dollar amount of his cash compensation, the dollar amount the

---

[2] See Chapter 14.

[3] See Chapter 11.

[4] See Chapter 7.

company spends for his benefit for group insurance, medical plans, and so forth, the amount the company contributes on his behalf to pension plans and profit-sharing plans, and the cash value of stock, services or other benefits the company gives him or makes available to him. In this reporting, use actual dollar amounts, not net amounts after taxes.

Rethinking the company's compensation package

Many major new rules have come into effect during the 1970s. Policies and programs developed in earlier years may now be dangerously outmoded. Among the new rules affecting the compensation picture for the 1970s are:

Federal wage controls: These can limit the amount of cash compensation that may be paid and most forms of noncash compensation, for firms subject to these controls.

Increased capital gains taxes: These can adversely affect compensation plans involving direct payments in stock, stock options, and stock purchase plans. They also affect lump sum withdrawal from pension, profit-sharing and similar plans. The decision to make a lump sum withdrawal has been further affected by denial of capital gain treatment for a portion of the withdrawal.

Reduced tax on current compensation: This can encourage increased cash compensation (where wage controls permit), and tend to discourage certain forms of compensation involving a postponement of benefit, such as deferred compensation and stock options.

Tax on "tax preferences": This has an adverse impact on certain stock options.

These and other new and changing rules are considered in depth in the following chapters, and their full impact on compensation planning is reflected. Also considered are the new and developing compensation devices (such as financial counseling and the fringe benefit "supermarket"), and not-so-new devices (such as phantom stock) now taking on added importance.

Planning for the owner himself

All too often, the business owner overlooks himself in the compensation planning operation. Yet if he holds down a job in the corporation, as president or otherwise, compensation planning is at least as important for him as for any other present or prospective employee. Compensation planning factors in this book apply to stockholder-executives—including controlling stockholders—as well as other executives. Any problems or special considerations arising because the executive is a stockholder (or controlling stockholder) are pinpointed, with suggestions for surmounting difficulties.

chapter 2 The ideal cash compensation for executives

O<small>NE</small> of the foremost problems currently facing top business management is the need to determine the proper or correct amount to pay key personnel, and to justify that amount to government authorities and stockholders. In practice, this means the ability to select and justify an amount which is not too much pay for the services rendered. True, executives can be paid too little as well as too much. An underpaid executive may hurt his employer by underperformance. Nonetheless, it is allegations of *over*payment that invite adverse publicity and the danger of legal action. Avoidance of overpayment and the appearance of overpayment is therefore a primary concern.

If the company can take a tax deduction for the compensation it pays its executives and employees, its true cost of what it pays is, in most cases, only 52 percent of the actual payment. But the company can deduct only a reasonable amount as compensation. Anything in excess of that amount is nondeductible and therefore sharply increases the company's true cost of executive salary. Reasonableness is also the standard to be employed if a stockholder or group of stockholders questions a salary as being excessive. Thus, if a reasonable salary for a particular executive would be about $80,000, and he was paid $200,000, the company could tax-deduct only $80,000. Therefore, the true cost of this compensation to company would be $161,600. Furthermore, stockholders might be able to recover the excess $120,000 for the company from the officers involved. Directors or officers authorizing executive salary should therefore be prepared to prove that the amount involved is reasonable.

From a business standpoint, the ideal cash compensation is the one that, at lowest cost to the company, leaves the executive in a kind of aggressive contentment. The exact amount depends on the particular individual and company involved, and cannot be found by formula. But granting that this amount must vary from case to case, a constant feature of all compensation planning should be the aim to keep the federal tax collected on a compensation arrangement at not more, or not much more, than 50 percent. Putting the same goal another way, the amount that the executive nets after taxes should not be less than the company's after-tax cost. Assuming sizeable amounts are involved, this goal is achieved only if compensation is found to be reasonable. This is true from the executive's standpoint as well as from the company's. If the company's payment is reasonable, 48 percent of that amount is, in effect, recovered by the company as a reduction in its income tax. And if it is reasonable, the executive cannot be taxed on any of it at more than 50 percent (with some qualifications).

Example: If a $100,000 salary is "reasonable," the $100,000 deduction saves the company $48,000 in taxes and its true cost is $52,000. To the executive who receives it, the tax on reasonable salary of $100,000 (disregarding other income and deductions and assuming a joint return) is $42,060. Thus, the executive gets $57,040 at a cost to the company of $52,000.

But if only $50,000 of the $100,000 salary is reasonable, the company's tax saving is only $24,000 and the executive's tax bill is $45,180. Here, the executive nets $54,820 at a cost to the company of $76,000—a bad bargain, which underscores the need for careful advance planning to establish that amounts paid are reasonable compensation.

• Understandably, reasonableness depends on the circumstances of the particular case. But the key factors to be considered are:

1. Compensation being paid to executives in comparable positions by comparable companies. This is probably the most important factor, and one which seems easiest to establish. If the company pays what its competitors are paying, this is a very strong indication that its compensation is reasonable.

2. The executive's qualifications for the job. His previous experience in this particular job is probably his most important qualification. Other qualifications would include his experience in other jobs with this company, and in similar or different jobs in other companies. Education, degrees, professional licenses and other credentials would also be relevant.

3. The nature and scope of his work. The more responsible and demanding his job, the more compensation he deserves.

4. The size and complexities of the business. Running a large firm, or a large part of a large firm, tends to justify a sizeable salary.

5. A comparison of salaries paid with the gross income and the net income. If gross income is substantial but salaries to executives essentially eliminate or greatly reduce net income, this indicates that salaries are unreasonable.

6. General economic conditions. Good times tend to support liberal compensation.

7. Comparison of salaries with distributions to stockholders. Large salaries as against small dividends tend to indicate that salaries are excessive.[1]

---

[1] Actually, they may also tend to indicate that amounts designated as salaries are in fact something else, if the recipients are also stockholders. See page 14.

8. The company's salary policy as to all employees. There is something of a tendency to find that executives' salaries are not excessive if other employees are liberally paid. It is a sign that compensation is excessive if stockholders or the owners' families get more than other employees for the same work.

9. In the case of a small corporation with only a few officers, the amount of compensation paid to the particular executive in the previous year. A substantial increase over last year's compensation tends to show that this year's compensation may be excessive.

Compensation planning professionals and legal authorities agree that no single factor is decisive. Compensation may be justified though only a few of these conditions are met. But management and other company decision-makers should be aware that their salary judgments will be subject to review by stockholders or the Revenue Service, or both, and possibly by courts as well. These second-guessers may well apply all nine standards listed above. Therefore, the directors or officers should be prepared to show which conditions indicating reasonableness of salary were satisfied, and which need not be satisfied, and why. It is wise to make and preserve a written record of this decision (say, as part of the minutes of a directors' meeting), which will be available to answer possible future challenges by the Revenue Service or by stockholders.

For the company whose directors or officers are seeking to set and justify a particular level of compensation for a particular executive, the author recommends the following approach:

First, find out what other firms in the same line of business are paying comparable executives (test 1, above). While this will already be known in a general way, dig deeper. Compensation ranges and norms can be obtained from a number of sources, such as: trade associations and their publications; periodicals directed to personnel officers; newspaper ads; and executive recruiters and employment agencies. Today's figures are essential. Ignore the tables of comparable salaries prepared by tax publications—they will be based on cases decided years ago, involving compensation paid years before that. While the principles used in these cases may sometimes be relevant to your situation, pay no attention to the dollar amounts which were found reasonable (or unreasonable) in those cases.

Second, establish the executive's qualifications for his job. If his qualifications are about standard for his position, and he is paid about what comparable executives of comparable firms are paid, it is virtually certain that his compensation will be considered reasonable.[2]

But suppose the executive will draw a larger than normal salary. This could be justified by showing his superior qualifications (more than usual experience or training, for example), or that his responsibility is greater than his counterparts in other companies usually have, or that this business is larger than is typical in the industry, or that he has shown outstanding performance. Any one of these factors could support a higher-than-usual salary, though it would be impossible to specify just how much higher. But where it is essential or important to pay an executive substantially more than would clearly be justified under the above considerations, it may be wise to use a bonus arrangement, such as is described in Chapter 3.

Paying an executive substantially more this year than last is especially likely to excite Revenue Service suspicions that he is being overpaid. Therefore, be prepared to justify the raise, for example, by citing new or widened duties, or specific individual or company achievements. One justification for increased salary expressly approved by the U.S. Supreme Court is: making up for past undercompensation.

Payments this year for services performed in past years can be

---

[2] But if he is also a stockholder, there is a danger that, regardless of reasonableness, the payments may be considered dividends, not deductible for tax purposes. See page 14 on this.

reasonable even though the executive also drew salary in those past years. Reasonableness here would require a determination that the executive was underpaid in past years, and current pay is to cover that past undercompensation as well as to provide adequate pay for this year. It is comparatively easy to establish that he was underpaid if the business was in its start-up phase, was caught by a general economic depression, or was subject to governmental wage controls. It is also wise to specify in advance of payment, in a board of directors resolution or other company document, that this year's pay is intended to cover past undercompensation. A sample resolution appears at the end of this chapter.

This justification of high current pay on the grounds of past underpayment is a rule of tax law. It may prove harder to satisfy dissident stockholders than the Revenue Service that further payment for past services is in order. Advance planning can help, though. If the company is currently unable to pay what its directors consider an appropriate salary to its executives, the board can express its intention to make up for this when circumstances improve. This could prepare the ground and would tend to still complaints against salary increases from both stockholders and the Revenue Service.

Remember that if the justification for the current high rate of compensation is that the executive was underpaid in the past, that justification disappears once undercompensation is taken care of in the current year. To protect deductions in future years, future compensation should be reduced below the current level (though it can still be above levels in undercompensated years), or a new justification must be found.

Bonuses may be made to depend on an executive's performance, or on the performance of the company as a whole. Or they may be given more or less automatically, as further compensation—some Christmas bonuses, for example. When judging whether an executive's compensation is reasonable, reasonableness is determined on the basis of his entire compensation—salary, bonus, and any other taxable item he collects. There is no separate inquiry as to whether any particular bonus is unreasonable. Thus, if a salary of $90,000 and a bonus of $10,000 is reasonable for a job, then a salary of $10,000 and a bonus of $90,000 is equally reasonable for that job.

Some reasonableness-of-compensation disputes are in fact something other than an argument over whether an amount is reasonable. Rather, they are quarrels over whether an amount described as compensation is really entirely compensation, or partly compensation and partly something else. The problem usually arises where the executive is also a stockholder (or a relative of a substantial stockholder) and the "something else" is usually a distribution of earnings—a dividend. Even an amount which would be reasonable if paid as compensation is not deductible for tax purposes, whatever label it is given by the company, if it is in fact a distribution of earnings. Also, a stockholder who is not an employee would be entitled to object to a distribution to stockholder-employees of company earnings in the guise of compensation. Considerations and planning action in this area are set forth in Chapter 4.

Preparing for IRS challenge

It is understood that Revenue agents, when checking whether compensation is reasonable, are especially alert to:

1. Salary for the current year which is substantially more than the executive was paid in the preceding year.
2. Bonuses paid close to the end of the company's taxable year.
3. The fact that no dividends, or only a small amount of dividends, were paid in recent years.
4. Salary in proportion to stockholdings.

While no particular step is necessary to protect against an IRS challenge that salary is unreasonable, and no particular step guarantees success against such a challenge, the author suggests these measures:

1. Fix a specific dollar amount of salary, before the year begins. (If the salary is to be contingent, or there is a contingent bonus, the *formula* should be fixed in advance. For more on this, see Chapter 3.)

2. Set forth a complete explanation of why the salary is what it is. Where the salary corresponds to what other companies are paying, reflect this fact and use the most recent salaries. If this year's compensation includes an element making up for past undercompensation, say so. Recite the executive's qualifications and achievements, and so forth. Note the fringe benefits which this executive *does not* get which executives elsewhere may enjoy. Point out that he is expected to do some unreimbursed business entertaining (if that is the case), which would tend to support a higher compensation level.

3. Put this in writing, as part of an employment contract or board of directors resolution. If too bulky for inclusion in a contract or resolution, reflect key points there and make the complete documentation a part of company records.

The part time executive

Many small companies have executives who divide their time among several enterprises. Also, in some companies, a veteran executive may cut down his time at the office as he gets older. As a general proposition, part-time services cannot be as liberally compensated as full-time services. But courts face reality here. They recognize that a part-time executive may be worth more to the company than a full-time clerk. And they do not seek to make an hour-by-hour proration of pay. That is, assuming that one company's president who works a 50-hour week draws $50,-

000, the president of another comparable company who puts in a 20 hour week there could be worth much more than $20,000. In language that should be welcomed by every executive, Federal Circuit Judge Mahoney said "It is well accepted in the business world that an executive's salary is not dependent upon the amount of time spent on the job. An executive may do some of his most creative work while relaxing at home."[3] But be ready to show the part-time executive's grasp of his duties, and satisfactory results from his efforts.

Payments for future services

It is comparatively rare for a company to pay a sizeable cash compensation substantially before the services are rendered. (But it might pay in stock or other property. For considerations here, see Chapter 6.)

Prepayment for services would sometimes be criticized by stockholders. It therefore should be cleared with them in advance when possible.

From a tax standpoint, a company can deduct only the compensation paid for services which were actually rendered by the end of the taxable year for which deduction is claimed. Amounts paid before services are rendered are deductible pro rata over the period in which they are rendered. Thus, if a calendar year corporation paid $24,000 in 1974 for services to be rendered in 1975, it could not deduct anything until 1975, but the entire amount would be deducted in 1975 if the services were actually rendered then. If it paid $24,000 in February 1974 for services rendered April 1974 through March 1975, it could deduct $18,000 in 1974 and $6,000 in 1975. This rule applies whether the company uses the cash or the accrual accounting method, and regardless of

---

[3] *Lydia E. Pinkham Medicine Co.* v. *Commissioner of Internal Revenue*, 128 F.2d 986.

stockholder approval of the prepayment or any contractual obligation to prepay.

An executive on the cash method (as virtually all are) reports the payment when he gets it, even though he has not yet earned it and even though the company cannot yet deduct it.

The executive's tax picture

Amounts an executive receives from his employer for his services are compensation income. This income is subject to full, regular income tax rates, without relief or reduction except that under the earned income rules, discussed below, it generally cannot be taxed at more than 50 percent.

An executive or other employee reports his compensation in the year he receives it or it is made available to him so he can withdraw it at will. If he is paid by check, he reports the amount in the year he receives the check, even though he does not cash it until the next year.

Around year's end, executives may be advised, by unsophisticates, to have their salaries for the last few weeks of the year postponed to the following year. This would be done to postpone for a year the need to pay tax on the salary (apart from withholding tax). For example, suppose an executive draws $4,000 a month. Instead of taking down his December 1974 salary in 1974, he postpones receipt of that salary until January 1975, when he collects both his December and January salaries. The check for the December 1974 salary is not made out until 1975. Therefore, tax on the amount collected in 1975, it is claimed, is not due until the 1975 return is filed in 1976. Legally, this advice is unsound. If the company is solvent and the executive is entitled to the money, the Revenue Service will tax him as if he received it when it was due.

Executives are sometimes given advances or drawing accounts.

For executives, the term drawing account is usually just a syno-nym for regular salary, implying that other payments may be made later, as a bonus or division of profits. If so, the drawing account is taxable when received, as regular salary. If the execu-tive is not absolutely entitled to the advance or "draw," but must repay all or part of it if he does not earn it through performance of services (for example, if he is a sales manager and must repay any advance in excess of his share of sales commissions), he is taxable on it only when he earns it.

A bonus, like regular salary, is taxable to the executive when he receives it or it is made available to him. If a bonus based on this year's performance is not legally payable, under the terms of the bonus arrangement, until next year, it is not taxable until next year. This is so even though the executive may be in a position to withdraw the funds this year, because of his management position and controlling stock interest, if such an early withdrawal would violate the arrangement and is not actually made. For rules specially applicable to incentive bonuses, see Chapter 3.

The executive's compensation income includes amounts the company pays to someone other than the executive, which are paid for the executive's benefit, unless those amounts are expressly tax-exempt or tax-deferred (such as pension or hospitalization contributions). Thus, he must report and pay tax on company payment of his taxes or living expenses (reimbursing commuting expenses, for example). Amounts withheld from the executive's salary and set aside for his benefit—such as his voluntary pension or savings plan contribution—are also included as his income.

Earned income relief is the most important innovation in the taxation of salaries since wage withholding began in 1943. But the relief is limited to persons with relatively high incomes—chiefly, executives, managers, professional men, business owners or coowners, and entertainers. Since earned income relief puts a ceiling of 50 percent to the tax on compensation, it only applies where tax rates would otherwise exceed 50 percent. Thus, it never applies unless the compensation exceeds:

$52,000—in the case of a married person filing a joint return
$38,000—in the case of a single person
$26,000—in the case of a married person filing a separate return

Because of various computation factors, earned income relief does not in practice produce benefits unless earned income is somewhat above these figures. If salaries (and other compensation) fall below the above figures, the following discussion of earned income rules can be ignored.

For an executive, earned income is the sum of the taxable amounts paid him or for his benefit: salary, bonus, payments in company stock or other property or bargain purchases of such items, taxable insurance premiums, and so forth. But the Revenue Service does not recognize excessive or unreasonable compensation as earned income. Thus, if an executive is paid $100,000 but $35,000 is considered unreasonable, that $35,000 does not qualify for earned income relief and is taxed at more than 50 percent. What is reasonable compensation for purposes of earned income relief is decided according to the same tax principles as apply for purposes of the company's compensation deduction.

Revenue Service procedures for denying earned income relief for excessive compensation have not yet been announced and may not yet be developed. It can be expected that the Revenue Service will not challenge an executive's earned income relief for excessive compensation unless it also challenges his company's deduction for that excess.[4] Presumably, if some compromise figure is worked out during the audit of the company's return, the executive could also compromise at that amount. But if it comes to litigation, the

---

[4] It could happen that an executive will claim as compensation what the company treats as something else: dividends or rent, for example. Only in unusual circumstances would the executive's claim be upheld.

figure treated as reasonable for the company may differ from that for the executive, who is a different taxpayer.

It must be recognized that most executives will not benefit from the 50 percent tax ceiling; their earnings just are not large enough. For those few who do, a new approach should be adopted toward a number of company benefits and outside investments.

In recent years, compensation income could be taxed at up to 70 percent, while capital gains were taxed at not more than 25 percent. But now, compensation income is taxed at no more than 50 percent, while capital gains (in excess of $50,000) are taxable at up to 35 percent. This means that wherever large risk is involved, the balance may have shifted in favor of present cash compensation over future capital gain.

For example, the reward, the benefit, in a qualified stock option is the prospect of capital gain more than three years in the future. A few years ago many executives in top brackets would have preferred a qualified stock option over a current cash payment equal to the amount of the expected capital gain benefit, because they could keep 75 percent of it (after capital gains tax) instead of 30 percent of it (after tax at ordinary rates). Now, with only a 15 percent difference (between 50 percent and 35 percent) instead of 45 percent (between 70 percent and 25 percent), many more will prefer current cash compensation. The same consideration applies where the executive will buy or be paid in stock which is expected to rise in value. The prospective appreciation in value, which would be capital gain, is relatively less important now, since a cash payment equal to that appreciation would be taxed at no more than 50 percent.

It has also become less attractive for an executive who is a major stockholder to underpay himself for his services. In past years this was done in the hope that the corporation's increased income would raise the value of his stock; he could realize this increased value by selling it at capital gains rates, or in other tax-favored ways. This has always been risky, for several reasons, and the changes in tax on compensation and on capital gains sharply reduce its advantages.

So-called deferred compensation has also been undermined. This is basically an arrangement to postpone receipt of compensation until after retirement, to reduce total tax collections on compensation. Such arrangements (analyzed in Chapter 5) are somewhat less attractive now, thanks to the 50 percent tax ceiling.

And tax sheltered income has become less important. The basic idea behind the tax shelter is that a substantial part of the investment can be deducted against ordinary income in the investment's early years, while profits from the investment come in as capital gains or with other tax benefits. Thus, when ordinary compensation income was taxable at up to 70%, tax shelter deductions offsetting such income were sought even if they involved high-risk ventures. The risks may seem less worth running now that deductions save only 50 cents instead of 70 cents on the dollar, and now that capital gains profits and certain other types of investment income are in effect taxed at higher rates.

Deductions and profits connected with some tax shelter investments also are tax preferences, which can cut down further on the saving available from earned income relief.[5]

What the executive may net after taxes

In determining what to pay or offer an executive, the compensation planners should be able to compute, at least roughly, what tax the executive is likely to have to pay, so they can project what the executive will have left in spendable funds *after* taxes.

---

[5] It is the author's opinion that tax shelter activity did not in fact diminish when earned income relief was enacted. The relief was enacted at a time of growing awareness of tax shelters and of more aggressive marketing of them. Many executives turned towards tax shelters because of a sluggish or erratic stock market.

Tax and after-tax income can be approximated as follows:

Total compensation income	$_____
Add 10 percent of compensation income for outside income (dividends, interest, etc.)	$_____
Deduct 15 percent of compensation income for itemized deductions (state taxes, interest expense, etc.)	$_____
Deduct $3,000 for personal exemptions	$_____
Balance: Taxable income (approximate)	$_____

If taxable income is less than the amount qualifying for earned income relief ($52,000 for most married persons), the tax can be obtained from the tax table. (The table is reproduced at the end of this chapter.) The executive's spendable after-tax income[6] would roughly approximate taxable income minus the tax. Thus, an executive with a salary of $40,000 would have a spendable after-tax income ranging somewhere around $25,080.

If compensation will qualify, or might qualify, for earned income relief, the computation becomes much more complicated, and cannot easily be summarized.

The figures below show what the tax and after-tax amount on various salaries would be using the above assumptions about outside income and itemized deductions:

Salary	Tax	After-tax income*
30,000	6,200	19,300
40,000	9,920	25,080
50,000	14,310	30,190
60,000	19,120†	34,880
80,000	28,889††	44,110
100,000	38,802††	53,198

* See footnote no. 6.
† Though salary exceeds $52,000, earned income relief is not available because of the taxpayer's itemized deductions.
†† Reflects tax savings from earned income relief ($481 on $80,000, $1,578 on $100,000).

---

[6] This spendable after-tax income is also after reduction for assumed itemized deductions and personal exemptions ($750 each for a family of four).

BOARD OF DIRECTORS RESOLUTION TO MAKE UP FOR PAST UNDERCOMPENSATION OF CORPORATE OFFICER

This meeting having been called for the purpose of acting upon the proposal for a grant of further compensation to _____ for his past services to the company,

It is the determination of this Board that said _____'s services were not adequately compensated for in past years because (<u>reason</u>), and it is hereby

RESOLVED, that this Board authorize and direct the payment of _____ dollars ($_____) to _____, as further compensation for his past services to this company as an officer thereof and in any other capacity.

How to compensate executives

TAX RATE TABLES

The tables below show the income tax due on an individual's taxable income (gross income less allowable deductions and exemptions).

Single Taxpayers Not Qualifying for Rates in Schedule Y or Z				Unmarried (or legally separated) Taxpayers Who Qualify as Heads of Household			
Over—	But not over—		of excess over—	Over—	But not over—		of excess over—
$500	$1,000	$70+15%	$500	$1,000	$2,000	$140+16%	$1,000
$1,000	$1,500	$145+16%	$1,000	$2,000	$4,000	$300+18%	$2,000
$1,500	$2,000	$225+17%	$1,500	$4,000	$6,000	$660+19%	$4,000
$2,000	$4,000	$310+19%	$2,000	$6,000	$8,000	$1,040+22%	$6,000
$4,000	$6,000	$690+21%	$4,000	$8,000	$10,000	$1,480+23%	$8,000
$6,000	$8,000	$1,110+24%	$6,000	$10,000	$12,000	$1,940+25%	$10,000
$8,000	$10,000	$1,590+25%	$8,000	$12,000	$14,000	$2,440+27%	$12,000
$10,000	$12,000	$2,090+27%	$10,000	$14,000	$16,000	$2,980+28%	$14,000
$12,000	$14,000	$2,630+29%	$12,000	$16,000	$18,000	$3,540+31%	$16,000
$14,000	$16,000	$3,210+31%	$14,000	$18,000	$20,000	$4,160+32%	$18,000
$16,000	$18,000	$3,830+34%	$16,000	$20,000	$22,000	$4,800+35%	$20,000
$18,000	$20,000	$4,510+36%	$18,000	$22,000	$24,000	$5,500+36%	$22,000
$20,000	$22,000	$5,230+38%	$20,000	$24,000	$26,000	$6,220+38%	$24,000
$22,000	$26,000	$5,990+40%	$22,000	$26,000	$28,000	$6,980+41%	$26,000
$26,000	$32,000	$7,590+45%	$26,000	$28,000	$32,000	$7,800+42%	$28,000
$32,000	$38,000	$10,290+50%	$32,000	$32,000	$36,000	$9,480+45%	$32,000
$38,000	$44,000	$13,290+55%	$38,000	$36,000	$38,000	$11,280+48%	$36,000
$44,000	$50,000	$16,590+60%	$44,000	$38,000	$40,000	$12,240+51%	$38,000
$50,000	$60,000	$20,190+62%	$50,000	$40,000	$44,000	$13,260+52%	$40,000
$60,000	$70,000	$26,390+64%	$60,000	$44,000	$50,000	$15,340+55%	$44,000
$70,000	$80,000	$32,790+66%	$70,000	$50,000	$52,000	$18,640+56%	$50,000
$80,000	$90,000	$39,390+68%	$80,000	$52,000	$64,000	$19,760+58%	$52,000
$90,000	$100,000	$46,190+69%	$90,000	$64,000	$70,000	$26,720+59%	$64,000
$100,000	....	$53,090+70%	$100,000	$70,000	$76,000	$30,260+61%	$70,000
				$76,000	$80,000	$33,920+62%	$76,000
				$80,000	$88,000	$36,400+63%	$80,000
				$88,000	$100,000	$41,440+64%	$88,000
				$100,000	$120,000	$49,120+66%	$100,000
				$120,000	$140,000	$62,320+67%	$120,000
				$140,000	$160,000	$75,720+68%	$140,000
				$160,000	$180,000	$89,320+69%	-$160,000
				$180,000	....	$103,120+70%	$180,000

2   The ideal cash compensation for executives

Married Taxpayers and Certain Widows and Widowers							
Married Taxpayers Filing Joint Returns and Certain Widows and Widowers				Married Taxpayers Filing Separate Returns			
Over—	But not over—		of excess over—	Over—	But not over—		of excess over—
$1,000	$2,000	$140+15%	$1,000	$500	$1,000	$70+15%	$500
$2,000	$3,000	$290+16%	$2,000	$1,000	$1,500	$145+16%	$1,000
$3,000	$4,000	$450+17%	$3,000	$1,500	$2,000	$225+17%	$1,500
$4,000	$8,000	$620+19%	$4,000	$2,000	$4,000	$310+19%	$2,000
$8,000	$12,000	$1,380+22%	$8,000	$4,000	$6,000	$690+22%	$4,000
$12,000	$16,000	$2,260+25%	$12,000	$6,000	$8,000	$1,130+25%	$6,000
$16,000	$20,000	$3,260+28%	$16,000	$8,000	$10,000	$1,630+28%	$8,000
$20,000	$24,000	$4,380+32%	$20,000	$10,000	$12,000	$2,190+32%	$10,000
$24,000	$28,000	$5,660+36%	$24,000	$12,000	$14,000	$2,830+36%	$12,000
$28,000	$32,000	$7,100+39%	$28,000	$14,000	$16,000	$3,550+39%	$14,000
$32,000	$36,000	$8,660+42%	$32,000	$16,000	$18,000	$4,330+42%	$16,000
$36,000	$40,000	$10,340+45%	$36,000	$18,000	$20,000	$5,170+45%	$18,000
$40,000	$44,000	$12,140+48%	$40,000	$20,000	$22,000	$6,070+48%	$20,000
$44,000	$52,000	$14,060+50%	$44,000	$22,000	$26,000	$7,030+50%	$22,000
$52,000	$64,000	$18,060+53%	$52,000	$26,000	$32,000	$9,030+53%	$26,000
$64,000	$76,000	$24,420+55%	$64,000	$32,000	$38,000	$12,210+55%	$32,000
$76,000	$88,000	$31,020+58%	$76,000	$38,000	$44,000	$15,510+58%	$38,000
$88,000	$100,000	$37,980+60%	$88,000	$44,000	$50,000	$18,990+60%	$44,000
$100,000	$120,000	$45,180+62%	$100,000	$50,000	$60,000	$22,590+62%	$50,000
$120,000	$140,000	$57,580+64%	$120,000	$60,000	$70,000	$28,790+64%	$60,000
$140,000	$160,000	$70,380+66%	$140,000	$70,000	$80,000	$35,190+66%	$70,000
$160,000	$180,000	$83,580+68%	$160,000	$80,000	$90,000	$41,790+68%	$80,000
$180,000	$200,000	$97,180+69%	$180,000	$90,000	$100,000	$48,590+69%	$90,000
$200,000	....	$110,980+70%	$200,000	$100,000	....	$55,490+70%	$100,000

chapter 3 Planning the cash bonus

Bᴏɴᴜsᴇs and other incentive awards have long been a feature of executive compensation planning. The legendary bonuses of the early 1900s are still being echoed, if not exactly duplicated, in the 1970s—for example, in Ford Motors President Iacocca's bonus of $610,000 in 1972, and ITT Chairman Geneen's 1972 bonus of $411,000, down from $430,000 in 1971.[1]

Incentive pay is a practical form of stimulus and reward for the smaller company as well as for the giants. And with the smaller firm, it is often easier to tailor incentive pay to the performance of particular executives. The incentive awards we will consider in this chapter are those which are decided on before they are earned. Usually they will be expressly covered in an employment contract or board of directors resolution. If the incentive pay arrangement is not worked out beforehand, the amount paid is simply additional compensation for past services, and will risk difficulties with the Revenue Service and the stockholders, as noted in Chapter 2.

There are two differing views on what to cover under an incen-

---

[1] Despite federal wage controls in those years.

tive compensation arrangement with any particular executive. Under one theory, the regular salary is set at a fairly high, or at any rate, competitive, level, and the incentive is geared so that bonuses are slight unless company performance is outstanding. Here the thought is that regular salary is compensation enough for a workmanlike job, and that bonuses should be paid only for extraordinary achievement.

Another theory is that the executive should be paid a basic minimum salary plus a bonus which directly reflects the position of the company for that year. In this case, the executive's total compensation will more or less follow the year-to-year rise and fall in the company's fortunes.[2]

Either approach is acceptable from a legal standpoint. The selection of either depends on what the company prefers and what its executives insist on or will settle for. The company and the executive must of course agree on what should be the proper measure of an executive's performance under an incentive plan. In most cases, the test is profits. Thus, the bonus might be some percentage of profits. It might be a percentage of profits above some predetermined dollar amount, or a percentage which varies with the amount of profit. Or, it might be a percentage of the profits in excess of some predetermined rate of return on invested capital.

Sometimes, the award is made to depend on the price of company stock over a period or at year-end. Occasionally, it can depend on other items, such as dividends, sales (especially for sales, marketing or advertising managers) or costs (for production managers or comptrollers). And executives charged with special, short-run tasks may be rewarded on some basis connected with

---

[2] Practice often departs from theory when this approach is adopted. Directors and management may take the approach that when an incentive plan is adopted, regular salary may therefore be reduced. In practice, however, many companies with bonus plans eventually come to pay higher-than-normal salaries as well as bonuses.

that task. For example, an executive negotiating an acquisition may receive a bonus based on the amount of purchase cost saved through his efforts. Usually though, the incentive award is dependent on profits. This raises the danger that payment of such an award might be considered a distribution of profits rather than compensation for services. Distributions of profits are not deductible by the company.

Nonetheless, the Revenue Service is willing to recognize an incentive bonus based on profits as compensation. As such, it can be deducted by the company if it is reasonable pay for the services rendered. Furthermore, if it is reasonable pay, the high-bracket executive can make use of the 50 percent tax ceiling on earned income analyzed in Chapter 2.

But what is reasonable pay? Standards of reasonableness are stretched a bit when incentive or contingent compensation is involved, but the basic rules covered in Chapter 2 remain applicable. The principal factor is that determination of reasonableness requires consideration of all the executive's pay—his regular salary, his incentive or contingent award, and any other compensation he receives from that employer. A base salary of $50,000 and a $20,000 bonus is no more or no less reasonable than a base salary of $20,000 and a bonus of $50,000. In either case, compensation is $70,000.

Management's problem here is to design a plan calling for an incentive bonus which will be accounted reasonable (as part of the executive's overall compensation) whatever that amount may prove to be. Suppose the company will pay its executive vice president a salary of $60,000 plus 2 percent of profits in excess of $500,000. When drawing this plan, the company cannot know how much he will get, because it cannot be sure whether profits will be $400,000 or $4 million. His compensation could be $60,-000, or $130,000, or something else. The company therefore may be foreclosed from using the strongest argument that his pay is reasonable, the claim that he got no more than comparable executives in comparable companies. Instead, its main argument would have to be that his work contributes so much to profits that whatever he earns under this arrangement represents fair reward for his services. Company profits reflect the value of his services; the higher those profits, the more he must have done to produce them.

The Revenue Service accepts this argument in principle. The fact that the contingent deal may result in a higher compensation than would ordinarily be paid does not prevent treating it as reasonable compensation. The IRS will honor the arrangement if it represents what amounts to an arm's length and fair bargain, agreed to before the services are performed. In determining what is reasonable, the IRS looks to the circumstances at the time the agreement was made, not those at the time it may be questioning reasonableness on a tax audit.

The exact portion of profits to be paid the executive is generally a matter for negotiation between him and his company, just as his regular cash salary may be. (Indeed, the definition of profits may be a matter for negotiation.) But the following approach should be considered where there is concern that the compensation might be considered unreasonable.

Suppose it is planned to pay an executive a regular salary of, say, $30,000, plus an unspecified percentage of the profits. Check the salaries of executives in comparable companies. Assuming their salaries exceed $30,000, compute what percentage of the profits of their companies that excess represents. The percentage to use for your executive might represent an average of the percentages from those companies which most resemble yours, or those executives whose work most resembles your executive's work.

But those executives will be drawing straight salary.[3] Since your executive's compensation is to some extent at risk, the percentage of profits decided on could be slightly inflated to compensate for this risk. Courts have recognized that if an executive's compensation is contingent or partly contingent, it is reasonable to pay him a little more than persons with fixed salaries receive for the same work.

Defining profits

We should recognize that when an incentive agreement is being drafted, "profits" needs to be carefully defined. They can be defined in any way the executive and the company may choose, but definition there must be. Profits could be defined as the amount shown as profits under the method of accounting currently being used by the company in its financial statements. But if accounting principles are changed, this could require the company to keep a special set of books just for the bonus plan. Or profits could be defined as taxable income for federal income tax purposes, before or after federal income taxes. Here, compensation might have to be adjusted (additional amounts received, or amounts refunded, by the executive) if tax liability is later changed following IRS audit. Also, the profit picture could change in future years as Congress changes the rules on what items are income or deductions.

If the company has corporate affiliates, the parties must decide whether profits are to be this particular company's profits or consolidated profits (usually preferable). If other executives will also be granted an incentive bonus, will profits be computed before or after their bonuses? Will profits include or exclude extraordinary gains and losses?

---

[3] Some may be drawing salary plus incentive pay. If their incentive arrangement is known, it may serve as a guide to your own.

No method of determining profits for this particular purpose is wrong. But the parties should realize that profits is a flexible concept and should be careful to design a definition they can live with. A sample incentive plan, employing its own definition of profits, appears at the end of this chapter. The author also suggests that the agreement contain a provision for arbitration of any disputes over the definition.

Bonus arrangement needs time limit, periodic review

Now suppose that the parties have agreed on a plan to pay incentive compensation for 1974 and after. The plan clearly defines the basis on which the incentive pay is to be computed (profits, sales, or whatever). And suppose that the compensation to be paid the executive under this plan is reasonable according to standards prevailing in 1974. Does this mean that compensation he collects under this plan in 1975, 1976 and thereafter will be accounted reasonable?

Not necessarily. Circumstances may change, so that a payment under the agreement in 1976 may be unreasonable even though payments in 1974 were reasonable and fully deductible. For example, if the executive worked full time in 1974 but part time in 1976, the 1976 pay clearly could be excessive. And a number of court cases from World War II developed the point that if the economy or the market sharply changes after the agreement was written, incentive pay can become unreasonable. During the war, some of a particular company's profits could still have been produced by executive efforts, but other profits were simply the result of wartime scarcities. The executive did not produce these profits and compensation based on them was not reasonable or deductible.

Of course, the employment contract may oblige the company

to make payments based on profits, regardless of what causes the profits. This, however, does not make company payments deductible. The company deducts reasonable compensation and no more; it does not matter that larger amounts are legally required.

This suggests that incentive plans should last only a year or two. Where a longer term arrangement is desirable, the plan should leave some opportunity for renegotiation, so that the company need not continue paying amounts it cannot deduct. The contract might be made to terminate, or to bar further increases in pay, upon the occurrence of war, national emergency, disaster (for federal disaster relief purposes), consumer or commodity price rises of more than a stated percentage, or other events which could affect profits but which the executive did not cause or contribute to.

Early deduction

If the company is on the accrual method of accounting, it can deduct the incentive compensation for the year the bonus is earned, even though it is not paid or even computed until the following year. Incentive compensation will normally be based on company profits for a particular year. The exact amount of these profits will not be known until the year ends. Thus, the bonus cannot be computed until after the year is over. Yet the company can deduct the bonus on the return for the year the profits in question were made.

Example: Company and executive both report on the calendar year. The executive's incentive compensation is 1 percent of company profits. On February 14, 1975, company accountants determine that its 1974 profits were $2,000,000, and the executive is paid his $20,000 of 1974 incentive compensation on February 27, 1975. The company deducts the $20,000 of incentive compensation on its 1974 return, if it is on the accrual method. The executive reports the compensation as income for the year he gets it, in this instance, 1975.

To qualify to take the deduction for the year before it is computed, the accrual method corporation must be committed to make the payment; committed, that is, to pay a bonus under some particular bonus computation method or formula. The commitment must be made before the end of that year. Also, the company must make the payment reasonably promptly in the following year. (If the executive is a controlling stockholder or a close family member, the payment must be made in the first 2½ months of that following year.)

In this chapter we have assumed that the incentive arrangement was worked out before the start of the year. Thus, the requirement of a bonus commitment is met automatically.

But deduction is available even if the bonus is not a contractual arrangement with the executive, but is decided on by the company as additional compensation only well after the year began. If so, the bonus commitment should be put in writing. This is usually done at a board of directors meeting, and the commitment is written into the minutes.

The commitment need not be to make incentive payments to any particular individual. The company could commit itself to a bonus formula in, say, 1974, and decide in 1975 which executives will receive a bonus. Bonuses distributed in 1975 would still be deductible on the 1974 return if distribution is reasonably prompt in 1975.

Remember that an incentive arrangement worked out before the year begins is somewhat more likely to be deductible as reasonable compensation than a bonus decided upon late in the year, after the profit picture for the year becomes discernible. When the bonus decision comes late in the year, there is a somewhat greater tendency to treat the bonus as a distribution of profits rather than as compensation for services.

The bonus fund

Incentive bonuses need not be separately designed for or negotiated with each individual executive who will receive a bonus. Instead, some companies have a bonus fund, based on profits, in which each executive, or selected executives, will share. For example, a company could agree to contribute to the fund an amount equal to 2 percent of company profits. The executives who will share in this fund would normally be determined in advance, though this is not always so. The portion of the fund each executive will receive could also be determined in advance. Thus, his share could be made proportionate to his salary, or his share could be decided on only after the year is over, and based on his performance. Here, his share might be determined by a compensation committee, which would base the award on what committee members think he contributed to profits that year. Such a committee could include nonemployee directors or others not employed by the company.

Bonuses paid out of a bonus fund can be deductible as part of reasonable compensation, just as separately negotiated bonuses may be. A bonus award based on an appraisal of the executive's performance for the year can, of course, look like a nondeductible distribution of profits, rather than compensation for services. But this danger is lessened when the award is made by a committee which is not subordinate to the executive in question.

The author doubts the value of the bonus fund device as an incentive to executive performance. Its incentive value appears weakest where the number of executives who may benefit is large, and where the bonus award to covered executives is proportionate to their salaries.

Reporting bonuses received

The executive reports the bonus award in the year he receives it (or in the year it is made available to him so he can withdraw it at will, if this is earlier).

Suppose Euclid Company and Stewart, its president, both use the calendar year. And suppose that at the start of 1974 they agree to a salary of $45,000 a year, plus an incentive bonus of 2 percent of the profits, to be determined and paid in the first 60 days of 1975. For 1974, Stewart receives only $45,000, all salary, and reports only that amount. Profits in 1974 were determined to be $2 million. Stewart's bonus of $40,000 is paid February 26, 1975. For 1975, Stewart reports his $45,000 of 1975 salary plus the $40,000 bonus received that year. The company deducts 1974 salary in 1974 and 1975 salary in 1975. If it uses the accrual method, it deducts the bonus in 1974; if the cash method, it deducts the bonus in 1975.

Assuming compensation is reasonable, the executive's maximum tax rate cannot exceed 50 percent under the earned income rules discussed in Chapter 2. The Revenue Service may occasionally seek to deny earned income benefits, on the claim that compensation is excessive. While no pattern of IRS attack using this theory has yet been developed (because the earned income rule is still comparatively new), it is probable that the executive's earned income benefit will be attacked only after the corporation's deduction for that excessive part has been attacked. A bonus arrangement makes the picture more complicated than where only straight salary is involved, because reasonableness would be determined for a year other than the year in which the bonus is received or paid. The company which paid the bonus in 1975 would claim that the bonus (together with 1974 salary) represented reasonable compensation for 1974 services. The executive who received the bonus in 1975 would make the same claim—that is, that $85,000 was reasonable pay for 1974, though he collected only $45,000 that year.

Bonus advances

Companies occasionally make advance payments during the year of a bonus based on the year's profits, before the year's profits have been determined. These advances are treated like the executive drawing accounts discussed in Chapter 2. That is, if the executive must repay any bonus not earned, he is not taxable on the advance until the amount of his bonus is finally determined, and then only to the extent of the amount he may retain.

SAMPLE INCENTIVE COMPENSATION AGREEMENT

AGREEMENT made this _____ day of _____ between _____ (hereinafter, "the company") and _____ (hereinafter, "the employee").

WITNESSETH

1. [Employee's duties, term of contract, etc.]

2. As compensation for the employee's services hereunder, the company agrees to pay the employee: (a) a salary of $_____, per annum, payable semimonthly, and (b) an additional amount (hereinafter, "incentive compensation") equal to _____% of the amount of consolidated net earnings of the company and its subsidiaries,* except that in no event shall incentive compensation exceed _____% of salary.

Consolidated net earnings of the company shall be such earnings as are determined by the independent accounting firm employed by the company as its auditors, and shall reflect deduction for federal income taxes, compensation of all kinds paid to the employee, and all other proper charges. The determination of consolidated net earnings made by such accounting firm shall be final and binding on company and employee, and no adjustments in incentive compensation shall subsequently be made because of adjustments in federal income taxes or other items. The consolidated net earnings for purposes of this incentive computation shall be computed not later than 60 days after the end of the company's fiscal year and distribution of any incentive compensation shall be made not later than 75 days after the end of that fiscal year.

3. et seq. [Clauses unrelated to incentive compensation]

IN WITNESS WHEREOF the company and the employee have executed this agreement as of the day and year first written above.

[company]

———————

by _____

[title]

———————

———————

[employee]

---

* Alternative clauses for determining the amount to be paid appear on the following page.

How to compensate executives

Alternative clauses based on profits:

A. _____% of the first _____ of profits [consolidated net earnings or other definition]

_____% of the next _____ of profits

_____% of the next _____ of profits

and so on.

In some agreements, the percentage of profits to be paid drops as profits rise; in others, the percentage rises. The author prefers the latter arrangement—for example, 2% of the first $500,000, 3% of the next $1,000,000, and so on.

B. _____% of the profits in excess of _____% of the sum of the company's average amount of capital stock outstanding during the year.

This bases the award on profits which exceed some predetermined rate of return on invested capital.

C. _____% of profits in excess of $_____.

This is somewhat similar to the preceding clause, basing the award on profits which exceed a predetermined dollar amount.

chapter 4 Special considerations in compensating the stockholder-executive

THE need to establish that compensation for an executive is reasonable, and techniques for doing so, are covered in Chapters 2 and 3. This chapter will cover other problems peculiar to the cash compensation of the stockholder-executive.

Protection against IRS disallowance

Suppose that in 1974 Bell Corporation pays a salary of $100,000 to Carlisle, who is Bell's president and 15 percent stockholder. An IRS agent, on auditing the company's 1974 return in 1976, decides that only $80,000 of Carlisle's salary is reasonable compensation for his services; the $20,000 balance is not deductible. Bell might challenge this determination administratively within the IRS, in court, or in both ways. But assuming it accepts the agent's finding (or loses any challenge), the result is that Carlisle actually collects $100,000 but the company can deduct only $80,000, and is fully taxable on the $20,000 balance.

A solution to this problem, from the company's standpoint, is to require the stockholder-executive to repay any amount it paid him as compensation for which it cannot take a tax deduction. The foresighted company would make this requirement a condition of Carlisle's employment, and impose it before the services are performed. If the stockholder-executive has a binding legal obligation to repay, the Revenue Service will allow him to take a business expense deduction for his repayment. If such a repayment obligation had existed in the Bell-Carlisle situation, and Carlisle had repaid the $20,000 in 1976, the tax picture would be: For 1974, Carlisle would be taxable on $100,000, of which $20,000 is later determined to be not reasonable compensation and therefore is disqualified for the earned income tax relief discussed in Chapter 2. Bell Corporation would be taxed in 1974 on the nondeductible $20,000 (plus its other 1974 income). For 1976, Carlisle could deduct the $20,000 repayment he makes that year against his other income. The company is not taxed in 1976 on receipt of the $20,000 on which it was already taxed.

This repayment arrangement is widely known among professional practitioners, and they often recommend it. But these points should be noted to put such arrangements in perspective:

1. They are practical only for stockholder-employees and, for the most part, only for those with substantial holdings. An executive derives no benefit from repaying compensation. He is worse off economically by repaying and taking a tax deduction than he would be by keeping the money. Thus, an executive is not likely to agree to such a repayment arrangement unless he will continue to have an interest in the amount repaid, as a stockholder.

2. The repayment arrangement was first recognized (allowing an executive to deduct his repayment) in a court case in which the repayment requirement was set forth in a board of directors resolution. Some practitioners therefore recommend that the repayment requirement be put in a board resolution. The author

instead recommends putting the repayment requirement in an employment contract. In the author's view, a board of directors resolution will not always be effective as a binding obligation to repay. (A legally binding obligation is not always a prerequisite to a business expense deduction, but it seems advisable to try for one in this area.)

3. Even stockholder-officers may be reluctant to agree to repay excessive compensation. They may fear that the company's knowledge that it will recover any excessive amount from the executive may weaken its incentive to fight for the deduction in IRS negotiations. An amount treated as excessive compensation would not get earned income benefits in the executive's hands. Thus, before agreeing to repay, some stockholder-executives might insist that the repayment agreement oblige the company to contest the reasonableness issue in good faith through all levels of the IRS, or allow the executive to do so on its behalf.

4. Some practitioners are nervous about using such repayment arrangements, fearing that the Revenue Service is especially likely to attack compensation deductions once it knows that a repayment arrangement exists. The thought here is that the mere existence of a repayment arrangement tends to show, in the revenue agent's mind, that compensation is excessive. To this attitude, the author has these comments:

Some agents do conclude that if a repayment arrangement exists, compensation is probably excessive. Thus, where the agent learns of the arrangement, deduction is somewhat more likely to be challenged than where no such arrangement is made.

The agent sometimes will not learn of the arrangement. This will depend on the agent's routine in doing his work. Some agents make it a practice to examine board of directors minutes as part of their tax audit. This way, they can learn of repayment arrangements reflected in directors' resolutions. This approach would not necessarily disclose repayment requirements in employment contracts, though, of course, the agent might ask to see those as well. Agents who don't approach their corporate tax audits in this manner might not learn of the repayment arrangement for the year the deduction was taken. But if some compensation is ruled nondeductible anyway, they may learn about the repayment arrangement in a later year, when auditing for the year the excessive amount is repaid.

It is therefore understandable that some practitioners avoid using repayment arrangements, fearing that they excite suspicions of unreasonableness. Despite this, the author is willing to use such an arrangement when representing the company.

"Best salary" considerations

Some tax advisors and compensation planners suggest setting the salary of stockholder-executives at that exact level which will minimize tax collections. This advice can fit only limited situations. It presupposes that any amount the stockholder-executive foregoes as current compensation can be later withdrawn, by him or his heirs, in some tax-favored way.[1] The plan, sometimes called a "best salary" plan, therefore requires that the stockholder-executives be substantial stockholders and that they be prepared to act in concert. In fact, the best salary plan works best (assuming it works at all) where the stockholder-executive is effectively the principal or sole stockholder.

Just which amount of salary is "best" under this theory will depend on the amount of the corporation's income before compensation to the stockholder-executive. For simplicity, we will assume that only one stockholder-executive is involved, and that he will file a joint return. Some of the corporate income will be

---

[1] Tax-favored ways to withdraw corporate funds would include tax-free merger with a larger firm, sale of stock at capital gains rates, or transfer of stock by bequest (free of income tax).

paid as compensation, and some will be retained by and taxed to the corporation. The compensation advisor will determine the exact amount of salary which produces the lowest total tax on stockholder-executive salary paid and corporate income retained.

For example, if corporate income (before the stockholder-executive salary) is $30,000, the best salary would be $12,000, with the corporation retaining the $18,000 balance. This produces the lowest total tax take since the corporate tax bracket is 22 percent and the stockholder's tax bracket is the same. Increasing the stockholder's pay would increase the total tax paid, since he would be in a higher bracket on every dollar over $12,000, while the corporation's bracket would not decline. Decreasing his pay would not save tax, and would result in an increased tax if pay were reduced below $8,000, since this would forfeit part of the benefit of the 19 percent tax rate on income between $4,000 and $8,000. On corporate income of $65,000, the best salary would be $40,000, with $25,000 retained by the corporation.

The best salary concept requires a major adjustment where large amounts are involved. Following the concept strictly, the best salary for a married person filing a joint return would never exceed $44,000 (or, more precisely, a salary which would leave a taxable income of $44,000 or less). But there is slight difference between the maximum corporate income tax (48 percent) and the maximum individual income tax on compensation income (50 percent, with some qualifications, see Chapter 2). Even though the immediate individual tax cost of salary over $44,000 may be a bit more than the corporate tax cost of retaining those added salary dollars, it is wiser on the whole to pay the extra salary (assuming it will be considered reasonable compensation). This way, the stockholder-employee will have the immediate use of the after-tax salary, without having to wait until some tax-favored withdrawal can be structured. Also, withdrawal may involve some additional tax cost (capital gains tax, for example), which immediate salary payment avoids. Thus, where corporate income (before stockholder-executive salary) exceeds $69,000, the best salary is one in which the corporation retains $25,000 (taxed at 22 percent) and pays the rest as salary (taxed at up to 50 percent or so, assuming it is reasonable compensation).

The same principles apply, though the corporate income figures would be different (higher), if there are two or more stockholder-employees to be covered.

Though the best salary concept is fairly widely known among tax practitioners and other compensation advisors, the author considers it of limited value in practice. It can occasionally suit the small business. It works best for the entrepreneur conducting two or more businesses, who does not currently need much income from one or more of those businesses and therefore can tailor his withdrawals to suit his tax advantage.

"Best salary" is not necessarily deductible salary. In fact, deductibility is an especially serious problem here. For most corporations, it is impossible to know in advance what the year's income will be. Thus, the exact salary for the year can be set only during the year, and often only late in the year. Also, since corporate income may fluctuate from one year to another, salary may fluctuate as well. Revenue agents auditing corporate tax returns are trained to notice these factors. To the IRS, salary fluctuations tend to indicate that at least part of the amount designated as salary is in fact a nondeductible dividend. Another factor with the same tendency arises where two or more stockholder-employees are paid salaries proportionate to their stockholdings. Probably the heaviest blow to the best salary concept arose in a court case in which the judge concluded that the fact that stockholder-employee was paid the "best" salary, the salary that bore the least overall tax cost, tended to show that part of what he received was not reasonable compensation.

The departing stockholder-executive

A number of complex factors arise when a company decides to buy out a particular stockholder or group of stockholders.[2] These factors aren't properly part of a book on executive compensation. But one important factor worth considering here arises when buying out a stockholder who is also an executive with an employment contract. If the corporation wants to buy him out, it ordinarily wants to terminate his services; the stock buy-out is subordinate to that.

In any buy-out involving an employment contract, the corporation and the stockholder-executive will have conflicting interests from a tax standpoint as well as an economic standpoint. The executive of course will want to collect as much as possible while the company wants to pay as little as possible. But besides differing over amounts, they have a tax incentive to differ over what the payments are for. The executive has two things to sell: his stock holding, which will go to the corporation, and his employment contract, which will be cancelled. Anything he collects for cancelling his employment contract would be fully taxable ordinary income. What he collects for his stock would be tax free as return of capital, with any excess treated as capital gain. The executive therefore wants most of what he gets treated as for stock (tax free and capital gain) and only a small amount treated as for the employment contract (ordinary income).

The company, however, wants most of what it pays treated as for the employment contract, since such a payment is deductible as a business expense. Any amount it pays for the executive's stock is a nondeductible capital expenditure. Ordinarily, the tax treatment of the payment will be determined by the way the company

)

---

[2] The company decides because there are tax advantages in having the company do the buying. The initial decision is of course made by other stockholders.

and the stockholder-executive allocate the total payment in the buy-out arrangement.

Example: Suppose Redgrave is the president of Hewitt Corporation and owns 15 percent of its stock, which cost him $150,-000 six years ago. He also has an employment contract paying him $60,000 a year, which still has four years to run. Following a policy dispute with other stockholders, it is decided that he will sell all his stock and agree to cancel his employment contract for a total payment of $400,000. The buy-out deal might allocate, say, $330,000 of this to the stock and $70,000 to the employment contract. Or it might allocate $180,000 to the stock and $220,000 to the contract. Which allocation is chosen makes a sizable difference to each party. In the first method, Redgrave has $180,000 capital gain and $70,000 ordinary income, and the company deducts $70,000. In the second method he has $30,000 capital gain and $220,000 ordinary income, and the company deducts $220,-000.

Redgrave is much worse off—he gets to keep much less of the $400,000 paid him—with the second allocation than with the first. But one party's detriment is the other's benefit. The deal is much less costly to Hewitt under the second allocation. Thus, if one party is tax-conscious and the other is not, a benefit approaching a windfall can result, to the tax-wise side.

This is not to say that the party who is aware of the tax factors should keep those to himself, and design a wholly selfish allocation of the agreed amount. It sometimes happens that the other side (for instance, the executive) later realizes the tax detriment to him in the allocation and refuses to abide by it. He reports the allocation for tax purposes as he would like it to be. For example, though the agreement may have allocated $300,000 to the employment contract and $100,000 to stock, he might report it for tax purposes as $350,000 for stock and $50,000 for the employment contract. This maneuver is usually unsuccessful. That is, the parties generally are held for tax purposes to their agreement as written. But this is not always so. The IRS is not a party to such agreements and is not obliged to follow them. It can provide its own interpretation of the deal, or deny tax benefits to both parties, forcing them into court. Thus, even if the tax-conscious party's allocation is upheld, this may only happen after extensive tax audits and expensive litigation.

Some practitioners therefore prefer to spell out the tax costs and consequences to their less-informed adversaries, to reduce chances of reneging later. This can still leave some room to design the transaction to meet the parties' tax and financial convenience. For example, if deduction is especially important to the company this year, the executive might agree to a heavy allocation to the employment contract but might insist on a higher overall settlement amount.

The final agreement might include a clause requiring each party to report the deal for tax purposes as it is set forth in the contract. The IRS is not bound by this either. Thus, if one party deviates from the agreement, he could be upheld for tax purposes, but the other party would then have a claim for damages resulting from the former's breach of contract.

Postponing payment of controlling stockholder

A tax technique involving corporations using the accrual method deserves examination here. An executive who controls such a corporation sometimes notices that it can take a tax deduction for compensation owing to him which he need not yet report as income. A corporation on the accrual method can deduct compensation it owes but has not yet paid. The stockholder-executive, on the cash method, is not taxable on compensation owed him until he gets it. The apparent result is a tax deduction with no corresponding taxable income.

But the tax law strictly limits this technique. The corporation is allowed the accrual deduction for compensation to a more-than-50 percent stockholder only if the compensation is actually paid within 2½ months after the end of its taxable year. Thus, if corporation and executive are both on the calendar year, the corporation can deduct compensation due but unpaid for 1974 only if it pays that amount by March 15, 1975, and the executive is taxable when he gets it, in 1975. If payment is not made within that 2½ month period, the corporation's deduction is denied forever.

But deduction is allowed if the amount, though not actually pocketed by the executive, is made available to him (*constructively received* by him) during the year or within 2½ months thereafter. The executive is taxed in the year he constructively receives it. So a corporation may take the deduction and then, when subjected to a tax audit, claim that the compensation was constructively received. One difficulty with this is that the IRS may not accept a constructive receipt claim unless the corporation withheld tax on the amount in issue. At current withholding rates, up to 36 percent, and under today's rules requiring speedy deposit of tax withheld, a sizeable part of the amount being deducted must be parted with promptly, in cash, in any case. This withholding requirement therefore effectively undermines reliance on constructive receipt as a means to avoid actual collection by the controlling stockholder-executive.

Subchapter S stockholder-executives

The *Subchapter S*[3] corporation is a tax saving mechanism for closely-held corporate business. A Subchapter S corporation is in every respect a real, legal corporation under state corporate law. But it is exempt from U.S. corporate income tax, except in rare

---

[3] The term refers to Subchapter S of the Internal Revenue Code, specifically 26 U.S. Code sections 1371–1379.

cases. Its stockholders are taxable directly on their share of corporate income whether or not it is actually distributed to them as dividends. And they can deduct their share of corporate operating losses.

There is an important tax saving consideration for stockholder-executives of such corporations. Until recent years, it made no tax difference whether they took their share of corporate income out as salary or as dividends. For that matter, it seldom made a difference if they left their share of income in the corporation, since they were taxable on undistributed corporate income as well. Now it makes a big difference. Now there is a 50 percent tax ceiling on earned income, but other income, such as dividends, is taxable at rates up to 70 percent. It is therefore important for stockholder-executives of Subchapter S corporations to maximize the amount which they take out of their corporations in the form of compensation (salary, bonus, and so forth), and thereby minimize the amount taxable to them as dividends or undistributed earnings. For example, a stockholder-executive who now collects $64,000 in salary and $36,000 in dividends from his Subchapter S corporation could reduce his tax bill by up to $1,560 if he instead collected $88,000 in salary and $12,000 in dividends, though both represent a $100,000 income.

Increasing compensation (and decreasing other income from the corporation) is a practical consideration only if executive employees (or some of them) hold or control substantially all the stock. Stockholders who are not employees would not benefit from this arrangement, and might either block it outright or sue to undo it later. Also, the arrangement produces no benefit unless corporation income is such that the corporation could pay salaries large enough to qualify for earned income relief. Thus, for a married stockholder-executive filing a joint return, increased salary would have to be somewhat above $52,000.

Earned income relief is available only for amounts representing reasonable compensation for services. But the possibility that the Revenue Service may treat some or all of the increase as excessive (unreasonable) should not deter the stockholder-employee from seeking the salary increase. He has nothing to lose by this move. If the increased amount is ruled excessive compensation, he is taxable on that amount at ordinary rates, up to 70 percent. If he had not taken it as compensation but as a dividend, or had left it in the corporation, he would have been taxable on it at ordinary rates, up to 70 percent.

Of course, increased compensation saves taxes only if at least some of the increased amount is reasonable. The company should take all available steps to establish that the amounts paid are reasonable. For suggestions on this, see Chapters 2 and 3.

CLAUSE COVERING REPAYMENT OF EXCESSIVE COMPENSATION

Any payment made to _____ [the executive] as salary, commission, bonus or other compensation for personal services, which shall be disallowed in whole or in part as a deductible expense by the Internal Revenue Service, shall be reimbursed by _____ to _____ [the company] to the full extent of such disallowance, not later than _____ days after demand for reimbursement is made by _____ [the company]. In lieu of such reimbursement by _____, the Board of Directors of _____ [the company] may at its discretion direct that amounts be withheld and deducted from _____'s compensation until the amount owed to _____ shall be recovered.

chapter 5 Why high-salaried executives may favor deferred compensation

Actor William Holden reportedly was paid $1 million for starring in the movie *The Bridge on the River Kwai*. For tax reasons, he chose to take this sum in annual $50,000 installments over a 20-year period. Texas attorney and politician John Connally's fee for serving as executor to the Sid Richardson estate came to $750,000. For tax reasons, he arranged to receive this in installments of varying amounts over 11 years.

Tax savings are the motivation behind the deferred compensation arrangements to be considered in this chapter. The scale of compensation, and of tax saving, when dealing with company executives will seldom approach that for movie stars or high-powered Houston lawyers. But deferring compensation is to some degree easier to arrange for executive employees than it is for self-employed persons.

Deferred compensation arrangements are products of the tax laws and, in particular, of progressive tax rates. The higher a person's taxable income, the larger the proportion of that income which must be paid in taxes. Deferred compensation plans are designed to postpone payment of some of an executive's compensation from the year he earns it, when he is in a high tax bracket, to some later year, when he is expected to be in a lower bracket. They are not the same as pension or profit-sharing plans (analyzed in Chapter 12). For one thing, deferred compensation normally is tailored to fit one particular executive or a few executives. Unlike pension or profit-sharing plans, rank-and-file employees are never covered by deferred compensation plans.

Deferred compensation arrangements have declined in importance in recent years, as a result of changes in tax laws. Effective for 1972 and after, compensation cannot be taxed at more than 50 percent (with some qualifications, see Chapter 2). Formerly, when compensation was taxable at rates up to 70 percent, it seemed wise to postpone a certain amount of that income into retirement years, when effective rates might otherwise range around 25 to 32 percent. The advisability diminishes when the 70 percent rate is reduced to about 50 percent. Also, there are the income averaging rules which were adopted in 1964 and liberalized for 1970 and after. These rules permit a taxpayer with windfall income or a sharply rising income to compute his tax somewhat as if all income for a 5-year period were received in equal annual installments over that period. Such averaging, an alternative to earned income relief, is another way to reduce the tax on current pay.

These recent changes do not eliminate the tax advantage of deferred compensation arrangements. But they reduce the advantage by reducing the tax cost of current compensation. There is less to lose by maximizing current cash pay than by deferring some.

With this background, deferred compensation is still worth study by compensation planners and some executives. Some tax saving benefit remains, even where earned income relief (or, alternatively, income averaging) is available. It must be decided whether the benefit of the various types of deferral arrangements justifies postponing the receipt of cash which is otherwise available currently. Also, earned income relief is not available if compensation is excessive. That is, tax at rates up to 70 percent (instead of 50 percent) apply to that part of compensation which is ruled unreasonable. Thus, if the executive suspects that part of his compensation might lose earned income relief, he could seek to have it deferred to a later year. Earned income relief is generally unavailable for amounts received as deferred compensation. But this will not matter if the deferred amount is received in a year when total taxable income (of a married executive) is $52,000 or less.

Types of deferred compensation

Compensation planners recognize two basic types of deferred compensation arrangement. In the first and much more common type, the company is willing to pay a high cash salary now, but the executive for tax reasons prefers to postpone receipt of part of this amount until a later year. This type is often called an "unfunded" plan, for reasons which will appear later.

In the second type, the executive will be paid an amount at some future time if certain conditions are met. These conditions usually relate in some way to services to be performed by the executive in the future. This type is called a "forfeitable" plan.

In both situations, the executive wants to avoid being taxed now on amounts to be received in future years. The obstacle to this is the tax concept of constructive receipt of income, the rule that if income is set aside for a taxpayer so he can collect it at will, it is taxable to him when set aside for him, regardless of when he actually collects it. Successful deferred compensation plans are those that avoid constructive receipt. The discussion that follows shows how to draw up successful deferred compensation plans—

what features they must have, may have, and cannot have. A sample plan appears at the end of this chapter.

Unfunded plan

Two requirements must be met in designing this type of deferred compensation plan:

1. The company's obligation to pay the deferred amount must be no more than its contractual promise to pay. The executive cannot have a right in or claim to any specific fund or property, but just a contract right to be paid. The company must not be obliged to pay any amount into a trust for the executive's benefit, set up an escrow account for him, or acquire any particular item of property out of which the future payment must be made. The company's promise is therefore said to be unfunded.[1] If it were funded, so that the executive had a claim to particular property or to any fund, he would be taxable on it in the current year (unless it was a forfeitable plan, discussed later in this chapter).

2. The deferral of compensation must be agreed to before the compensation being deferred is earned. But would this rule prevent reducing future pay and deferring *that* amount? For example, why not amend a present employment contract calling for $70,000 currently, and instead pay $50,000 currently and a deferred $20,000? There seems to be no rule against this, though the author finds no specific Revenue Service approval either. An arrangement which results in an increase in total pay, for example, $51,000 currently and $20,000 deferred, or $50,000 currently and $21,000 deferred, seems safer.

---

[1] Companies often in fact set up funds or buy property (insurance or annuity policies) to cover liability to pay deferred compensation in the future. This is acceptable and maybe even desirable (see below) as long as it is not required. These are sometimes called informally funded plans. For our purposes, they are unfunded.

The Revenue Service has accepted deferral agreements made after the amounts deferred were earned, where they were not yet due to be paid. This situation seldom arises in executive compensation planning. One setting where it could be used arises when the executive is to receive, say next July, a bonus based on this year's profits. Company and executive could agree, after the bonus is earned but before it is due, that instead of paying the bonus in a lump sum, it would be paid in equal installments over, say, five years. (They could, of course, have made this arrangement in the first place.)

How deferral works

Example: Grumble Corp. contracts to employ Blake in an executive capacity for five years. Compensation will be at the rate of $50,000 a year, plus $10,000 a year credited to a bookkeeping reserve. Amounts so credited will be distributed in annual installments of one-fifth of the total, starting with the year Blake's employment is terminated, or the year of his death or disability if earlier. On these facts, the $10,000 a year qualifies as deferred compensation. It will not be taxable until Blake receives it, which presumably will be when he retires. (If he died before then, it would be taxed to his heirs.) The agreement was made before the monies were earned, and no funding is provided; there is only a contractual promise and a bookkeeping entry.

Note that for unfunded plans there is no requirement that amounts being deferred be subject to forfeiture by the executive at any time. Also, it doesn't matter that the company may have been willing to pay the entire $60,000 currently. The amount to be deferred need not be known in advance. It could, for example, be a percentage of the profits for the year the services are performed.

The deferral payout pitfall

The most serious practical mistake in deferred compensation planning arises in designating when the deferred amounts should be received. Almost every executive wants the deferred amounts to be paid in installments after his retirement, when his tax bracket is expected to be low. Yet the deferred amounts often are paid before retirement, in high-income years, so that the tax advantage of deferral is lost.

The biggest trap here, from the executive's standpoint, is the contract clause which pays the deferred amount after the executive terminates his employment with the company. Many an executive will terminate his employment with the company, not by retirement, but by taking a job with another firm at a higher salary. He will get this new salary, which in itself could put him in a higher tax bracket, plus the deferred amount from his former employer, which will now bear a tax higher than if there had been no deferral at all. And deferred compensation under an unfunded plan ordinarily does not qualify for earned income tax relief.

For example, suppose Peters receives $60,000 in 1974 and a further $20,000 is deferred until termination of his employment. In 1976, Peters leaves for a new job, which pays $80,000 plus a deferred $25,000. The $20,000 deferred from his previous job increases his 1976 income to $100,000. This $20,000 bears a tax of $11,840, or up to $1,840 more than if it had been received in 1974.

Another, more obvious, trap, but one some executives fall into, is the deferral for a specified number of years, where the executive is still working when that deferral period has expired.

A properly drafted deferral agreement can avoid these traps. The deferred payments could become payable only after the executive has reached the age at which he expects to retire, for example, age 65.

Some executives may not be sure of the age at which they will want to stop work. In this case, deferral could be until such time as the executive "ceases substantially full-time gainful employment, but for a period of not less than _____ years."

Another possibility for avoiding the worst impact of timing mistakes is this: Suppose an executive is scheduled to receive $20,000 next year, earned for services performed in past years, but he does not want to collect this next year, since he will still be working at a high-salaried job. Presumably, the Revenue Service would accept as valid an agreement made now which defers the $20,000 until after retirement. The problem is that this further deferral requires a new contract (at least as to these amounts). The company might not be willing to accommodate the executive with a further deferral if, for example, the deferred amounts are becoming due because the executive is leaving to join a competitor. There is, of course, the alternative of taking the deferred $20,000 next year as scheduled, and deferring a corresponding amount out of next year's salary until retirement. The drawback here is that deferred amounts normally does not qualify for earned income relief. Thus, the $20,000 received next year can be taxed at a rate of more than 50 percent. This would not happen if it could be deferred until after retirement.

Assuming deferred amounts are not due until after retirement, a further technical point should be checked. It can be wise to make sure that deferred amounts do not become payable until the year *after* retirement has occurred. This will avoid receipt of this amount during the executive's final year of employment, when he could still be in a high tax bracket. This postponement might not be necessary if he will work only a few weeks during the year in which he retires. Thus, payout could be made to begin in the year following retirement except that it would begin within a month after retirement if retirement occurred in, say, the first four months of the year.

Timing when payout should begin should also take account of

the fact that the executive may want to make a lump-sum withdrawal of the amount standing to his credit in a company pension or profit-sharing plan. Lump-sum withdrawal qualifies for tax benefits, which can in some cases be maximized if the executive has comparatively little other income. The best timing might be: first year, retirement (near year-end); second year, lump sum pension or profit-sharing withdrawal; third year and thereafter, installments of deferred amounts.

Other planning aspects

Deferred compensation agreements often run for long periods. Every effort should therefore be made to foresee the future, for both executive and company, and to cover anticipatable events in the agreement, perhaps with provision for independent arbitration of disputes.

The deferred compensation agreement typically requires the company to make one or more payments of deferred amounts already earned if the executive's employment is terminated by death or disability. Payments to the estate or heirs of a deceased executive are taxed as follows: The commuted or present value (as of the date of the executive's death) of his right to deferred payments is included in his estate for estate tax purposes. (For estate tax considerations in general, see Chapter 15.) Amounts received by the executive's estate or heirs under an unfunded plan are also subject to income tax at ordinary rates. But any estate tax attributable to deferred amounts can be deducted against the amounts included in income.

Funding for company convenience: Insurance

There is no rule barring the company from buying property out of which it intends to fund any obligation it might have under the deferred compensation agreement. But deferral is lost if the company is *required* to obtain such property, and it is unwise to hint that the company ought to obtain it.

In practice, companies sometimes do acquire property to fund their deferred compensation obligations. In so-called phantom stock plans, this may be stock (see the discussion on this under phantom stock, below). In other situations, it is usually an insurance policy. Funding through insurance would work this way: The company would take out a policy on the executive's life to cover its deferred compensation liability to him, naming itself as the beneficiary. The executive would have no rights in the policy, and would not be taxable on company payments of premiums. The company could not deduct the premiums since it is the beneficiary.

If the executive dies before he is due to receive the deferred compensation installments, the company would collect the insurance proceeds. These proceeds are tax-free to the company. Many deferred compensation arrangements require the company to pay any earned deferred amounts to named heirs of the executive if he should die before installments are fully paid. Where this happens, the company would deduct its payments (assuming they are reasonable compensation).

If the executive survives to receive his deferred compensation in installments, the company normally would cash in the policy. Any profit the company received on the policy (that is, surrender value less premiums) is ordinary income; loss, if any, is not deductible. The company may deduct amounts it pays the executive (assuming they are reasonable), and the executive pays tax at ordinary rates on what he collects. To summarize, funding with insurance means: (*a*) no company deduction for insurance premiums, (*b*) no tax to company on insurance proceeds, (*c*) ordinary income (or nondeductible loss) to company on policy cashed in before death, and (*d*) company deduction (to the extent reasonable) for payments to executive or heirs.

The executive's receipts are ordinary income; so are receipts by heirs, and there is also an estate tax.

Company deduction for deferred compensation

Deferred unfunded compensation is deductible by the company, just as other compensation is. The company deducts only when the compensation is paid, and not when it is earned by the executive, even if the company uses the accrual method of accounting. Only reasonable compensation for the executive's services is deductible.

In practice, few questions have arisen about the reasonableness of deferred compensation paid an executive under a plan. But the problem might arise in this way: Coleman's contract calls for $50,000 this year plus another $20,000 to be paid five years hence. The company will deduct only $50,000 this year, so this year's deduction might not be questioned. Five years from now, the company will pay and deduct an additional $20,000. This additional $20,000 might be challenged as unreasonable. If Coleman has retired, any payment would seem unreasonable at first glance because Coleman rendered no services that year. If Coleman is still an employee, the $20,000 on top of his other salary could seem excessive.

To counter IRS challenges, the company must show that the payment represents compensation for services performed in the past. It should therefore have ascertained in the year the services were rendered that the current pay plus the deferred compensation was reasonable. That is, it should have applied the tests for determining reasonableness set forth in Chapters 2 and 3, and it should have retained full documentation as part of company records to support its claim of reasonableness.

Inflation has probably tended to protect deferred compensation arrangements from challenge. For example, $70,000 of compensation for 1973 might seem excessive if looked at in 1974. But if looked at in 1979, after the compensation had been paid in installments of $50,000 in 1973 and $20,000 in 1978, it might well seem reasonable. This may help to explain why the reasonableness of deferred compensation has not yet become a serious issue in executive compensation planning.

Phantom stock

Phantom or *shadow* stock as a compensation device has come to serve as a way of investing deferred amounts for the executive. Suppose an executive's employment contract calls for $50,000 this year and an additional $10,000 in ten years. This $10,000, deferred for ten years, is worth much less than a present payment would be. The executive loses ten years of investment increment by opting for deferral. He would prefer to have that $10,000 put into some income-producing or growth investment for his benefit. Yet if the company were obliged to put the deferred $10,000 into some investment in which the executive had an ownership interest, it would not qualify as deferred compensation but would be taxable currently, when earned.

The solution here is the phantom stock plan. The $10,000 is considered for purposes of the deferred compensation agreement as if it were put into some particular investment, designated in the agreement. At the end of the deferral period, the executive is paid the value of that "as if" investment. Deferral is not jeopardized because the company is not obliged to make that investment, or any investment. It is just that the value of that "as if" investment becomes the measure of the amount to be paid when deferral ends. The make-believe investment could be in a bank account, an annuity, stock of any company, or any bond. This arrangement was given the name phantom or shadow stock because usually the deferred amount is treated "as if" invested in stock of the company paying the deferred compensation.

Example: Cowell, President of Hedake Corporation, is paid $50,000 this year, and an additional $10,000 is credited to a deferred compensation account. This $10,000 is considered under the employment contract as if invested in Hedake shares. When deferral ends, ten years hence, Cowell will receive an amount of cash equal to the value at that time of the number of shares which the deferred amount would have bought when deferral began.

Assume Hedake Corporation shares are currently selling at $50. Thus, it is as if Hedake invested the deferred $10,000 in 200 Hedake shares. Ten years from now, Hedake shares are at $225 each. Cowell therefore is entitled to $45,000 (200 x $225). Cowell has no right to the Hedake *shares,* just their cash equivalent.

The amount he collects is ordinary income and would normally not qualify for earned income relief. The company's payment is deductible as compensation, to the extent that it, coupled with regular salary, is reasonable (a point we will further examine below).

If Hedake stock stood at $40 when deferral ended, Cowell's $8,000 would have been treated the same way: ordinary income without earned income relief, and company deduction if reasonable.

So far, we have been considering phantom stock arrangements simply as a way of investing deferred amounts for the executive's benefit, so he does not lose investment increments during the deferral period. Here, company and executive can agree on what kind of investment shall be the measure of the payout. Thus, they could agree that the deferred amount should be treated as if invested in IBM stock, a Bank of America savings account, or anything else. The executive might be entitled to receive an amount equal to any dividends on the make believe investment, with or without the right to receive the value of the investment itself. He might also be given the right to alter the make-believe investment during the term of deferral. Thus, company and executive could consider the initial investment as if sold when the executive so elects, and the proceeds put into some new "as-if" investment he designates.

Another practical use of the phantom stock plan is as a substitute for paying the executive in stock of his employer company. Paying an executive with stock may provide him with an incentive to improve company profits, in which he will share as stockholder. On the other hand, Chapter 7 points out that paying with stock can be more expensive to the company than paying with cash, without any greater financial benefit to the executive. A solution to this problem would be to pay in phantom stock. This way, he would benefit from any rise in value of the stock. (The arrangement could pay him the value of the stock plus the value of all dividends in the interim, if this is desired.) He would therefore have a stockholder's incentive to improve company profits. Yet he would be paid in cash rather than in stock, so that the company would have full deduction for the amount paid (if reasonable), and not the limited deduction that arises if there is a payment in stock which the executive later sells at a capital gain. Of course, company deduction is taken only when the company pays. Deduction therefore comes later under phantom stock plans than under straight stock payment arrangements.

Will a payment equal to the value of phantom stock be considered reasonable compensation? For example, suppose the amounts deferred in 1974–78 total $80,000. At the end of the deferral period (say 1983) the "as if" investment is worth $270,-000, so the executive is entitled to receive cash in that amount. Is the $270,000 reasonable compensation?

This question arises under tax law, for purposes of the company's deduction, and under state corporate law, as a possible dissipation of company assets against the interests of the stockholders. There are as yet no clear answers for either tax law or corporate law purposes.

Remember that the phantom stock is used as a measure of an amount to be paid later. In tax law, we are used to arrangements which measure the executive's bonus by this year's or last year's profits, sales, and so forth. Such measuring rods will often directly reflect the value of the executive's services. The same could be said of a payment in stock which is subject to forfeiture by the executive until he has earned it, maybe years later, through his services. But basing compensation on the value which investment property may achieve several years after the right to receive this value has been earned is something quite different, even where that property is stock in the employer corporation.

To the author it seems that reasonableness of compensation in a phantom stock plan would be hard to establish, for purposes of the company's compensation deduction (or, where this is relevant, the executive's earned income relief). The difficulty is in establishing that the value of stock in, say, 1980, reflects the value of services in 1974. Fortunately for deferred compensation planners, the IRS may not share the author's concern on this matter. There is apparently no instance of an IRS challenge to reasonableness of phantom stock reaching the courts. (This also means, of course, that reasonableness has never been officially confirmed.)

But as a matter of state corporate law, reasonableness is plainly in question. The author has unearthed two cases asking whether phantom stock results in excessive compensation which the stockholders can recover on the company's behalf. One case found it reasonable; the other found it unreasonable. The true balance of opinion among professional advisors may not be 50–50, but may be tilted in favor of reasonableness. Still, doubt remains.

Forfeitable plans

Another form of deferred compensation, other than the unfunded variety discussed above, is the *forfeitable* kind. In this case, the executive is not taxable on deferred amounts because he has not yet fully earned them. In unfunded compensation, the amount being deferred has been earned but is not currently taxable because payment is postponed and there is no trust, escrow, or other specific fund to which the executive has a claim. In the forfeitable arrangement, there may be a trust fund or other property for the executive, but he is not currently taxable because his interest may be forfeited by future action or inaction.

Forfeitable deferred cash compensation is rare. Where it exists, it serves company needs rather more than the executive's needs. That is, though it accomplishes a postponement of current salary, the delayed payment is intended as an incentive to continued executive performance rather than as a tax-saving move to delay income and tax until retirement age.

An example would be an arrangement to pay Johnson, the advertising manager, $50,000 for 1974 plus an additional $10,000 paid into a trust of which Johnson is beneficiary, to be distributed to him in 1979 if he shall perform the duties of advertising manager on a substantially full-time basis from 1974 through 1978.

Such an arrangement is recognized as providing an effective deferral only if:

1. The executive's interest in the trust is subject to *substantial* risk that he will forfeit it.
2. Assuming he transfers his interest, that interest remains subject to substantial risk of forfeiture in the hands of his transferee.

At this writing, there is no official indication or example of any deferred compensation paid into a trust which satisfies this twofold requirement. In the author's opinion, this is not because it is impossible or unusually difficult to satisfy the requirement,[2] but

---

[2] The requirement here is a modification of that for compensation paid in restricted stock, discussed in Chapter 8.

because there has as yet been no significant interest in the matter in the business community. This is another way of saying that achieving deferral through this device is technically possible, but in practice attracts no one.

Unfunded, forfeitable deferred compensation would be possible as well—and even less interesting to executives. In forfeitable arrangements, though the company may pay into the trust this year on an executive's behalf, it can't deduct for its payment until the executive is taxable on it—that is, when deferral ends. The notion that the company parts with funds now which it gets no tax benefit from for several years ought to discourage company interest in this device.

LETTER AGREEMENT FOR EMPLOYMENT AND DEFERRED COMPENSATION

Dear Mr. _____,

The following shall constitute the agreement between us regarding your employment by _____ [hereinafter, the company]:

The company will employ you during the period _____ through _____.

Your base salary during this period shall be at the annual rate of $_____, payable in equal monthly installments.

In addition to this base salary and in further consideration for your services under this agreement, the company agrees to accrue as deferred compensation in each month during the period of this agreement, an amount equal to $\frac{1}{12}$th of $_____ and to credit that sum to a special account on its books.

Neither you, nor any legal representative or beneficiary designated by you, shall have any right (except as an unsecured general creditor) against the company with respect to any portion of the account.

The deferred compensation due you, consisting of the total amounts so credited to the special account, shall be paid to you in ten equal annual installments, beginning on the _____th day of January following the year in which you shall have terminated your employment with the company on a substantially full time basis [or, following the year in which you shall have attained age _____ or shall have ceased substantially full-time gainful employment, whichever is the later (earlier)], with further installments on the _____th of January of succeeding years.

If you should die before payment of the last installment, unpaid installments shall be paid on the due dates as above set forth to the beneficiaries designated by you in writing, or, failing such designation, to your estate.

. . . [Other clauses]

Your acceptance by signing in the space below will constitute our agreement with respect to your employment by the company.

Very truly yours

_____[Company]

by _____

[title]

Accepted:

_____

[employee]

CLAUSES COVERING PHANTOM STOCK
PROVISION FOR INVESTMENT IN SECURITIES
SELECTED BY EXECUTIVE

[Certain amounts are credited periodically to deferred compensation account]

The amount in the account shall be deemed invested in such securities as you [executive] shall designate which are traded on a national securities exchange. You shall have the right, on the first business day of each quarter of the calendar year, to designate the securities deemed sold or purchased for the account on that date. The account shall further be credited with the dollar amounts equal to the amount of dividends or interest paid on securities deemed held by the account.

The company is not required to purchase or sell any securities designated by you. If it should purchase any such securities, they shall remain the sole property of the company and will not become part of the account, nor will you or any legal representative or beneficiary designated by you have any right (except as an unsecured general creditor) against the company with respect to any portion of the account.

As of the first date on which an installment of deferred compensation shall become due from the account, your right to designate investments shall cease. The account shall be valued by adding the fair market value of all securities deemed part of the account to the dollar amounts in the account which are not deemed invested in securities. The fair market value of securities shall be the mean between the high and low prices for the day on the largest national exchange on which such securities traded for that day, or absent any trade that day, on the first preceding business day on which trades occurred. As each installment shall be paid, the balance in the account shall be reduced by the amount paid. The balance in the account (less each installment payment as it occurs) shall be deemed invested at interest at an annual rate of _____ percent, and an amount equal to such interest shall be credited to the account.

If in doubt about whether your own deferred compensation will be considered a valid deferral by the Revenue Service, you may ask it to issue a ruling on the subject, before the contract in question becomes effective. Such rulings requests are normally prepared by company or private attorneys or accountants.

chapter 6 Paying executives with stock or other property

THE executive may demand or may be awarded property in addition to cash and fringe benefits for his services. Usually, this is stock of the company, but may be a car or some other asset. Or, the company may give him the opportunity to buy stock or other property from it at a bargain price.

This chapter will cover the basic rules governing payments of property and bargain sales of property to executives. The rules given here apply to all types of property paid over or sold—stock, real estate, or anything else. But a number of special legal, accounting and other considerations arise when the property involved is stock of the corporation the executive works for. These special considerations are explored in Chapter 7. Thus, both this chapter and Chapter 7 should be consulted by the compensation planner who is contemplating a payment or bargain sale of company stock, or is choosing between a payment (or a sale) of stock or, on the other hand, of some other property.

Additional special considerations are involved if the company plans to pay or sell stock or other property but with strings attached. This is the situation where the executive actually receives the property now, but will not get complete legal or practical ownership of it until some months or years in the future. These special considerations are covered in Chapter 8.

An executive is subject to tax when he receives property for his services. This is true regardless of the nature of the property he receives: stock of his employer corporation, stock of another corporation, land, or whatever (with a minor exception for items of nominal value, see below). And it is true whether his company pays him in cash and property or—the rare case—in property only.

Usually, the executive is taxable on property in the year he receives it (for exceptions to this rule, see Chapter 8). This is important. Tax ordinarily is imposed when he gets the property and is not postponed until he converts it into cash. The amount he pays tax on is the fair market value of the property, regardless of what the property may have cost the company making the payment.

Example: Suppose Williams, Globe Corporation's production manager, received a $36,000 salary during 1974 and in addition a bonus of 50 Globe shares worth $125 each. Williams' compensation income for the year is $42,250 ($36,000 plus $6,250).

The taxable amount is the property's *fair market value.* This may occasionally be hard to determine. These are the guidelines to apply in determining the amount on which the executive will be taxable.

1. In most cases, the property is stock. If the stock paid as compensation is traded in an established market (including over-the-counter), the value of the stock generally is the mean between the high and low price of the stock in that market on the date payment is made. This is true whether the stock paid as compen-

sation is stock of the employer corporation or of some other corporation.

But if the trades in the market are infrequent, or in very small quantities, or the amount of stock being paid exceeds the amount usually traded, or if, as often happens, there is no established market in the shares, determination of their fair market value is a complex task. The company should first check whether any determination of the shares' value has been made recently for some other purpose—for example, determinations for purposes of personal property tax, gift tax, estate tax, or inheritance tax. The value as so determined may be used if realistic and recent enough, and assuming the number of shares in question does not involve a major or controlling interest. If no such recent determinations have been made, a professional practitioner should be consulted. He will consider a number of factors, such as book value, earning power and earnings history, size of the block of stock in question and its effect on corporate control.

2. For other types of property, fair market value may be easier to determine. Thus, for such items as automobiles, boats, and TV sets, the prevailing retail price (including the used price if the item isn't new) should be used. If in doubt, have the property appraised (cost of appraisal is deductible). If large amounts are involved, the careful taxpayer may seek several appraisals and use the average of the appraisals. Real estate usually should be professionally appraised to determine its value. Valuations for real property tax purposes are seldom acceptable.

Bonds traded on an established market would be valued the same way stock so traded is valued. Otherwise, bonds or notes usually are considered to be worth their face amount, but may be assigned some other value, higher or lower than face amount, if justified by the facts (chiefly, the credit rating and the interest rate).

The value of any property received as compensation from the company is earned income. It therefore generally can't be taxed at *more* than 50 percent. (For details on this earned income ceiling see Chapter 2.)

Where a company distributes Christmas turkeys, Easter hams and other holiday gifts of nominal value to its employees, such gifts are tax-exempt—if the distributions are made to employees generally, to promote employee goodwill. Limiting such gifts to executives would make them taxable. Therefore they are not an element of executive compensation planning.

Bargain purchase: Another compensation device, closely related to the payment of compensation in stock or other property, is the grant to the executive of an opportunity to buy stock or other property at a bargain. Bargain purchases should be distinguished from options to buy property. As used in compensation settings, an option means the right or privilege to buy the stock or other property under an offer continuing for a stated period of time. A bargain purchase offer would be one without a stated duration which the executive could count on, one which might be withdrawn or modified at the company's discretion or to reflect changes such as rises or falls in the value of the offerred property.

Sometimes there may be no practical distinction between bargain purchase opportunities and nonstatutory options. It is a rare employer that will offer an executive a bargain purchase opportunity without allowing him a few days or weeks to think it over; this could be the practical equivalent of an option extending for that period.

But most compensation planners, and all executive optionees, prefer to see some substantial exercise period, months or years, written into the option. Chiefly for that reason—the need to provide for events and contingencies months or years hence—stock option arrangements are more likely to involve corporate documentation and formality. Stock options are analysed in detail in Chapter 9.

The tax rules for an executive's bargain purchase of property from his employer are in essence the same as those for payment received in property. The only change in the picture is that he pays something for the property, and the only tax difference this makes to him is a dollar for dollar reduction in the amount he is taxed on.

If he receives a payment in stock or other property, he reports the fair market value of the property as compensation income in the year the property is received.

If he buys stock or other property from his company at a bargain—which means for any amount less than its fair market value—he is taxed in the year the property is received, at its fair market value less the amount he paid for it. Thus, if in 1974 an executive is given the opportunity to buy 100 shares worth $90 each for $75 each, he has compensation income of $1,500 in the year his purchase is made ($9,000 value minus the $7,500 purchase price he pays).

The executive is not taxable on a bargain offer if he foregoes it.

Courtesy discounts: Employees are not taxed on their bargain purchases of goods from the company, under a company policy of granting courtesy discounts on purchases of items of relatively small value, to employees generally, to promote employee goodwill, health or efficiency. Limiting such discounts to executives would make them taxable. They therefore are not elements of executive compensation planning.

Sale by the executive

Stock or other property which the executive received as compensation or bought in a bargain sale from his company normally is a capital asset to him. His profit or loss on a later sale of the item is capital gain or loss. Gain is tax-favored *long-term* capital gain if he held it more than six months from the day following receipt of the stock or other property to the day it is sold. *Receipt of the stock* refers here to the day the executive becomes legal owner of the stock, regardless of any delay in delivering stock certificates to him, and even if such certificates are never delivered.

For tax purposes, gain (or loss) is the amount by which the sales proceeds in an arm's length sale exceed (or fall below) the amount on which the executive is taxed as compensation. Thus, if Broder received 100 shares worth $100 each in 1974 which he sold for $14,000 in 1976, he would have $10,000 of ordinary conpensation income in 1974 and $4,000 of capital gain in 1976. If he had sold them for $10,000 immediately upon receipt in 1974, he would have $10,000 of compensation income in 1974 and no capital gain at any time.

If the executive had bought the property at a bargain, his gain (or loss) is the amount by which the sales proceeds in an arm's length sale exceed (or are less than) the sum of the amount he paid and the amount he was taxed on.

Withholding on property payments

The company must withhold income tax on property it pays as compensation. Just how withholding is to be handled is left to the company's own ingenuity. The Revenue Service provides no rules or suggestions. The author suggests the following alternatives, from which the company can choose the one which best suits the circumstances:

1. Pay out a smaller amount of property and use the balance to satisfy the withholding amount. For example, suppose Wales Company intends to pay Bowker, its president, a bonus of 200

shares worth $100 each, or $20,000. If Bowker's withholding bracket (not the same as his tax bracket) is 36 percent, Wales could simply pay him 128 shares and deposit $7,200 as the tax withheld on $20,000. Bowker would report a bonus of $20,000 and claim a $7,200 withholding credit against tax due.

This method for meeting the company's withholding obligation works best where the property is readily divisible, with each unit of equal value, as in the case of shares of stock.

2. Reduce the executive's cash salary by an additional amount (in addition, that is, to regular tax withholding on his salary) representing the tax to be withheld on the property. For example, if an executive is paid $4,000 a month regular salary and is also paid a bonus of stock worth $2,000, the regular income tax withholding on salary could be increased by $720, representing the withholding on $2,000 at the 36 percent withholding rate.

3. Where the executive intends to sell all the stock or a substantial part of it immediately after acquisition, the sale proceeds can provide the funds needed to cover the withholding obligation. Thus, if the executive is paid 100 shares worth $100 each and he immediately sells 40 shares for $4,000, he can draw on this fund to cover the withholding, paying over to the company the amount required to be withheld (assume it is $3,600).

The immediate sale would normally eliminate the problem of valuing the property received. It would be worth what the executive got for it, unless the sale was not at arm's length (e.g., a sale to a family member or nominee).

4. Where the executive will keep the entire property, he can pay over to the company the cash equivalent of the withholding amount out of his own funds. He may need to borrow for this. For considerations involved in company loans or company-sponsored loans to executives, see Chapter 13.

The company's viewpoint

A company takes a compensation expense deduction for the compensation it pays in stock or other property, just as it does for compensation paid in cash. It deducts the amount the executive is taxed on, the property's fair market value, except that, as with cash compensation, it can't deduct any unreasonable or excessive part of compensation paid. (For a detailed analysis of unreasonable compensation, see Chapter 2.)

Thus, if Wye Corporation pays its vice president Bonner 150 shares of Wye Corporation stock worth $80 a share, Wye Corporation would deduct $12,000 (subject to reasonable compensation limits) regardless of its basis for the stock. The same deduction rule applies if Wye Corporation pays in shares of some other corporation, or in some other property such as land, a boat or a car.

The company deducts on its tax return for the year in which the executive's taxable year ends. If company and executive both use the calendar year, the executive reports a 1974 payment on his 1974 return and the company deducts on *its* 1974 return. But if the company uses a fiscal year, this rule is a bookkeeping nuisance. Suppose the company has a fiscal year ending September 30 and pays the executive in property on July 1, 1974. The executive reports it on his 1974 return, but the company cannot deduct until its return for October 1, 1974—September 30, 1975 is filed, since this is the year in which the executive's tax year ends.

Where the corporation pays compensation in property other than its own stock, it will also have gain or loss for tax purposes. This is because the delivery of property to satisfy a debt, including a debt for compensation, is a taxable sale of the property. Gain or loss is usually capital gain or loss, but is ordinary income or loss if the property involved is in the nature of the corporation's stock in trade. Loss is not deductible if the executive to whom the loss property is paid, or his family (brother, father, children, wife, etc.), owns more than half the corporation's stock.

The amount of the company's gain or loss is the property's fair market value less the company's basis for it. To determine that value, follow the guidelines at pages 74 and 75. (Occasionally, the property is paid for services which were rendered at a stipulated price. Here, the fair market value of the property can be treated as equivalent to that price, absent better evidence of value.)

Example: Crown Corporation pays 50 shares of duPont stock to its president, Koenig, as a bonus. Crown bought the stock at $140 a share two years ago, but it was worth $200 a share when paid to Koenig.

With respect to this payment, Koenig has $10,000 of compensation income. Crown has $10,000 of compensation expense deduction (assuming total compensation to Koenig is reasonable) and $3,000 of long-term capital gain ($10,000 less $7,000) on the "sale" to Koenig.

• For the company as well as for the executive, the bargain sale rules are essentially the same as for a payment in property. Its compensation expense is the fair market value of the stock or other property transferred to the executive reduced by the amount he pays for it. This amount is deductible assuming that, when added to the executive's other compensation from the company, it is reasonable compensation. Deduction is taken on the company's returns for the year in which the executive's year ends.

If the property bargain-purchased is company stock, the company has no taxable gain or deductible loss from the transaction. If it is property other than company stock, the company's gain or loss is the property's fair market value less the company's basis for it. The amount the executive pays is not relevant in figuring gain or loss, but only in computing the compensation deduction.

Property is sometimes paid *now* for services to be rendered in the future. Technically, a company can only deduct compensation for services already rendered. Thus, if services to earn the property are to be rendered over a period of years in the future, the company theoretically must prorate its deduction over the period the services are rendered.[1] While it does not clearly appear that this deduction limitation is actually enforced, companies for which a full, present compensation deduction is an important element in the decision to pay in property should consider one of these alternatives:

1. Ask the Revenue Service for a ruling on when the company may deduct for its payment, or
2. Set up a forfeitable, nontransferable arrangement to pay restricted property (see Chapter 8), which will give full deduction when restrictions lift.

---

[1] This assumes the property is not forfeitable *and* nontransferable under the rules for restricted property in Chapter 8.

BARGAIN SALE TO EXECUTIVE OF PROPERTY OTHER THAN COMPANY STOCK

EXAMPLES OF TAX TREATMENT

Example 1

Assume:

Property's value	$10,000
Selling price	$ 6,000
Company's basis	$ 2,000
Executive's income	$10,000 − $ 6,000 = $ 4,000
Company's deduction (if reasonable)	$10,000 − $ 6,000 = $ 4,000
Company's gain (or loss)	$10,000 − $ 2,000 = $ 8,000 gain

Example 2

Assume:

Property's value	$10,000
Selling price	$ 6,000
Company's basis	$12,000
Executive's income	$10,000 − $ 6,000 = $ 4,000
Company's deduction (if reasonable)	$10,000 − $ 6,000 = $ 4,000
Company's gain (or loss)	$12,000 − $10,000 = $ 2,000 loss

chapter 7 Special rules for payments in company stock

THE rules in Chapter 6, on paying an executive in property or selling him property at a bargain price, are fully applicable when the property in question is the stock of his employer. But there are additional tax, legal, accounting and practical considerations when paying or selling stock in stock bonus, stock award, stock purchase, or stock thrift or savings plans. These considerations are discussed in this chapter.

Not that the rules are significantly different. The executive who receives or buys stock is subjected to exactly the same tax rules as apply where he receives or buys other property. True, there is one important difference affecting the *company:* It has no taxable gain or deductible loss on its stock (see below). But in other respects, it is additional rather than new rules that come into play when payment or purchase is in the company's stock.

Stock of the employer corporation has a two-fold use in compensation planning. It can be a payment or reward for services already performed, and in this respect does not differ from payment in cash or in other property of equal value. But it also operates as an incentive to further productive work for the company. It gives the executive a stake in the company, and he will benefit, apart from his salary, in the increases in company profits or net worth to which he contributes.

Executive incentive plans may be structured to pay out bonuses in stock in direct response to particular executive achievements. Historically, the executive team would be rewarded with a predetermined amount of stock if company stock as a whole attained a certain value, or a certain level or percentage of profits was achieved. While this method is still widely applied at present, there is a trend in the larger companies towards gearing stock bonuses more closely to each executive's own performance— hence the name *performance shares* for stock received under these arrangements. The performance share concept represents the company's recognition that it can be unrealistic to hitch an executive's reward to the record of the company as a whole. The award of performance shares to a particular executive therefore may be made to depend on the showing of that area of company activity which is under his control. In the author's view, it will often be difficult to pinpoint particular areas of executive responsibility where success can clearly be seen and measured. Still, individual performance can often be recognized in such areas as sales, production, cost and quality control, and investment profits.

The plan discussed here contemplates that the executive is paid the stock after performance is shown. (Plans in which the executive is currently paid in stock which can later be forfeited if performance is not shown may seem similar in concept but are subject to differing rules, discussed in Chapter 8.) In such a plan, the executive reports the value of the stock as income when he gets it.

Incentive plans for paying stock as a bonus are often designed to make half the payment in stock and the other half in cash. The executive could use the cash part to pay the tax on the award, and it would also provide the funds to cover any withholding obligation. Half in cash would seldom be too little, since the executive's federal tax on the stock generally couldn't exceed 50 percent. For executives in brackets below the 50 percent bracket (less than $44,000 of taxable income for married executives), some smaller cash proportion could be preferred, with a larger proportion of stock. But where state or local income tax is imposed, it may be desirable to pay half in cash in any case, to cover state or local tax obligations in addition to the federal take.

Company tax and cost factors: When a company pays an executive in company stock, it takes a compensation expense deduction for the fair market value of the stock, assuming compensation is reasonable. It has no taxable gain or deductible loss on the payment in stock, unlike the case where the payment is in property other than its stock. (If it had sold the stock to the executive at less than its market value, it would deduct the difference between value and what the executive paid, if compensation is reasonable, but still would have no taxable gain or deductible loss.) Thus, a company can pay with its own stock worth $10,000, and take a $10,000 deduction, without any capital gains tax even though it has little or no basis for the stock.

But this is no free deduction. When a company pays stock with a $10,000 market value to an executive, it is thereby surrendering $10,000 which it could have collected on a sale of that stock to an outsider.[1]

Moreover, any amount collected on sale of its own stock to an outsider is tax-free, just as its payment of compensation using such stock is tax-free. Thus, a company's payment of compensation in its own stock costs the company (before taxes) an amount equal

---

[1] As a practical matter, the market value used for tax purposes sometimes differs from the amount an outsider would actually be willing to pay for the stock. It may be worth more to an executive who has a continuing intimate involvement with the corporation than to an outside portfolio investor. The corporation might not actually be able to collect as much on sale of the stock as the figure it uses to compute its deduction.

to the stock's fair market value, since it could collect that amount tax-free by selling it instead. This cost is reduced by the tax value of the company's deduction for the compensation payment, so that the after-tax cost of payment in stock usually is 52 percent of the stock's value.

In deciding whether to make such a payment, the corporation will weigh whether the after-tax value of the stock payment to the executive justifies the after-tax cost to the company. In most cases, payment in company stock meets this condition. After-tax value depends on the executive's tax bracket. But he can not be taxed at more than 50 percent, so cost will never greatly outrun value. If the tax bracket were 42 percent (taxable income between $32,000 and $36,000 on a joint return), a $4,000 stock bonus could cost the company $2,080 but would be worth $2,320 ($240 more) to the executive.

But the cost-value balance may shift against the payment-in-stock device if the executive's capital gains on the sale of the stock are considered. For example, suppose an executive receives stock worth $10,000 this year which he sells two years hence for $22,-000. This year, the stock's value to the executive may well exceed its cost to the company, thus making it a worthwhile compensation device. But if the sale two years later is also considered, the picture changes. Then the executive will pay a capital gains tax, of $3,000 or thereabouts. The company, of course, has no income or deduction from the executive's sale. But if the company had held on to the stock and had itself made the sale then, the $22,000 it collected would have been completely tax free. Thus, it has surrendered $12,000 of capital gain to the executive which is worth more to it than to him.

Example: Whelp, Inc. pays Brown 100 shares of Whelp stock worth $10,000. Whelp's deduction reduces its after-tax cost to $5,200. Assume Brown's tax on the 100 shares is $4,500 (after-tax value is therefore $5,500) which he pays out of his own pocket and without selling his shares. Two years later Brown sells all 100 shares for $22,000, keeping $19,000 after $3,000 of capital gains tax.

Brown's total take after taxes is $14,500 ($22,000 minus the sum of $4,500 and $3,000). Whelp's true after-tax cost (since it could have taken the $12,000 gain free of tax) is $17,200—that is, $5,200 plus $12,000. In this case, a $22,000 outlay costs the company $2,700 more than the outlay is worth to the executive.

Where a capital gain is foreseen, payment in cash instead of stock will give the executive the same amount as with stock, at less cost to the company. A cash payment of $29,000 would be needed to yield $14,500 after taxes to an executive in the 50 percent[2] bracket; $26,364 if he is in the 45 percent[3] bracket. The after-tax cost to the company of a $29,000 cash outlay is $15,080 ($13,709 after taxes on a $26,364 outlay), which is less, obviously, than the $17,200 cost of the $22,000 outlay of stock and capital gain in the above example.

Nonetheless, paying more cash instead of stock is not always a satisfactory solution from either a tax or a business standpoint. First, a payment of $10,000 in stock (plus regular salary) this year could be fully deductible as reasonable compensation. A payment of $29,000 or $26,364 in cash (plus regular salary) might be partly nondeductible as unreasonable. This might be so even if the payment were spread out over two or three years. The after-tax cost to the company increases by 48 cents for each nondeductible dollar of cash compensation. Thus, the company that prefers to pay increased cash compensation should be especially well pre-

[2] The terms 50 percent bracket and 45 percent bracket are technically inaccurate in this context. Read them to mean that the effective tax rate on the amount involved is 50 percent or 45 percent.

[3] See footnote 2, above.

pared to prove that compensation is not unreasonably large. (See Chapter 2 for how to prove that compensation is reasonable.)

Also, in some situations, the executive who receives compensation in stock is significantly responsible for the subsequent appreciation in stock values. As a stockholder (or larger stockholder), he may make mightier contributions to the corporation than if he drew only cash.[4] This is a factor which only corporate management can judge. But despite a higher cost potential to the corporation, payment in stock instead of cash can be recommended where a valued executive would quit unless given a share of the business, or where stock ownership would substantially stimulate productivity or cost consciousness.

Installment sale plans

From the company's standpoint, the sale of company stock to the executive for a price payable in installments can have benefits not found in stock options. From his first installment payment, he begins to feel he has a stake in the business, and has an incentive to improve its performance. Also, the installment obligation, while it lasts, tends to tie him to the company. Furthermore, the privilege to pay for the stock in installments rather than all at once is, from the executive's viewpoint, an economic advantage in itself. It may not be necessary to include any bargain element in addition (as it is with stock options).

The executive pegs the price he must pay when he agrees to the installment purchase arrangement. He pays this price, in installments, even though the stock's market value rises. Assum-

---

[4] Shadow stock will sometimes be an attractive substitute for actual stock. The company would treat the executive as if he owned 100 shares, agreeing to pay him, in two years, what 100 shares would be worth at that time. The executive would have an incentive to cause company stock to rise in value. And the company could deduct the stock's value when it makes the payment two years hence. For details on shadow or phantom stock arrangements, see Chapter 5.

ing a bona fide purchase, the spread between the price he agreed to pay and the value when the stock is fully paid for is not compensation income, and it is not taxable until the stock is disposed of. At that point, the executive has capital gain (capital loss, if the stock declined in price) equal to the difference between the amount he paid for the stock and its selling price. (From the company's standpoint, surrendering to the executive capital gain on its stock is an economic disadvantage, as discussed above in connection with stock paid as compensation.) An installment purchase plan, therefore, need not result in any compensation income to the executive, or in tax consequences of any kind until the stock is sold. What causes earlier tax to the executive, and generates a deduction opportunity to the company, is the company's action in selling the stock at a bargain, or letting an executive buy it without an absolute personal commitment to pay for it. That is:

a. If the stock will be sold to the executive at a bargain, the rules for bargain purchase of company stock will apply. The executive will be taxable on the market value of the stock at the time he makes a binding commitment to buy it, less the amount he agrees to pay for it. He is taxable in the year it is transferred to him, though he hasn't yet paid for it (assuming it is not restricted stock as described in Chapter 8).

b. The Revenue Service considers the arrangement a genuine installment purchase only if the executive is personally obligated to pay the purchase price. If he can cancel out (say, because the stock's market value falls), or if the purchase price is paid only out of dividends, the IRS treats the arrangement as an option. For the executive, this means that he is not the owner of stock for tax purposes until it is paid for. His holding period for long-term capital gain purposes does not start to run until he becomes the owner. This sharply limits his chance at capital gain benefits. Worse, if the market value has risen between the time he entered into the agreement and the time the stock is paid for, the spread between the stock's value at the time he pays for it and the amount he pays is compensation income at that time. (For the rule where he does not acquire full ownership rights even after paying all installments, see Chapter 8 on restricted stock.)

Many companies setting up installment purchase arrangements today want a plan which avoids tax consequences until the executive disposes of his stock. Most of the remaining companies are willing to grant a bargain purchase opportunity which has tax consequences, but do not want an arrangement which the executive can back out of. Such an arrangement leaves his situation, and the company's, unsettled until the installment price (which the IRS would call the option price) is paid. In the author's view, the company that wants a clear, bona fide predictable installment arrangement should make sure the plan meets each of the following requirements:

1. The executive is obligated to pay the full installment purchase price. This, however, does not preclude a provision that the debt to the company for the unpaid installment balance is to be satisfied first out of the stock itself, and it does not prevent requiring the stock to be pledged with the company as collateral.

2. The executive has full rights over the stock immediately upon his agreement to buy it. This means he has the right to receive dividends on the stock. (This is not an absolute IRS requirement, but is advisable.) But check for possible state corporate law limits on the right to receive dividends on stock not fully paid for.

3. A substantial downpayment should be required, with payment of the balance over a reasonable period. *Substantial* and *reasonable period* will depend on the amounts involved. But the author inclines towards a downpayment (or first year's payment) of not less than 20 percent, with payment completed within five years.

4. Interest should be required on the unpaid balance. This interest will be interest income to company, and deductible by the executive. If the interest rate is less than 4 percent simple interest, the company normally will be treated as if it received interest at a 5 percent rate, and the executive will be allowed an interest deduction at that 5 percent rate, even though he actually paid at a lower rate, and even if no interest was provided.

If these tests are met, the executive becomes the owner of the stock when he enters into a binding contract of purchase. His holding period for long-term capital gain purposes begins then, and any appreciation over the price at that time comes to him as capital gain on sale. (If the installment price is a bargain, below the stock's value at that time, the spread between price and that value is compensation income in the year he contracts to buy.)

Example: Caleb is granted the opportunity to buy 100 shares of stock of Pfalz Corporation, his employer. Present value of Pfalz Corporation shares is $60 each and Caleb buys at that price, which is payable 25 percent down and the balance in installments—25 percent in each of the following three years—for which he signs a binding promissory note. By the time Caleb makes the final payment, the stock is worth $150 a share and he sells his shares at that price. He has a profit on the sale of $9,000, that is, $15,000 sales proceeds less his $6,000 cost. This profit is capital gain, and is all long-term, since his holding period began when he entered into the installment purchase contract. Caleb has no taxable compensation income, and there is no compensation expense deduction for Pfalz Corporation.

If the executive should be taxable on the installment purchase, either because the initial price was set below value at that time or because he was not personally obligated to buy, the company is allowed a compensation expense deduction. This deduction is taken in the year the executive realizes his taxable income (that is, in the company's tax year in which the executive's year ends), and in an amount equal to that income (but deduction for that amount plus other compensation to the executive cannot exceed reasonable compensation).

The company has no taxable gain or deductible loss with respect to its installment sale of its stock.

Installment purchases of stock are occasionally subject to federal margin limitations. These are rules designed to limit purchase of stock on credit. They apply only to stock traded on a national securities exchange and to certain stock traded over the counter (called OTC margin stock). This OTC stock is stock which the Governors of the Federal Reserve System have determined to have a degree of national investor interest. Thus, the limits don't apply to small or closely-held companies. A list of OTC margin stock can be obtained from any Federal Reserve Bank.

The margin rules would require the executive to make a substantial minimum downpayment for the stock, but the rules are eased for certain plans.

State law obstacles

Issuance of stock for services occasionally poses problems for the employer under state corporate law. While issuance of stock for services already performed presents little difficulty, issuance of stock for services to be performed in the future may violate state law. Three possible solutions to this problem are:

1. Issuance of shares which are not transferable by the employee until fully paid for through performance of services could satisfy local law requirements, but would be restricted stock, see Chapter 8.

2. A present contract calling for delivery of shares in the future, after the services have been performed, could also meet local

law requirements. This would be a deferred compensation arrangement, covered in Chapter 5.

3. Payment of compensation with treasury stock (stock which was lawfully issued and later repurchased by the corporation) would not violate local law.

In practice, stock is issued or paid for future services in practically every case, in the sense that the transfer of stock would not be made unless the company expected that the executive would continue to perform services for the company.

A company should seek professional advice on compliance with local corporate law requirements before adopting a plan to pay or sell stock to executives.

Accounting for stock plans

Stockholders and management occasionally voice concern about how plans for paying compensation in stock, or making bargain sales of stock, may affect the stock's earnings per share. Normally, the immediate tendency is to decrease earnings from an accounting standpoint. The value of the stock is an expense (decreasing earnings), unless the executive will pay an amount for the stock which equals its fair value (or its quoted market price if available) at the time the stock is offered to him.[5] Thus, it is an expense factor in direct payments and bargain sales of stock, but not in noncompensatory installment sales (or in the qualified stock options discussed in Chapter 9). This expense factor is somewhat offset by reduction of income tax expense, to reflect the compensation deduction for a stock payment or bargain sale. Still, the immediate net effect is an increase in expense and therefore a decrease in earnings.

---

[5] Such plans also reduce earnings per share by increasing the number of shares. This is also true of qualified stock options and noncompensatory installment sales.

The company, of course, expects that the executive recipients of compensatory stock, inspired by their new stock interests in the company, will soon drive company earnings up.

Stockholder pays executive in stock

It sometimes happens that stock is paid to the executive or sold to him at a bargain by a controlling or substantial stockholder rather than by the corporation itself. From a practical standpoint, it may be necessary to arrange this payment outside the corporation, because the corporation has no treasury or unissued stock, or because other stockholders will not agree to the payment, or because of some private agreement between executive and stockholder.

But payment of stock by a stockholder should be avoided wherever possible. It is of no tax benefit to the executive that he receives his stock from a stockholder rather than from the corporation. It is fully taxable ordinary income to him. It is not tax-exempt as a gift, because the stockholder expects value in return—the executive's services, enhancing the value of the stockholder's stock.

It is not yet certain that stock received from a stockholder would always qualify for the benefit of the 50 percent tax ceiling, described in Chapter 2. For employees, that benefit is limited to amounts received as compensation for personal services actually rendered, that is, services already performed. In practice, stockholders often pay stock to executives to induce them to render or continue to render services in the future. While the theory or intent of the 50 percent tax ceiling seems consistent with allowing its use here, such allowance might be prevented under a strict or literal interpretation.

The stockholder is not allowed a compensation expense deduction for the value of stock he pays the executive, since the executive's services are not rendered to him. He is treated as having made a contribution to the corporation's capital.

The corporation is allowed to deduct the payment, in the amount the executive must report as income, to the extent compensation to the executive is reasonable.

Any stockholder who intends to pay stock to an executive should inform company management of this fact so that the company will know when and how much it can deduct. The company would not necessarily learn of its deduction opportunity simply by learning that stock was transferred from stockholder to executive, since that could have been an ordinary sale. It can also be wise for stockholder and management to confer before the amount of stock to be paid is decided upon, to be sure that the executive's total compensation won't exceed reasonable limits. The fact that the stockholder gets no deduction, and that the executive might not qualify for the 50 percent earned income tax ceiling, are reasons to have the corporation make the payment wherever possible.

If the company lacks stock, it could purchase (redeem) some of the stockholder's stock. This ordinarily would result in capital gain (sometimes capital loss) to the stockholder, but he would also be collecting cash from the corporation, which does not happen, of course, if he is simply paying stock to the executive. There is a danger that his redemption will be taxable to him as a dividend instead of as a gain or loss. But the danger is slight if the only purpose for the redemption is to provide the corporation with needed stock, and especially if there are other large stockholders.

If the stockholder sells stock to the executive at a bargain (instead of simply paying it over to the executive), the executive presumably has taxable compensation income equal to the amount of the bargain and the company presumably deducts that amount, subject to reasonable compensation limits. But rules here are even less well developed than where the stockholder just pays over the stock. Thus, there are no specific rules governing tax treatment of the stockholder on such a sale. Also, it can occasionally happen that an executive will buy without suspecting he will be taxable—without knowing he is getting a compensatory bargain, in other words. For all these reasons, a sale of stock from stockholder to executive is risky from a tax standpoint and should be avoided wherever possible.

STOCK PURCHASE PLAN

_____ (hereinafter, the company), to encourage the purchase of common shares of its stock by selected employees, hereby adopts the following stock purchase plan:

1. Officers and other executive personnel (hereinafter, "executives") of this company, as designated by a committee consisting of the company's president and two other members of its board of directors, shall be eligible to participate in the plan. The number of shares to be issued to any executive under the plan shall be determined by the committee, but not more than _____ shares in all may be issued and not more than _____ to any individual.

2. The price at which the shares may be purchased shall not be less than the fair market value of such shares on the date the contract of purchase between executive and company shall be executed. The committee shall exercise due diligence in determining that value, and is hereby authorized to engage the services of professional appraisers and consultants in this effort, all reasonable costs of determining value to be borne by the company.

3. Each executive selected for participation in the plan shall be notified of his selection and of the number of shares which he may purchase under the plan. The executive may refuse to participate, or may agree to participate in full or as to a lesser number of shares (but not less than _____ shares). An executive choosing to participate shall enter into a purchase contract for his shares.

4. Payment for shares shall be made concurrently with the execution of the purchase contract, as follows: A check payable to the company representing not less than _____ percent of the purchase price, and a promissory note for the balance of the price, payable in quarterly installments (commencing _____ months after execution of the contract) of not less than _____ percent of such price at each installment date, with interest on any unpaid balance at the rate of 4% per annum.

5. Immediately upon receipt of payment of the purchase price as described above, title to the purchased stock shall pass to and vest in the executive purchaser. The executive shall have all voting rights with respect to such stock, and the right to all dividends thereon. However,

certificates representing purchased stock may be retained by the company as security for payment of the note.

6. The rights and obligations of executive and company under the purchase contract shall not be affected by termination of the executive's employment, for whatever reason, following execution of the contract.

chapter 8 Restricted stock and other restricted property

Companies often want to make strings-attached payments or sales to their executives. Thus, a company may want to give (or sell) stock to an executive now, but withhold from him the right to sell or vote the stock until some future date. In the usual case, full rights in the property are withheld as hostage for further performance of services. That is, the executive might be denied full rights to the property until he has worked an additional number of years in his executive capacity, or until some level of profits, sales, and so forth have been achieved. Failure to reach the desired goal could cause the executive to forfeit the stock or other property in question. Where the executive receives or buys stock or other property from his employer but acquires less than complete ownership of it at that time, he is said to have *restricted stock* or *restricted property*.[1]

There are no legal barriers to the use of restricted stock or other

---

[1] The practical effect of restricted property can be somewhat similar to the effect of deferred compensation discussed in Chapter 5. But the motivations behind the two devices differ: Restricted plans usually are designed to suit company business needs; deferred compensation plans are designed to suit the executive's tax situation.

property as a compensation device. Legally, it is no more alarming to make the executive's right to full ownership of property depend on satisfactory performance of his duties—as the company or the employment contract defines "satisfactory"—than it is to make his cash compensation depend on satisfactory performance. There is no legal objection to the fact that the stock or other property in his name or in his possession on restricted terms is taken from him if requirements for full ownership are not met. In fact, this forfeitability device is a sound arrangement to avoid complaints by stockholders against the board's sale or transfer of stock for an inadequate consideration. Issuance of stock for future services may violate state law. But issuance of restricted stock, to be earned in the future by performance of valuable services and which will be forfeited if such services are not performed, would normally not be illegal, though state law should be checked on this. Here, when the executive acquires full rights to the stock, he will have paid the full value, through the services he performed (plus the cash he paid, if any).

Restricted stock can be an unattractive compensation device from the executive's standpoint. Depending on how the deal is drawn, he can be subject to tax on the full, current value of the restricted stock or other property in the year he receives it, even though he is legally prevented from selling any of it to raise money to pay the tax. He therefore may have to borrow on or sell other assets to pay tax on stock which he might forfeit in a later year anyway.

For example, suppose Hesburg receives a bonus of 100 shares of his employer, Global Corporation. He cannot vote or collect dividends on these shares for three years. Global shares are currently selling at $120 on the market. Hesburg can be currently taxed on $12,000 (100 X $120), even though his shares are not worth $12,000 because he cannot vote or receive dividends on them. Or suppose he was given the opportunity to buy the shares at $40 and he did so. He would be taxable on $8,000 (100 × $120 minus 100 × $40) even though to him the bargain is less than that amount because he cannot vote or collect dividends on the shares.

Global can take a compensation expense deduction for the amount Hesburg is taxable on when he receives the stock, assuming Hesburg's total compensation is reasonable.

On the other hand, the company can design a payment or bargain sale of restricted stock or other restricted property so that the executive is not subject to tax on it until he acquires full rights to it. (If so, the company won't be able to take a deduction for the stock or other property until then.) To do this, it must make the executive's rights to the stock or property:

1. *Forfeitable,* that is, subject to a substantial risk of forfeiture (explained below) *and*

2. *Not transferable* by him free of such risk. That is, if the executive sells or gives the restricted item away, there must be a substantial risk that the recipient of the item will also forfeit the property because of the executive's failure to meet the conditions for full ownership.

When a risk of forfeiture is substantial depends on the circumstances of the case. Certainty is difficult in this area. But the company that wants an arrangement which will let its executives postpone tax would insert one of the following requirements:

a. Oblige the executive to return the property if he does not complete some additional period of substantial services, say, three years' full-time future services in his executive capacity. A requirement that he return the stock if he commits a crime would not be a substantial risk of forfeiture, nor would a requirement that he resell it at book value or other reasonable price on termination of employment.

In addition to the requirement of forfeiture if the executive fails to work for a particular period, there could be a forfeiture of the stock if the company fails to attain certain earnings goals or if the stock fails to reach a certain market or book value. Whether this particular risk is substantial will depend on whether, when the agreement is made, the possibility of forfeiture is significant or negligible.

b. Forfeiture if the executive joins a competing firm. In the author's view, this is often a distinct possibility, especially in certain industries, and so the risk of forfeiture could be substantial. But the Revenue Service is a bit more cautious here. Its position is that the risk generally is not substantial, but can become so in certain circumstances. The executive's age, skills and health are factors in determining how substantial the risk is.

In judging whether a risk is substantial, the terms of the contract are important but not decisive. The contract may reflect a substantial risk and yet the risk may in fact be slight, because of the relationship between executive and company. The Revenue Service is aware of this. It says that if an executive owns more than 5 percent of the company's stock, this will be a factor in deciding whether the risk is really substantial. In other words, where the executive is a more-than-5 percent stockholder, there is a somewhat larger danger that the risk will be considered insubstantial and the executive taxed immediately.

Besides providing the substantial risk of forfeiture, the company which wants to postpone tax on its executives must arrange that the stock or other property is not transferable by the executive free of the risk that his transferee will forfeit it. *This* risk of forfeiture would be tested under state law, not tax law. The requirement is met if the company has the right under local law to reclaim the property from the transferee because it was forfeited by the executive. This requirement is not hard to satisfy in practice where the restricted property is company stock, as it usually is. The company may simply type the relevant restrictions or provisions of the employment contract on the share certificate itself, or type a legend on it that refers to the contract and bars or limits transfer.

If both requirements—substantial risk of forfeiture and nontransferability free of risk—are met in the company's plan, the executive is not taxed when he gets the property (unless he elects to be taxed, see page 106). And the tax exemption continues until the property first becomes nonforfeitable (no substantial risk of forfeiture), or becomes transferable (free of risk of forfeiture) if that happens earlier. In normal practice, this will mean he continues tax-exempt until he acquires full rights to the property, and can sell it or part of it to raise the funds to pay his tax. But he could be subject to tax earlier if, for example, the company cancelled some requirement that had made the risk substantial, or cancelled some limitation on his transfer of it.

Example: Muncie is allowed to buy 200 restricted shares of his company's stock July 1, 1974. The shares are subject to substantial risk of forfeiture—they would be forfeited by him if he failed to serve full time as financial vice president for the next three years. The shares are also nontaxable, that is, the share certificates are stamped with evidence of the restrictions. In addition, no dividends are payable on the shares until the restrictions are lifted.

Unrestricted shares of the company are selling for $100 each, but Muncie is allowed to buy them at $10 each. Muncie is not taxable on his acquisition of the shares on July 1, 1974.

On July 1, 1977, the substantial risk of forfeiture terminates and Muncie acquires full rights to the stock. On that date, unrestricted shares are selling for $250 a share. Muncie therefore has $24,000 of compensation income at that time, that is, the value when restrictions end ($25,000) minus the amount he paid ($1,000).

Example: Torres is paid a bonus of 100 shares of his company's stock on November 1, 1974. He must return these shares if he leaves the company's employ. But for each year he remains employed by the company, he ceases to be obliged to return ten shares.

The payment of 100 shares on November 1, 1974 is subject to substantial risk of forfeiture. But on November 1, 1975, ten shares are not subject to substantial risk of forfeiture and the fair market value of 10 shares on that date is taxable to him then. On November 1, 1976, he is taxable on another ten shares, at their 1976 value, and so on.

Any dividend or other income the executive receives on the property while it is forfeitable and nontransferable is taxable to him as compensation income (not as dividends, rent, etc.). This means it is earned income and cannot be taxed at more than 50 percent.

When stock or other property is taxable, the amount on which the executive is taxed is the fair market value of the property, less the amount he paid, if any. In determining fair market value in any restricted property situation, disregard all restrictions except those which by their terms will never lapse. Thus, even though stock may be subject to restrictions which affect its value, the value of stock which is not subject to restrictions is used to figure the taxable amount, unless those restrictions are nonlapse restrictions.

For example, if his company's shares are trading on the market at $80, but he can only get $76 for his shares because of the restrictions on it, he is still taxable on $80. A value of $76 could be used instead only if the restriction, which reduces its value, is one which by its terms will never lapse. Such a nonlapse restriction is given a narrow definition by the Revenue Service. To qualify, the IRS says each of the following tests must be met:

1. The restriction must limit the executive's right to transfer the property—for example, it must require him to resell the stock to the company upon a certain event.

2. It must set a price for property which the executive would collect on resale, or a formula for determining the price. And

3. The restriction must apply to and be enforceable against any person to whom the executive transfers the property, except the company itself.

Thus, if the executive is required to offer the stock for resale to the company when he terminates his employment, at its book value on the date he gets it, and his executor must offer it for resale at that value if he dies while employed, the stock is subject to a nonlapse restriction. Furthermore, the value to be used in computing tax on the executive is the price at which he is to sell—here, the book value.

An obligation to resell the property at its fair market value at the time of the resale is not a nonlapse restriction; it would not affect the stock's value.

The author agrees with the IRS that tests 1 and 3 must be met, but not that test 2 (formula price) must be met. That is, a formula price would qualify, but other restrictions (instead of formula price) would also qualify. These would include: restrictions on the executive's rights to dividends on the stock and limits on the class of persons to whom stock can be transferred—such as members of the executive's family (to keep stock ownership within the family), individuals who are U.S. citizens or residents (to avoid loss of status as a *Subchapter S* corporation), or, in the case of professional service corporations, persons licensed to practice that profession (which in any case could be a requirement of state professional corporation law). The Revenue Service does not at present agree that any of these is a nonlapse restriction.

The executive who manages to obtain a reduction in present tax because a nonlapse restriction cuts the tax value of property he receives may be subject to another tax if that restriction should be cancelled by the company. For example, if the company should later cancel the executive's duty to resell at book value, the executive would then (with some exceptions) be taxable on the fair market value after the cancellation less its value immediately before the cancellation.

For some sizeable firms, the key obstacle to awarding restricted stock lies in the IRS stand that *investment letter stock* is not subject to a nonlapse restriction. Under federal law, stock in many cases cannot be offered for sale to the public unless the stock issue is registered with the Securities and Exchange Commission. Registration involves detailed public disclosure and is a costly and lengthy process. But the shares can be transferred to private investors or other holders free of registration if these holders do not sell them to the public. In such private issues, the company typically requires the holder to represent in writing that he holds stock for investment and not for resale. The practical effect of such a representation (the investment letter) and the other circumstances is that stock subject to the letter can't be sold to the public for a prolonged (though unspecified) period, but only to other private investors, unless the issue should at some time be registered. Investment letter stock is therefore valued in the market place at large discounts below the price of registered stock of the same company.

The IRS stand that this discount must be ignored when valuing letter stock paid to executives has been sharply attacked by tax practitioners. In the author's opinion, however, the IRS here is justified, in the sense that its position appears to reflect the will of Congress.

In the author's view, then, investment letter stock is at present a highly unfavorable compensation device from the executive's standpoint, since it subjects him to current tax on much more than the true or realizable market value of what he gets.

The executive whose tax is deferred because of risk-of-forfeiture and nontransferability clauses can elect to be taxed at the time he gets the property instead of when deferral ends, if he wishes. He would make such an election if he thought the property (usually, company stock) would be worth a lot more when the restrictions end. If his estimate proves correct, his election can save substantial tax. He will be taxed on a low value now, and will not be taxed again when restrictions end.

Example: Casey is paid 1,000 shares of restricted stock worth $20 a share, which Casey believes will be worth $200 a share when restrictions go off five years hence. If his estimate is correct, he will have $200,000 of fully taxable compensation income at that time. If he instead elects to be taxed now, he is taxed on $20,000 and avoids the additional potential tax at ordinary (compensation) rates on the $180,000 increase in value. Of course, he would be taxed on this appreciation at capital gains rates if he sells the stock for $200,000.

There is the obvious economic risk that the stock may have dropped in value when restrictions go off. There is also an important tax risk. If for some reason the executive should forfeit the stock, he cannot recoup the tax he paid on it. He cannot get a refund or claim a tax credit or deduction for this tax.

Thus, the decision to elect calls for close calculation, weighing the possibility of forfeiture against the prospect of capital gain. Forfeiture will be a serious possibility. Remember that the election opportunity does not arise unless there is already a substantial risk of forfeiture.

Usually, the executive himself is the best judge of the extent of that risk. The election decision cannot be made as well by tax, investment or other professional advisors. Nonetheless, the author inclines against such election as a general proposition. Besides the tax and economic risks just mentioned, the election involves a prepayment of tax which many executives find a hardship. Moreover, the tax advantage of capital gains in employment situations has lately been lessened, now that the tax ceiling on compensation, including compensation in the form of restricted stock, has dropped to 50 percent while the tax ceiling on capital gains has risen to 35 percent.[2]

Selling restricted stock or property

Once the executive has been taxed on the restricted property, he gets capital gains treatment if he sells it at a profit, and has a capital loss if he sells at a loss. Capital gain is tax-favored long-term gain if he held it more than six months from the time he received it to the date of sale. His gain is the amount he received less the sum of the amount he paid for the property (if any) and the amount he was taxed on.

Example: Crawford's company sold him 200 restricted shares for $80 a share when the market value was $110 a share. Since there was no substantial risk of forfeiting his shares, Crawford was taxable when he got them. And since there was no nonlapse restriction on the shares, they were valued for taxing purposes at their market value of $110. Crawford therefore was taxed on a bargain of $30 a share ($110 minus $80), or $6,000.

Two years later, when the restrictions are lifted, Crawford's stock is worth $195 a share, and he sells all his shares at that price. He has a long-term capital gain of $17,000, that is, $39,000 less the sum of the $16,000 purchase price and his $6,000 of compensation income.

If an executive forfeits property after being taxable on it, he would have a capital loss deduction for the amount he was taxed on (and the amount paid for it if any).

The executive may find a buyer for his restricted property even

---

[2] More details on these tax ceilings may be found in Chapter 2.

though it is still subject to substantial risk of forfeiture and is not transferable free of such risk. Here, he has not already been taxed on receipt of the property (unless he has elected to be taxed). Thus, on his sale of the property he is taxed on the sale proceeds less the amount he paid for the property if any. This amount is compensation income, not capital gain. If the sale is made to a relative or otherwise is not an arm's length sale, the executive would be subjected to tax again when forfeitability or nontransferability ends (or if there is an arm's length sale of the property), on the value (or selling price) of the property at that time minus the proceeds of his non-arm's length sale. (If the non-arm's length sale had been for more than the stock's fair market value at that time, which rarely happens, he would have been taxable then only on its fair market value less any amount he paid for it, and this fair market value would be treated as his sale proceeds in figuring his second tax.)

For long-term capital gain purposes, an executive's holding period generally begins when he becomes taxable on the property. But if he has elected to be taxed currently, his holding period begins when the property is transferred to him.

Company's tax treatment

The company is entitled to a compensation expense deduction for restricted property in the amount the executive is taxed on, assuming that amount represents reasonable compensation. The author believes that reasonableness should be judged as of the time the property was transferred subject to restrictions, and not as of the time the restrictions end. Thus, full deduction should be available even though the value ultimately realized by the executive may be much greater than when the property was transferred. But the Revenue Service has not yet taken a public stand on the point.

The company takes its deduction for the year the executive becomes taxable (technically, the company's taxable year in which the executive's year ends). Thus, if the company intends to postpone tax on the executive, it must be willing to accept postponement of its deduction. The postponed deduction will be a larger deduction if the stock or other property goes up in value meanwhile. Any dividend or other income the executive collects on the property which is compensation income to him (see above) is deductible as compensation by the company.

Assuming the company decided on a plan which postpones the executive's income, it should still require him to notify the company if he elects to be currently taxed on the restricted item. Without this notification, the company would not know when the executive realized his taxable income from the property, and so wouldn't know when to take its deduction.

For the same reason, the executive should be required to notify the company if he sells the property while it is still forfeitable and nontransferable and, if that sale was not at arm's length, of any later arm's length sale.

If the company takes a deduction with respect to stock or other property which the executive later forfeits, the company would then (when forfeiture occurs) report as ordinary income the lesser of:

1. The property's fair market value when forfeited less any amount paid at forfeiture, or
2. If it was the company's own stock, the amount it deducted.

The company's gain or loss from transactions in restricted stock or other restricted property is computed under the rules in Chapters 6 and 7.

chapter 9 How to use stock options

Economic and tax developments in the past few years have muted corporate board room enthusiasm for the stock option as a compensation device. For decades, it offered an unmatched fortune-building opportunity for executive personnel. The business press regularly reported stock option profits in the hundreds of thousands of dollars going to executives of well-known companies, such as Chrysler and Columbia Broadcasting.

Even today, many executives can benefit handsomely from stock options. But the tax and financial climate has changed. The executive's profit potential is less, especially in terms of after-tax profit. And companies have come to realize that their own true cost of stock options is greater than previously supposed. Reappraisal of stock option policy is in order.

What a stock option is

A stock option is an opportunity to buy stock at a set price, sometime in the future. It must be distinguished from an opportunity to buy stock directly and immediately (at a bargain or in installments, or both) under some form of stock purchase plan. The term *stock option* means the right or privilege to buy stock under an offer continuing for a stated period of time. Stock purchases not involving options are analyzed in Chapters 6 through 8.

As stock options are typically used in executive compensation planning, the company grants its executive employee an option to buy stock in that company. Both company and executive expect—or at any rate, hope—that the value of the stock will rise. If it does, the executive exercises his option and acquires the stock. He profits from the deal because the price he pays for the stock under his option is less than the stock's market value. If instead of rising in value the stock drops in value after the option is granted, the executive declines to buy the stock and allows the option to lapse. Thus, if this were all there was to it, a stock option would give the executive a chance at a stock profit, with no risk of loss.

This simple example is enough to show why executives might want stock options. (There are other reasons, as we will soon see.) But why did companies give stock options? There are several answers: For one thing, they were cheap. The stock may have cost the company nothing to create, or at least management could have looked at it that way. Yet the company could collect something for it on a sale to the executive. Second, the executives prized stock options above other forms of noncash compensation, because of their tax advantages. Third, it gave the executive a stake in the company. His stock ownership tied him more firmly to the company and increased his incentive to produce profits for the company which he now would share.

Each of these reasons served to encourage management to grant stock options to executive personnel. *And each of these reasons has been undermined by recent developments.* The combined effect of these developments should be to limit, though not necessarily eliminate, the use of stock options. Executive enthusiasm for stock options has lessened as tax advantages have narrowed and stock market profits languished. Worse, executives have not hesitated to sell their stock as profit opportunities arose, thereby cutting this particular tie with their companies, uprooting one more executive stake in the company's success and prosperity. Worse still, the company now must recognize that through the stock option it has surrendered to the executive an asset worth far more to it, the company, than it is to the executive.

For example, suppose a company lets an executive buy stock for $20,000 which the executive later sells for $120,000. The company collects the $20,000 paid by its executive, whose profit on the deal, after taxes, may be about $70,000. If there had been no stock option, and the company had sold the stock for $120,-000, it would have kept the entire amount, free of tax.[1] The stock option arrangement therefore had a true cost to the company of $100,000 ($120,000 minus $20,000), but was worth only $70,000 to the executive, obviously a very bad bargain for the company.

This is not to say that stock options are always and everywhere a bad deal for the company. There are several kinds of stock option which the company might choose; some are better (or less bad) than others. But the true cost to the company is so high that management must be convinced it is getting full value for its option. Generally speaking, stock options are worthwhile from a company's standpoint only in the following situations:

1. Where the option is needed to retain the services of a valued executive who would resign unless given the chance to acquire a share of the business. For this purpose, use either a *qualified stock option* or a *nonstatutory option,* described below.

2. Where the option is needed to stimulate an executive's productivity or cost consciousness by giving him a share of the

---

[1] A company pays no federal income tax on profits on its own stock.

profits. Use a qualified stock option here or, if a nonstatutory option is used, limit his power to sell the stock. (See below.)

3. Where the option is a device to float a new stock issue among employees, avoiding underwriters' costs. Use the *employee stock purchase plan option.*

4. In limited cases where the amount of intended cash compensation would be unreasonably large and nondeductible. Reducing cash compensation, substituting a qualified stock option, would avoid this difficulty. But a qualified stock option has only a potential value, not a present value when granted, so that some executives would reject it and insist on full payment in cash.

Qualified stock options

The executive employee who is given the opportunity to buy stock under what is known as a *qualified* stock option will enjoy two special advantages:

1. Even though he acquires stock at a substantial bargain, he generally will not be obliged to pay any tax on the stock until he sells it. For example, suppose Franklin, an executive with taxable income of $44,000 a year, is given an option to buy 100 shares of stock at $100 a share. At the time he exercises the option the stock is selling at $180 a share, so that he acquires stock worth $18,000 at a cost of only $10,000. The $8,000 bargain is not subject to tax while he holds the stock.

2. When and if he should decide to sell the stock, his profit on the sale can qualify for favorable capital gain treatment. Thus, if Franklin had sold the stock after a suitable holding period for $180 a share, his $8,000 profit would have been a capital gain. Franklin's tax on this gain would usually be $2,000, so he would keep $6,000 of his profit.

In short, the executive given a qualified stock option enjoys both postponement of tax and reduction of tax. Contrast this with the typical result where the option isn't a qualified stock option: Franklin is taxed in the year he buys the stock, not later when he sells it. And his tax is $4,000, not just $2,000, so that if he later sells the stock at $180 a share, he nets only $4,000 of his $8,000 profit.

The company must pay a high price, in real economic terms, to make tax postponement and capital gains benefits available to its executive. The company cannot take a tax deduction for an amount which the executive can treat as a capital gain. This means the company may not take any deduction with respect to the option. Furthermore, the company would be exempt from tax on its profits on its own stock. Thus, if it makes $8,000 of stock profits available to its employee through a qualified option, the true cost to the company is the full $8,000, even though the true value to the employee is only $6,000. Looked at another way, surrendering $8,000 of profits on its own stock is equivalent to surrendering $11,429 in typical company capital gains or $15,385 in typical company operating profits.

But unlike the rule with some employee benefits, such as profit-sharing plans and employee stock purchase plan options, a company which grants a qualified stock option is not obliged to make the option available to employees generally. The company may if it wishes limit qualified stock options to any employees it pleases, and therefore may restrict options to one or more selected executive employees. Such limitation will serve to keep costs of the plan relatively low.

Moreover, with a qualified stock option, there is no benefit of any kind to the executive unless the market value of the stock rises after the option is granted. This can benefit the company by spurring the executive to enhance the stock's value.

How to qualify a stock option: The qualified stock option is legally one of the most complex devices known to compensation planning and should be established only with the assistance of

a professional practitioner. These are the more important requirements for qualification:[2]

1. The plan to make stock options available must be approved
by the stockholders. It cannot be done by the board of directors
alone.

2. The price the employee is to pay for the stock cannot
intentionally be set at less than the stock's market value at the
time the option is granted. For example, if the stock is selling
on the market at $100 a share when the option is granted, the
executive cannot be given the right to buy it for less than $100
a share. (He may accidentally be given the right to buy for less
than $100. This could happen where the company is unaware of
the true value of the stock when it grants the option. The executive does not lose all the benefit of a stock option in this case,
but must pay a tax penalty which increases his true cost of the
stock. If the price to the executive was intentionally set below
the stock's value when the option was granted, all benefits of
status as a qualified option would be forfeited.) This rule means
that the executive will benefit from the option only if the stock's
value rises after the option is granted him.

3. The executive may not own more than 10 percent of the
company's stock, including the stock he acquires under the option. If the company's equity capital exceeds $1 million, the
amount he is permitted to own may be reduced to 5 percent of
the stock.

4. The executive cannot have the right to transfer the option
to another person during his lifetime.

5. Once the executive exercises the option and pays for the
stock, he must be given all substantial rights of ownership over
the stock. The company may not impose special limits on his right
to sell it, or to receive dividends on it.

---

[2] A sample qualified stock option agreement appears at the end of this chapter.

6. The executive loses the right to capital gain treatment unless he holds the stock for at least three years before he sells it. If he sells within three years of acquisition, his profit is fully taxable ordinary income in the year of sale and the corporation is allowed a tax deduction for that amount in that year. This is the only situation in which the company is allowed a deduction with respect to a qualified stock option. Unfortunately for the company, its deduction depends solely on the executive's decision to realize a present profit rather than risk a future drop in price. The company has no control over whether it will be allowed a deduction, or the amount of the deduction. The company should require the executive to inform it of any sale of company stock he makes within three years after acquiring it under the option, and the selling price, so the company will know when and how much it can deduct.

7. The qualified stock option device can be rendered practically unusable where the market price of the stock under option has fallen. For example, suppose on March 1, 1974 a corporation grants an executive an option, exercisable any time in the next three years, to buy 200 shares at $80 a share. On March 1, 1974, the stock is selling at $78. If the price should rise above $80, the executive will consider exercising his option; if not, he is not interested.

Suppose the price should drop to $70, but the company believes the drop is temporary and the price will soon rebound. It might want to cut the option price to, say, $72. But such a modification of the option would forfeit the special tax benefits (for the executive) of status as a qualified stock option, and it would be treated as a nonstatutory option. (See below.)

Also, the company would be unable to make a new qualified option available to the executive during the period that any unexercised part of a prior qualified option granted to him remains outstanding. Thus, so long as the March 1, 1974 option remains

unexercised—because the market price of the stock is below the
option price and there is therefore no profit in exercising the
option—qualified stock option benefits aren't available to that
executive under any new option, until the March 1, 1974 option
expires. Exercise of a new option while the prior unexercised
qualified option is still outstanding is subject to the rules governing nonstatutory options, below.

Suppose the company, foreseeing a possible market slide, wants
to offer the executive a choice of options. It will set up a qualified
and a nonstatutory plan, and let him choose between them. Thus,
it might let him buy up to 200 shares under the qualified plan,
at $80 a share (assume the stock's market value is $78 when the
plan is set up), or up to 200 shares at 95 percent of market value
at the time the option is exercised, under a nonstatutory plan.
If the stock's market value rose above $80, the executive would
exercise the qualified option, reaping a bargain equal to the spread
between market value and $80, plus hoped-for qualified option
tax benefits. If the market price fell, he could exercise the nonstatutory option, reaping a bargain equal to the spread between
market price and 95 percent of that price, plus the prospect of
further profit on a price rebound, but without the qualified tax
benefits. Any shares taken under one option would reduce the
number of shares available under the other option.

Though before 1973 the Revenue Service accepted the "qualified" option part of such "tandem" options as genuine qualified
options, its present position is that no stock issued under a tandem
option can be given qualified status. This tandem plan thereby
becomes a nonstatutory plan with alternative ways of determining
option price.

It is probably clear to the reader by now that the author is no
fervent advocate of the qualified stock option as a compensation
device. Its complexity and high cost to the company strictly limit
its usefulness to the situations set forth at pages 113 and 114.

Furthermore, its attraction to the executive has in recent years been dimmed by a slack stock market. But it must now be recognized that three tax reform rules recently enacted to discourage or penalize large profits in qualified stock option transactions are not significant deterrents to the use of such options.

One of these provisions is the addition of a special minimum tax on tax preferences, which defines the bargain element in a qualified stock option as a tax preference subject to this tax.

The minimum tax is sometimes spoken of as a tax of 10 percent on the amount of tax preferences. Viewed that way, an executive would seem to owe a tax of 10 percent of the amount by which the value of the stock he bought under his qualified option exceeded the price he paid for it. Thus, if he paid $50,000 for stock worth $120,000, he would owe a minimum tax of $7,000 (10 percent of $70,000) on the exercise of the option. But in fact the minimum tax applies only if tax preferences exceed the sum of a $30,000 exemption plus the regular income tax for the year, plus special tax carryovers from preceding years. These exemptions and qualifications mean that only in the rarest cases should the minimum tax discourage executives' interest in qualified stock options.

Somewhat more serious is the provision which limits the executive's use of the 50 percent maximum tax on earned (compensation) income where he has tax preferences, including the bargain element on exercise of a qualified stock option. The earned income which can benefit from this 50 percent tax ceiling is reduced by one dollar for each dollar of tax preference in excess of $30,000. Thus, if the executive exercised a qualified option at a $40,000 bargain, $10,000 ($40,000 less $30,000) of earned income, which would otherwise be taxable at no more than 50 percent, becomes taxable at the ordinary rates, up to 70 percent. This is a more severe tax detriment than the minimum tax because the tax here can be an additional 20 percent, instead of the ten percent of the minimum tax, and because the $30,000 floor is the only limitation on its application (unlike the minimum tax, which has several exemptions and qualifications). Even so, only a few executives will be affected. These will be executives whose earnings put them substantially above the 50 percent tax bracket. For example, a married executive filing a joint return is unaffected unless his salary and bonus exceed $52,000 after reduction for deductible job-connected expenses and a proportion of his other deductions (based on his outside income).

For those comparatively few executives who would be subject to these taxing provisions, advance tax planning can limit or eliminate the Reform Act's added tax. Thus, suppose an executive with a $120,000 salary (in the 64 percent bracket) has a qualified stock option on 500 shares. His option, granted 18 months ago, lets him buy the stock at $320 a share at any time during the next three years. He may exercise the option all at once, or in install-ments of not less than 50 shares each. The stock is currently selling for $520 a share.

If he exercises the entire option now, his bargain is worth $100,000, that is, $200 ($520 less $320) times 500. He will lose the right to claim the maximum tax on earned income, since the earned income qualifying for that tax benefit (the $68,000 in excess of $52,000) is entirely offset by the $70,000 of qualified option bargain in excess of $30,000. This increases his income tax by $5,520. In addition, he is subject to a minimum tax of $1,242 (10 percent of $100,000 less the sum of $30,000 and the $57,580 tax on $120,000).[3]

The entire $6,762 of tax cost—$5,520 plus $1,242—is avoided if the executive takes up only 150 shares this year. The bargain on this is $30,000, which does not cause reduction in earned income for maximum tax purposes or trigger a minimum tax.

---

[3] For simplicity, this example has assumed that the executive's salary equals his earned taxable income, and that he was subject to minimum tax in the preceding taxable year.

On the facts assumed, the remaining 350 shares remain open for exercise in a later year. There is no economic risk in postponing this exercise—just the opposite, since the executive has no commitment on them. But it, of course, postpones his stock participation in the company to that extent, and defers his opportunity to realize capital gains on the optioned stock, since he must own the stock for three years before capital gain treatment is allowed him on sale.

A third tax reform provision is the increased tax on capital gains. For many years, capital gains tax could not be more than 25 percent of the gain realized. But now this 25 percent tax ceiling applies only to the first $50,000 of gain for the year; the ceiling rises to 35 percent on gain in excess of $50,000. Thus, the maximum tax on $200,000 of capital gain has gone from $50,000 to $65,000. This provision for higher capital gains tax was also considered a deterrent to use of qualified options (though it applies to all capital gain, and not just gain on stock acquired in a qualified option). Yet it now appears that its impact on qualified options will be slight. Like the minimum tax, it only affects taxpayers in the highest tax brackets. Furthermore, it will apply only when capital gains are large (more than $50,000) and even here can be avoided by arranging stock sales so as to spread the receipt of the sales proceeds over two or more years; for example, by selling some shares this year and some next year, or by selling shares on the installment method. (Capital gains are another tax preference theoretically subject to the minimum tax, but the tax applies only rarely.)

Employee stock purchase plan options

The *employee stock purchase plan* option is not recommended as a device for compensating executive employees. Options of this type must be made available to employees generally (with limited exceptions such as for temporary or part-time personnel) and cannot be restricted to executives. Such options may still be a practical method of providing additional compensation where the permanent work force is small. But in most cases the cost to the company of using an employee stock purchase plan solely as a compensation device is prohibitively high.

However, such options are sometimes made to serve a two-fold function: to compensate employees, and to raise corporate capital. They were so used until recently by the American Telephone and Telegraph Co.

Principal features of the employee stock purchase plan are these:

1. The employee pays no tax on the option or the stock until he sells the stock. Profit on sale can be capital gain. The company generally is denied a tax deduction.

2. The employee's chance to profit on the stock need not be made to depend on a rise in stock value after the option is granted. The company can give the employee the right to buy stock for less than its market price at the time the option is granted. For example, the company can let the employee buy stock for $90 a share even though the stock is selling publicly for $100 at the time the option is granted.

3. If the company is issuing the stock to obtain needed capital, and not simply to compensate employees, the true cost to the company is the amount it collects from employees minus what it would collect from a public sale or through underwriters of a stock issue. Viewed from this perspective, the company's true cost of such a stock issue could be negligible.

Nonstatutory stock options

A nonstatutory stock option is less complicated and more flexible than other options. Such an option can be tailored by the company to achieve practically any desired balance of company vs. executive benefit. Generally speaking, the capital gains opportunities for the executive are less than with other options, and the true cost to the company is also less. The company has complete freedom to decide who can be given nonstatutory options (assuming stockholders and state law impose no special obstacles), so that nonstatutory stock options can be offered executives on terms which would be forbidden as unduly favorable in other option situations.

Typical nonstatutory stock option

Acme Corporation grants a nonstatutory stock option to select executive employees, including Freeman, one of its vice presidents. The option is granted February 1 and is to remain open for eight months. Freeman is given the opportunity to buy 1,000 shares at $95 a share. On February 1, the stock is selling publicly for $100 a share. Freeman exercises the option on April 20, when the stock is selling for $120 a share. Thus,he pays $95,000 and buys stock worth $120,000. He sells the stock for $135 a share the following January 12, at a profit of $40,000 ($135,000 minus $95,000).

In the usual situation, Freeman would be subject to tax on his purchase of the stock. The taxable amount in the year of purchase would be $25,000 ($120,000 minus $95,000), and it would be fully taxable at ordinary rates. The exact amount of tax paid would depend on Freeman's other taxable income. If that were $60,000, tax would usually be about $12,500; even with higher incomes, it would seldom be much more than this.

Freeman would also be subject to capital gains tax on his sale of the stock. Since he already paid a tax on $25,000 of profit, he is not again hit with a tax on this $25,000. His taxable profit in the year of sale is $15,000 ($135,000 minus $120,000). Capital gains tax on this would be about $3,750. In a transaction which yields an overall gross profit of $40,000, Freeman would keep about $23,750.

Acme Corporation would normally be allowed to take a tax deduction of $25,000, equal to the amount which Freeman must report as ordinary income. With this deduction, Acme's true cost of Freeman's first $25,000 of profit is $13,000. Acme cannot deduct the $15,000 which Freeman treats as capital gain, so that its true cost for this amount is the full $15,000.

The total actual cost to the company of surrendering $40,000 of profit to Freeman is $28,000, while the actual value of this to Freeman is $23,750. Many compensation planners would consider this a reasonable balance of company cost to executive benefit and would go ahead with a nonstatutory option that could be expected to produce this sort of result.

This approach assumes the executive holds on to the stock hoping for (and in this case actually realizing) a long-term capital gain on a later sale. But in fact, compensation planners have found that the executive often exercises the option only to sell the stock immediately thereafter. If no capital gain element is involved, the nonstatutory option becomes even more attractive to the company (and less attractive, of course, to the executive). Thus, if Freeman, in the above example, were to sell the stock immediately after exercising the option, the company's cost would be $13,000 while the value to the executive would be $12,500, for a net cost of $500 ($13,000 minus $12,500), or 2 percent of the $25,000 compensation amount.

The company's deduction is central to the growing interest in so-called "seesaw" or "yo-yo" options, which might otherwise seem overly generous to executives. Here, the company might grant its executive an option to buy 200 shares any time in the next three years. Suppose the stock is selling for $60 a share on the date the option is granted. Under the option, the price of the stock to the executive is reduced (below $60) by $1 for every $1 increase in market value over $60. Thus, if the price rose to $70, the executive could buy for $50. Here, the executive gets stock worth $14,000 ($70 X 200) for $10,000, and has $4,000 of ordinary income. The company only collects $10,000, but also has a $4,000 compensation deduction (equal to the executive's ordinary income), which is worth $1,920 (48 percent of $4,000) in income tax saved. A corporation in the 48 percent bracket will collect, through the executive's payment plus the tax value of the deduction, almost as much as if the stock had been sold on the day the option was granted ($12,000 versus $11,920). A company whose executives' efforts directly and conspicuously affect the market price of its stock may want to consider the seesaw device.

The company has the duty to withhold tax with respect to the bargain element in a nonstatutory option, just as it must withhold tax on his salary. The Government has not prescribed any particular method for withholding in this situation. One method would be to reduce the dollar amount of salary to be paid the executive (after regular tax withholding on that salary) by an additional amount representing the tax to be withheld on the bargain element of the option. Another method, where large amounts are involved, would be to have the executive pay the company the required withholding amount out of his own separate funds, which the company would use to cover its tax liability. If the executive will sell the stock immediately after exercising the option, the sales proceeds will provide the funds needed to cover the withholding obligation. But if he intends to keep the stock, or is *required*[4] to keep it at least six months under "insider's rules" of the Securities Exchange Act (which apply to officers, directors and more-than-10 percent shareholders of listed corporations and

---

[4] He is not technically forbidden to sell, but must turn over to the company his profits on trades within this six month period.

other corporations required to file reports annually with the SEC), he may have to borrow needed withholding funds.

Under one company's option arrangement, an executive may exercise some of his options, receiving stock, and at the same time surrender other options to the company for a cash sum based on the value of the option (the stock's market value less the option price). The cash received is taxable income just as the exercise of the option is. But the cash provides funds out of which to satisfy the tax withholding liability on the exercised option and on the cash.

Other nonstatutory options

A nonstatutory option could be varied in ways which could increase or decrease the relative attraction of the plan to either the company or the employee.

For example, it is possible (though perhaps not easy) to increase the capital gain potential for the executive, which will somewhat increase the option's true cost to the company. To achieve this, the option should have a clear, determinable market value when it is granted. It will not have such a value unless the company makes the option transferable by the executive. He must be allowed to sell it and the company must be willing to recognize any purchaser of the option as entitled to buy the underlying stock. It will help if there is a fairly active market in the stock, on a local or national exchange or over the counter. If the option has what tax regulations describe as a readily ascertainable fair market value when it is granted, the executive is taxable on the bargain element in the option when the option is granted, and not later, when the option is exercised. Most executives should prefer tax-at-grant to tax-at-exercise, since tax at grant normally means a smaller total tax—that is, less tax at ordinary rates and larger capital gains.

This can be seen in the Acme-Freeman illustration above. If

the option to Freeman had a readily ascertainable market value of, say, $6 a share when it was granted, Freeman would have $6,000 of ordinary compensation income at that point, and would pay a tax of $3,000 then. He would not be taxed at exercise of the option, and his additional $34,000 profit on sale ($135,000 minus the sum of $95,000 and $6,000) would be subject to a capital gains tax of about $8,500. Thus, he would keep $28,500 of his profit, or $4,750 more than if the typical nonstatutory option rules were followed. The true cost to the company would be correspondingly higher.

Nonstatutory options can also be tilted to favor the company. This is most often done by some provision that prevents the executive from acquiring full rights to the stock even after exercising the option and paying the price for the stock. One such provision would cause the executive to lose his rights to the stock if he quit or was fired before some specified future date. The usual consequence of such a restriction is to increase the tax on the executive (as compared to other nonstatutory options) and to decrease the true cost of the option to the company. In many cases, the executive will pay no tax until the year he acquires full rights to the stock, but at that point all his profit is fully taxable as ordinary income. He has no capital gain, and the company takes a tax deduction for the entire profit.

Applying this result to the Acme-Freeman illustration, Freeman's tax would be about $20,000 and he would keep $20,000 of his $40,000 profit. The company's true cost would be $20,800, a low cost.

The nonstatutory stock option is comparatively easy to establish, though the author recommends that a professional practitioner be consulted beforehand. The key features of a nonstatutory option are noted below:[5]

1. A nonstatutory option may be granted to anyone the com-

---

[5] A sample nonstatutory option agreement appears at the end of this chapter.

How to compensate executives

pany chooses. It can thus be granted to selected executives; it need not be made available to employees generally. It does not matter how much or how little stock an executive already owns.

2. Tax rules do not require that stockholder approval be obtained. (Of course, company by-laws, company policy, or ordinary prudence may require such consent.)

3. The executive may be given or denied the right to sell the option. He *must* be given this right if the company intends the option to have a readily ascertainable fair market value (and so increase the executive's capital gain opportunity). If the option has such a value, the executive has immediate ordinary compensation income at the time of the grant equal to the bargain element, whether he sells the option or exercises it himself. But his *later* profit, from selling the option or exercising the option and selling the stock, is capital gain.

4. Federal tax law sets no maximum or minimum price for the stock. Stock worth $100 a share can be optioned at $1 a share or less, if the company chooses.

5. The property subject to the option need not be stock in the company, but could be stock in some other company, or other property. Executives of a small company would especially welcome an option to buy nationally-traded stock at a bargain. The chief drawback from the company's standpoint is that it will often be obliged to pay a tax on transactions involving stock other than its own stock.

6. The company may prevent the executive from enjoying full rights to optioned stock, by imposing any restrictions it pleases (local law and by-laws permitting) on the executive's right to sell, pledge or vote the stock or to share in dividends. These restrictions will often postpone tax on the executive until the restrictions are lifted, but in so doing will reduce his capital gain opportunities and increase the company's deduction.

7. There is no minimum period the executive must hold the

stock, but he can't qualify for favorable capital gains rates on the stock unless he holds it for more than six months. (An executive who sells the option must have held it more than six months to get capital gain benefits.) In very rare cases, capital gains in nonstatutory option situations may be subject to the minimum tax on tax preferences, but this tax does not apply to any other profit or bargain element of nonstatutory options.

8. Unlike qualified options, the nonstatutory option device can be fully effective as an executive inducement even during stock price doldrums. For example, suppose Clifford was granted a 5-year nonstatutory option to buy 200 shares at $95 when the stock was selling at $98, but before he could act on it the price fell to $89. Clifford, of course, has no incentive to pay $95 for stock selling at $89. But the company could modify the option, or grant a new option, to buy at any lower price, say, $86, thus restoring its effectiveness.

Or, instead of modifying the option price or issuing a new option, the company could cover the possibility of a market decline by allowing the executive to buy at some percentage, say, 90 percent, of the stock's market value at whatever time, during the period the option is open, he chooses to exercise it.

9. With a nonstatutory option, the executive has the power to choose when to realize his compensation income under the option. For example, if the option price for 200 shares is $80 a share and the stock is selling at $150 in December 1974, the executive can choose to exercise the option and take his $14,000 of compensation income either in December of 1974 or January of 1975 (assuming no drop in market price). The power to control the timing of income is unavailable in some other executive compensation situations, such as current bonuses or deferred compensation, and is therefore a factor favoring nonstatutory options over these other compensation devices from the executive's standpoint. (The company, of course, has no deduction until the execu-

tive exercises the option—which puts the timing of this significant deduction item outside company control.)

The author considers nonstatutory options somewhat more
desirable to the company than other stock options, in those relatively limited situations where stock options can be justified at
all. Benefits to the executive are less liberal than under other
options, but should be satisfactory.

For interest-free or low-interest company loans to enable executives to exercise their stock options, see Chapter 13.

SAMPLE QUALIFIED STOCK OPTION AGREEMENT

AGREEMENT made and entered into as of the _____ day of
_____, 19__, between _____, a _____ [state] corporation, hereinaf-
ter called the Company, and _____, hereinafter called the Employee.

Whereas, the Company having determined that its interests will be
advanced by enabling selected employees to acquire a proprietary interest in the company, and as a further incentive to such employees to
promote the Company's interests,

Now, therefore, in consideration of the premises, the parties agree
as follows:

1. The Company hereby grants to the Employee, as a separate inducement and not in lieu of salary or other compensation, the right and
option to purchase _____ of its common shares at _____ a share,
under the terms hereinafter provided.

2. This option may be exercised by the Employee during the period
of his employment, as to not more than _____ [¼ of total] at any time
after _____, not more than _____ [½ of total] after _____, not more
than [¾ of total] after _____, and as to the total _____ of such shares
after _____.

3. The Employee exercises the option by written notice to the Company, which notice shall specify the number of shares to be purchased,
and which shall be accompanied by a check in full payment of the option
price for such shares; and until such payment the Employee shall have
no rights as shareholder in the optioned shares.

4. This option shall be exercised only by the Employee during his
full-time employment with the Company and shall terminate forthwith
upon his separation from service, through resignation, death or otherwise, and in any case shall terminate not later than _____.

5. This option shall not be exercised while there remains outstanding
any option previously granted to the Employee.

6. The Employee agrees that all shares purchased by him under this
option are acquired for investment and not for distribution, and that
each notice of exercise of the option shall be accompanied by a written
representation, signed by him, to that effect.

7. To the extent that the number of common shares in the company

shall be increased or reduced because of the distribution of a dividend payable in shares, a split-up, or the like, the number of shares subject to this option shall be adjusted proportionately.

8. This option is granted pursuant to the terms of the plan adopted by the Company's Board of Directors on _____ and approved by the Company's shareholders on _____, which plan stated that _____ [number] common shares may be issued under the option plan, allocated in such proportion as the board of directors shall determine, among three (3) officers of the Company including the Employee hereinabove named.

IN WITNESS WHEREOF, the parties hereto have caused the agreement to be executed on the day and year first above written.

_____ Corporation

by _____

[title]

Attest:

_____

Secretary   Employee

SAMPLE NONSTATUTORY STOCK OPTION AGREEMENT

AGREEMENT made and entered into as of the _____ day of _____, 19__, between _____, a _____ [state] corporation, hereinafter called the Company, and _____, hereinafter called the Employee.

Whereas the Company having determined that its interests will be advanced by enabling selected employees to acquire a proprietary interest in the company, and as a further incentive to such employees to promote the Company's interests,

Now, therefore, in consideration of the premises, the parties agree as follows;

1. The Company hereby grants to the Employee, as a separate inducement and not in lieu of salary or other compensation, the right and option to purchase _____ of its common shares at _____ a share, under the terms hereinafter provided.

2. This option may be exercised by the Employee, in whole or in part, at any time within a period of 10 years from the day and year first above written.

3. The Employee exercises the option by written notice to the Company, which notice shall specify the number of shares to be purchased, and which shall be accompanied by a check in full payment of the option price for such shares; and until such payment the Employee shall have no rights in the optioned stock.

4. The Employee may transfer or assign the option herein granted, in whole or in part. Should the Employee make such a transfer or assignment, he agrees to give prompt notice thereof to the Company.

5. The Employee agrees that all shares purchased by him under this option are acquired for investment and not for distribution, and that any notice of exercise of the option shall be accompanied by a written representation, signed by him, to that effect.

6. The Employee agrees to promptly notify the Company of any and all sales made by him of shares acquired under this option, and of the amount of sales proceeds received therefor.

IN WITNESS WHEREOF, parties hereto have caused the agreement to be executed on the day and year first above written.

_____ Corporation

by _____

[title]

Attest:

_____   _____

Secretary   Employee

chapter **10 Executive expense accounts**

Some laymen hold the view that the expense account is the executive's tax-free passport to a life of luxury. This is definitely not the case. Expense accounts have a useful role to play in business life, but they should not be accounted a major element of the executive compensation package.

Expense accounts in recruitment and retention

A liberal expense account policy can help attract prospective executive employees. Most executives will expect to incur some entertainment expenses on their company's behalf, such as lunch with a client, and many must do occasional or frequent traveling. The executive will welcome the assurance that he need not bear any of these costs out of his own salary, that his company will cover all proper charges for meals in comfortable surroundings, for first-class hotels and plane accommodations, and so on.

The company that can offer the prospective executive employee a generous expense account has an advantage over other possible employers. And it takes something extra to attract an executive who already enjoys a liberal expense account.

To underscore the attractive power of the liberal expense account, one tax advisory publication poses this example: Two companies are competing for Brown's services. One offers him a $35,000 salary. The other offers him $30,000 and a $5,000 expense account. Assuming he will actually incur $5,000 in expenses in either job, which arrangement should he choose? The tax advisory service suggests the $30,000 + $5,000 job. Since the net income would be the same in either case, the chief attraction of the expense account arrangement is one of convenience. There would be no tax withholding on the expense account, and tax reporting of disbursements would be less detailed. But there are also small practical tax advantages in the expense account job. There, the executive is more likely to be able to establish to Revenue Service satisfaction that all his expense account items were business outlays, and that none were personal items generating taxable income. Thus, Jones of Ecks Corporation and Smith of Wye Corporation may incur exactly the same $5,000 of expenses. Jones has a salary of $30,000 and a $5,000 expense account. Smith has a $35,000 salary and pays his own expenses. It is more likely that the $5,000 covered by Jones's expense account will pass IRS review than the $5,000 deducted by Smith. The IRS might bar Smith's deduction for, say, $800 of his $5,000 outlay, so that Smith is taxable on $800 more than he actually has—an additional tax burden of about $250. Such a tax hardship for the executive whose costs are not covered by a company expense account or reimbursement arrangement could arise, for example, where the job involves travel abroad.

The IRS audit of Smith's deductions might arise as the result of a refund claim by Smith. Tax would have been withheld on Smith's entire $35,000, so his $5,000 deduction for business expenses could mean that he has overpaid his tax through withholding.[1] He would claim a refund of the overpaid tax, which could trigger an audit.

Another tax advantage of an expense account arrangement lies in the fact that expenses covered by an expense account are deducted in computing adjusted gross income. They are not itemized deductions. Thus, an executive can deduct such expenses and still claim the standard deduction. Most executives itemize anyway, so that this rule will make no difference. But it can mean a small tax saving for some executives (usually unmarried executives) who pay less than $2,000 in state and local taxes and other deductible items.

Expense account planning

Our concern in this chapter will be with planning how the company should set up its expense account for maximum advantage and protection for both company and executive.

Proper expense account planning must reflect awareness of these two rules: (1) company payment of an executive's personal expenses is taxable income to him, and (2) company payment or reimbursement of expenses the executive incurs on the company's behalf is normally tax-exempt to him. Depending on circumstances, tax exemption is achieved directly through being excused from reporting company-paid sums as income, or indirectly, through reporting such sums but taking an offsetting deduction.

From the executive's standpoint, the goal is to avoid having company payments treated by the Revenue Service as payments of his personal expenses, which will result in taxable income to him. The IRS should be convinced that all outlays were for business reasons on the company's behalf.

The company, for its part, will also want to prove that its

---

[1] In some cases, he could claim additional withholding allowances for his itemized deductions. These reduce tax withholding.

outlays were for business reasons and so are deductible. Technically, its motive need not always be the same as its executive's.
A payment of the executive's personal expenses is deductible by
the company as a compensation expense (if compensation is reasonable); the company need not prove the outlay was for business
entertainment or business travel. But as a practical matter, companies try to establish the business entertainment or travel aspect
to spare tax difficulties for their employees. This chapter therefore
will explore what expense account policies a company should
adopt to assure full tax deduction for all its outlays while at the
same time assuring tax exemption on those outlays for its executives.

What travel expenses can be covered

An expense account can properly cover the following travel
expenses:

1. Transportation costs from the home area to the away-from-
    home business location, such as plane, train or boat fare, or
    car rental
2. Meals and lodging while away from home on business
3. Transportation costs (cab fares or car rental costs), between
    airport or station and hotel, and between hotel and the busi-
    ness location, or between business locations
4. Cleaning and laundry costs
5. Baggage charges
6. Tips incident to any of these items

What entertainment expenses should be covered?

With entertainment expenditures as with travel expenses, the
company wants to be certain that the executive's outlays which

it covers or reimburses through the expense account device will be deductible as entertainment expenses. Executives should therefore be carefully instructed as to the ingredients of a deductible entertainment expense, so that they will know exactly what outlays they can make that will be deductible by the company and tax-free to them. The following material shows the categories of entertainment activities a company can authorize the executive to engage in with reasonable confidence that deduction and tax exemption will be available.[2]

"Directly related" entertainment: What is meant here is an outlay where: (*a*) the executive (on the company's behalf) expected to derive income or some other specific business benefit (not just goodwill) in the future, (*b*) business with the person being entertained was actually engaged in during the entertainment, and (*c*) business rather than entertainment was the dominant aspect of the meeting. This would recognize entertainment taking place at sporting events, night clubs, and so forth, if business is actually seriously considered during the entertainment. It would also recognize the costs of meals or drinks at home or in restaurants or bars, with the same business aspect (though cost of meals is deductible in other settings as well, and without the need for actual business discussion, see below). Business need not actually result, as long as it is seriously discussed.

The executive should be discouraged from expense account entertaining at cocktail parties or other gatherings where persons other than business contacts are present, since their presence would prevent or inhibit business discussion. Deduction would not be allowed unless business is actually discussed, and IRS

---

[2] We will not be concerned here with the detailed tax rules on entertainment expense deductions. The material given here is to indicate what entertainment expenses should properly be included in an executive's expense account. A readable account of the entertainment expense rules can be found in the Revenue Service publication *Tax Guide for Small Business.*

suspicions would be aroused by the presence of nonbusiness guests.

"Associated with" entertainment: Entertainment which precedes or follows a substantial business discussion would qualify. This rule contemplates the situation where, after a business discussion with a customer, prospect, or other business contact, the parties break off for entertainment. Costs of entertainment provided before or after a serious business discussion are deductible even though no business is considered during the entertainment. Ordinarily, outlays for entertaining the wife (or husband) of the business contact in the same gathering (and the executive's own wife, if other wives are there) are part of the deductible expense. Entertainment may take place anywhere—in the home, at sporting events, night clubs, theaters, restaurants, or elsewhere.

Example: Baker, sales V.P., is conducting negotiations with Whitlock, purchasing manager of a prospective customer from out of town. Following business discussions during the day, Baker, Whitlock, and their wives go out for drinks, dinner, and a hockey game, all at Baker's expense, borne by his company. The costs of these evening activities are deductible entertainment expenses even though no business is discussed. Baker could be properly authorized to incur such expenses under his expense account arrangement.

"Quiet" business meals: This recognizes the entertainment expense status of meals or drinks furnished "under circumstances generally considered to be conducive" to a business discussion. It is not necessary that business discussion actually take place or even be contemplated. It is necessary that the surroundings be appropriate to business discussion (a night club ordinarily would not be), and that the person being entertained has a significant business relationship to the company bearing the entertainment expense. Thus, the executive could be authorized under his ex-

pense account to take a regular customer to drinks or dinner, as a gesture to retain his goodwill, and without any need to discuss business. But reciprocal arrangements, where business associates alternate in picking up the tab for drinks or meals, would not be qualified entertainment.

The meals or drinks could take place in public restaurants and the like or in the executive's own home.

The executive's expenses: In all the situations set forth above, the executive's own expenses, his own meals or entertainment costs, are deductible by the company and not taxable to him, assuming the entertainment has business motivation.

Too luxurious?

The Revenue Service bars deduction for expenses of "lavish and extravagant" travel or entertainment. That is, deduction is denied to the extent that travel or entertainment is lavish or extravagant. This would suggest that the reasonable part of any outlay is deductible but that any more than that would be lavish and extravagant. The company could not deduct the entire sum, but only the dollar cost of reasonable accommodations or services. The executive enjoying the lavish and extravagant accommodations could also be required to report as taxable income (without offsetting deduction) the part the company could not deduct. The justification for taxing him would be that the lavishness and extravagance was probably incurred for his own gratification and lacked a business excuse. It would therefore be a company payment of an employee's personal expenses.

So much for what the law says and what professional practitioners might surmise about it. In fact, however, there is no recorded case or ruling holding any outlay to be nondeductible (or taxable) as lavish and extravagant. Just the reverse.

The Revenue Service says that expenses are lavish and extravagant if they are unreasonable, considering all the circumstances. But they are not lavish and extravagant just because they are for de luxe accommodations in a restaurant, hotel, night club, or resort.

This indicates that unless the amount spent is really ridiculous, it is deductible (assuming an adequate business connection). Haute cuisine at the town's grandest restaurant, a de luxe room at its finest hotel, the limousine between airport and hotel and between places where business is conducted, all would seem acceptable, under the present IRS position.

But this also indicates that the tax rules cannot be relied on to control or set a business standard for company spending. Management must decide on its own what it can reasonably afford to pay, consistent with executive comfort and company prestige. Decision-making here is an ongoing process, as travel and entertainment costs rise.

Club dues and expenses

In most cases, it will not be desirable to have the expense account cover an executive's costs of membership in a social or athletic club.

Membership or initiation fees are not deductible at all, if the membership lasts beyond a year.

Periodic dues or fees also are not deductible at all unless more than 50 percent of the executive's use of the club is for business purposes. Detailed records must be kept of the executive's use of the club. And even if the club is used more than 50 percent for business, the company deducts only that portion of the dues which is allocable to directly related entertainment and quiet business meals.

Amounts spent at the club for entertainment are deductible under the general entertainment expense rules already discussed.

For example, greens fees and caddy fees and tips of a round of golf are deductible if business is discussed. Costs of meals or drinks at the club, or of other club activities, could be deductible if they precede or follow substantial business discussion. And meals or drinks at the club could be deductible under the quiet business meals rule even though no business discussion takes place. These deductions are allowed whether or not club dues are deductible.

Dues and fees to businessmen's lunch clubs are normally exempt from the above rules on social clubs. They are deductible as ordinary business expenses and are not thought of as entertainment outlays. The dues are therefore often paid directly by the company, and would not be part of the expense account.

Such clubs are conducive to business discussion, so that meals or drinks furnished there would properly be part of an expense account arrangement, under the *quiet business meal* rule.

Business gifts

In the author's opinion, gifts to business contacts should come directly from and be paid for by the company; they should not be part of the executive's expense account. But some exceptions to this position can be justified: Gifts of candy or flowers to the wife of a business contact could appropriately be an expense account item. So could gifts of tickets to some entertainment activity which the executive himself will not attend.

Deduction for business gifts generally cannot exceed $25 per recipient, which should serve to keep expense account charges within bounds. Deduction for gifts of tickets can be taken either as entertainment expenses or as gifts. As entertainment expenses, they can exceed the $25 ceiling applicable to gifts, if they qualify under the *associated with* rule. But as gifts (subject to the $25 limit) they would not need to meet any of the entertainment tests.

A gift to the wife of a business contact is normally counted as a gift to her husband, in figuring the $25-per-recipient ceiling.

Record-keeping and substantiation of expense account charges

Company expense account policy is to make sure that it can deduct expense outlays and that its executives are not taxable on these amounts. Therefore the company should adopt procedures for full executive accounting to the company for travel, entertainment, and business gift expenditures. The material below sets forth what records and substantiation are needed.

If record-keeping and substantiation requirements are met, the executive is excused from the need to prove independently to a Revenue Agent that he is not taxable on a company payment or reimbursement of his expenses. Also, these records and supporting documents will give the company the materials it needs to satisfy the IRS that items labeled as travel, entertainment, or business gift expenses were actually that, and deductible as such, and not nondeductible dividends or unreasonable compensation.

The executive is excused from the need to include expense allowances or reimbursements in his income or otherwise report them on his return if: (*a*) the expenses equal the allowances or reimbursements, and (*b*) he is required to and does make an accounting to the company for receipts and outlays. The elements of a proper accounting are the records and substantiation set forth below.

Entertainment expense records should show:

1. The amount of each separate outlay for entertaining, except that such incidental expenditures as taxis and phone calls can be totalled on a daily basis. Tips may be recorded separately or included in the cost of the service rendered.

2. The date of the entertainment.
3. Name, location, and type of entertainment (dinner, theater, and so forth).
4. Reason for entertainment or nature of business benefit derived or expected and, except for business meals, the nature of any business discussion or activity. And
5. Data on person entertained which will establish his business relationship to the company: occupation, name, title, and so on.

For "associated with" entertaining, which precedes or follows substantial business discussion, instead of the information in (4) above, the records should show: the date, duration, location, and nature of the business discussion, the business reason for the entertainment or the business benefit derived or expected, and all persons entertained who participated in the business discussion. (The records for such entertaining would also cover items (1)–(3), and (5).)

Travel expense records should show:

1. The amount of each separate outlay for travel away from home (such as transportation or hotels), but the daily cost of incidental items may be aggregated and set forth in reasonable categories such as: meals; gasoline and oil; cab fares. Tips may be recorded separately or included in the cost of the service rendered.
2. Dates of departure and return home for each trip, and the number of days spent on business away from home overnight.
3. Destination or locality of travel, described by name of town or the like.
4. Business reason for the travel or the nature of the business benefit derived or expected.

Records of business gifts should show:

1. Cost of the item given.
2. When the gift was made.
3. Reasons for the gift or nature of business benefit derived or expected.
4. Data on person to whom gift was made which will establish his business relationship to the company: occupation, name, title, and so on.

Substantiating expense account records

The elements of travel, entertainment, or gift expense must be substantiated. This is done by an account book, diary, company expense statement, or similar record, whose entries are made at or near the time the outlay was made.

In addition, receipts, paid bills, or other similar documentary evidence is required for lodging away from home (regardless of amount) or for any other outlay of $25 or more, except that documentation is not necessary for a transportation expense where evidence of the cost is not readily available. Documentary evidence, where required, should show amount, date, place, and character of the expenditure. (A cancelled check alone would not be enough.) A hotel bill should show lodging, meals, and telephone charges separately.

Substantiation unnecessary for certain per diem and mileage allowances

Executive and company are excused from the need to provide the substantiation described above (account book, for instance, and documentation) for travel expenses in these situations:

a. The executive receives a per diem allowance of not more than $36 a day. This allowance would cover meals, lodging, laundry and similar items, and related tips; amounts for transportation (air fares, cab fares, and so on) could be covered outside the per diem. An employee who is "related" to his employer (that is, a more than 10 percent stockholder of a corporate employer or certain close relatives of an individual employer) would have to substantiate in any case; the per diem exemption would not apply to him.

b. The executive receives a mileage allowance of not more than 15 cents a mile. Substantiation of such mileage allowances isn't required even if employee and employer are "related." An executive may be given both per diem and mileage allowances or only one of these.

Companies which wish to ease the tax reporting burdens for themselves and their executives should adopt per diem and mileage policies, assuming they can be economically justified. The release from the substantiation requirement does not affect the company's duty to retain the travel expense records on time, place, and business purpose (travel expense items (2)–(4) on page 145). The amount of the expense would be the per diem and mileage allowances it pays.

Technically, an executive or other employee receiving a per diem or mileage allowance must report for tax purposes the excess of the amount he receives over his actual outlays. This would of course require him to keep a record of his outlays. In practice, the Revenue Service does not seem to require this reporting for the per diems and mileage allowances described here. Thus, in practice, records of outlays apparently are not necessary.

The company is expected to police the executive's expense account reporting, through "proper internal controls." Some responsible employee other than the executive himself must verify and approve the expense account.

According to the Revenue Service, the per diem allowance

given should be based on reasonable estimates of actual current costs in the localities where they are incurred. The idea behind this long-standing rule is that $36 may be a proper per diem in one area while $25 may buy the same accommodations and services in another area. In the author's opinion, the rule should now be considered inoperative because of inflation—that $36 is hardly likely to be an unreasonably high estimate of current costs of meals and lodging anywhere in the United States. (For travel abroad, higher per diems are allowed, up to those the U.S. government pays its employees for travel in the area.)

Companies which think a $36 per diem too little for travel in particular areas in the United States should apply for IRS approval of a higher rate. Requests for approval should give detailed information about the allowance to be paid, with the reasons why the company's situation justifies a higher rate. Address requests to: Commissioner of Internal Revenue, Attention: Income Tax Division, Washington, D.C. 20224.

What revenue agents check for

Revenue agents checking a company's travel and entertainment expense deductions are said to check these items specifically:

1. Was the entry made at or near the time the outlay was incurred (a substantiation item)?

    If it was a travel expense, who traveled? If it was an entertainment expense, who was entertained?
2. Where did the deducted event take place?
3. What was the business purpose?
4. Was the outlay in cash or by check? (This is a substantiation check, looking to the verifiability of the cost.)

5. Is there a receipt or other documentation, where such is
    necessary (another substantiation check)?
6. Is the person who incurred the outlay a stockholder? (This
    is essential only to per diem items of $36 or less, and is
    therefore a substantiation check. But the check is also part
    of an inquiry as to whether the outlay was for a business
    purpose or was a nondeductible personal purpose of a stock-
    holder.)

Expenses outside the expense account

Some firms find it unreasonable to try to cover every executive
entertainment outlay under its expense account policy. In some
businesses (advertising and public relations are examples), entertainment situations could be so numerous, or so widely varied,
as to resist codification in a company program or policing through
company accounting procedures.

A frequent solution is for the company to adopt an expense
account policy covering certain limited, easily definable expenses.
The company then instructs the executive that while many other
entertainment outlays are proper and encouraged, they will not
be covered by the company. Instead, the executive's salary is set
at a level intended to enable him to bear needed entertainment
outlays outside the expense account.

Reasonable, so far. The company has assured its own deduction: The easily defined expense account outlays will be adequately accounted for and deductible as entertainment expenses.
And the executives' salaries will be deductible as compensation
expenses. The executive will be tax-exempt on the expense account outlays. But he will have to be able to establish to Revenue
Agents his right to deduct entertainment expenses he bears out
of his own pocket (that is, out of the salary that was augmented

to cover his entertainment outlays). In other words, the company has shifted from itself to the executive the entire burden of accounting for entertainment expenses outside the expense account.

The company can ease this burden, without any cost or inconvenience to itself. A key difficulty when executives try to deduct entertainment expenses is the frequent Revenue Service claim that the deduction properly belongs to the company on whose behalf the outlay was made. For the executive to deduct them, he must show that they are expenses of his business as a company executive. The company can help here. It can clearly proclaim that its executives are expected to incur substantial entertainment expenses which are intended to be covered by their salaries and for which no company reimbursement will be made. The statement could be in an employment contract or other official company document circulated to executives involved and preserved in company records. A sample statement appears on the next page. Executives whose deductions are questioned can then produce such a statement to help establish that their outlays were required by their business.

MEMORANDUM FROM_____CORP. PRESIDENT TO
ALL CORPORATE OFFICERS

For guidance of_____Corp. officers, I wish to state company policy regarding reimbursement of entertainment expenses:

Executives of this company are expected to exercise initiative in promoting company objectives. Salary has been computed taking into consideration that the executive will incur expenses of a kind intended to benefit the company, but which will not be reimbursed by the company.

The company will reimburse costs of transportation, and related meals and lodging, on company business. It will also reimburse costs of lunches with present clients or customers of the firm, where business is conducted during lunch.

The company will not reimburse any other expenditures for entertainment of or gifts to present or prospective clients or customers.

chapter 11 Providing health care coverage for the executive and his family

Experienced compensation planners have learned that executives face a special handicap when trying to deal on their own with family medical and dental bills. Many executives find that the real cost of health care is higher for them than it is for rank-and-file employees.

Tax deductions reduce the true cost of medical care. If a $42,000 a year executive could deduct $1,200 of medical expenses, the real cost of medical care to him would be about $660. But in fact, few executives can deduct their dental and medical bills. This difficulty is an unwelcome by-product of their high salaries. An individual can deduct only the amount of his medical and dental bills which exceeds 3 percent of his income. Thus, the higher a person's income, the less chance he has of taking a tax deduction for his medical and dental expenses. The high-salaried executive therefore must bear, out of his own pocket, a larger share of his and his family's medical costs than other employees do.

Wise compensation planning on the part of company personnel officers or other management decision-makers can overcome this difficulty. The company can set up a plan to pay or reimburse the medical and dental bills the executive incurs for himself and his family. This can be accomplished at no tax cost to the executive and at comparatively low cost to the company. Specifically, the amount the executive receives from his employer to cover medical or dental outlays for himself and his family is exempt from income tax, while the company takes an income tax deduction for the full amount of medical or dental bills it pays or reimburses.

There is no requirement that the executive's sickness or injury be work-connected, though the company can insert this limitation if it wishes (very few do). The company may limit coverage under the plan to executives as a class, or to particular executives, or otherwise, as it chooses. This can keep total costs relatively low. Moreover, it may fix a dollar ceiling on the amount or type of expense which it will reimburse, to keep costs lower still.

From an economic standpoint, a plan to reimburse the executive's medical expenses should be preferred to simply increasing his salary by the amount of his medical bills. Though a salary increase would not affect the before-tax or after-tax cost to the company, the added salary would be subject to tax in the executive's hands, at his own high tax rates. The amount of the tax would reduce the amount of funds available to cover medical bills.

Example: Howard earns a salary of $60,000 a year, and has $5,000 of dividends and other taxable income. Family medical and dental bills total $1,800 a year, but Howard can not deduct any of this because it is less than 3 percent of his income (3 percent of $65,000 is $1,950). Thus, Howard must pay the full $1,800 with after-tax dollars.

But assume Howard's company adopted a plan to reimburse

medical and dental expenses of Howard and his family. The $1,800 Howard received as reimbursement does not increase his income tax, so that the entire amount goes to pay the medical and dental bills. Also, his company can deduct the entire amount, which reduces its income tax by $864 (48 percent of $1,800), making its net cost $936 ($1,800 minus $864).

Suppose that instead of covering Howard's medical bills under its medical plan, the company had awarded Howard a $1,800 bonus. The company's net cost ($936) is unchanged, but Howard's tax bill is increased by about $900. Thus, only $900 of the $1,800 is left to pay medical bills, and Howard must provide the balance out of his own pocket.

Health insurance coverage

Instead of directly reimbursing the executive's medical expenses, the company could pay all costs of health insurance coverage (hospital, medical-surgical and major medical) for him and his family. The company can tax-deduct insurance premiums, just as it would for direct cash reimbursements. The premiums are not considered taxable income to the executive, nor is he taxed when insurance proceeds are used to pay his actual medical bills.

An acceptable variation of this insurance arrangement would have the executive select and pay for his own health insurance but receive full reimbursement of premiums from his company. Here, too, the executive would not be taxed on company reimbursements of premium costs or on his collections under the policy to pay medical bills, and the company could deduct its reimbursements. On this type of plan, the Revenue Service insists that the company receive proof that the executive's insurance is in force and that he actually paid the reimbursed amount for health insurance premiums.

The company can set any limit it pleases on the type of health insurance cost it will reimburse and the amount it will pay.

Some companies may fail to reimburse health insurance premiums because they believe that the executive himself can deduct such premiums. This company policy should be reconsidered. The special deduction allowed individuals for health insurance costs seldom is enough to do much good at executive levels. One-half of health insurance premiums is automatically deductible by individuals up to a maximum deduction of $150. The balance of the premium is treated as an ordinary medical expense, deductible only if the individual's other medical and dental bills are at least 3 percent of his income. Thus, an executive may pay $420 for full accident and health coverage but deduct only $150. His actual after-tax cost for this insurance would be about $345. If his company paid the $420 for him, there would be no cost to him at all and the company's deduction for the full $420 would cut its actual cost to $218.40.

Combination plans

For many companies, the author would advise using a combination of insurance coverage and reimbursement of expenses. Typically, the company under study already provides employees—rank-and-file and executives—with coverage of some expenses under an insured plan, such as Blue Cross-Blue Shield. Covered employees may be expected to contribute towards the cost of coverage, at least to the extent of covering their family members.

It is easy and economical for the company to widen tax-favored health care coverage for its executives while continuing any existing plan it may have. First, the company could pick up the cost of the executives' contributions, if any, paying and deducting the premium. In addition, the company can directly pay or reimburse the executive for medical expenses not covered by insurance, such as: expenses falling below some deductible limit in the policy; preexisting conditions; cosmetic surgery; dental bills; medicines; health care equipment such as wheelchairs or contact lenses; added cost for a private room; travel or transportation to doctors' offices or treatment centers, including ambulance service; physician's home or office visits; and routine or periodic medical examinations. The company could also provide special insurance coverage for executives only, such as major medical coverage. It would deduct all its payments while the executive would escape tax on all of them.

Even if the company does not have or intend to have a plan covering employees generally, it may decide to provide the executive with insurance coverage for normal or major health risks and direct payment or reimbursement of other medical bills. When selecting an insured plan, the compensation planner should keep in mind that executives would prefer one which lets them choose their own physician.

It is wise to spell out to each executive exactly what the company is providing in the way of health care coverage. This can be advisable for legal reasons, as will be seen later, but should be done in any case so they will not feel a need to provide coverage on their own. This is important, since they might pay more than their company does for the same coverage, and might not be able to collect on their policy if already covered by the company's. And the company should emphasize whenever applicable that the executive's wife and children are covered as well, so that these individuals need not buy health insurance on their own.

Salary continuations during illness

Most companies continue to pay the salary of any executive who is absent from his job because of sickness or injury. Companies which have not yet adopted a plan for providing such continuations (called a sick pay or disability plan) should consider doing so. The company can take an income tax deduction for the full amount it pays the executive directly as sick pay, or for amounts it pays on insurance policies providing sick pay coverage for executives.

In addition, a special but limited tax exemption is available for the executive. Though his salary is in most instances fully taxable, salary he receives while away from work more than 30 consecutive days because of sickness or injury is partially exempt from tax. The exemption is for the first $100 of salary per week, beginning with the 31st day of absence from work. It is available only if paid under a preexisting plan of the employer to continue salary during sickness or injury. The same tax exemption is available if the executive gets his salary continuations from an insurance company under a policy paid for by his employer, and he is not taxable on any of the insurance premiums paid by his employer.

Example: Lamont, a $600 a week executive, falls ill September 1 and is away from work until November 12, drawing full salary throughout that period. For his last six weeks of absence, he is taxable on only $500 a week of his $600 weekly salary; the $100 a week balance is exempt from tax.[1]

The company may wish to limit the period for which it provides salary continuations, or the amount it pays. This is not necessary for purposes of the employee's exemption. The Revenue Service allows the sick pay exemption up to $100 a week, regardless of the amount the employee collects (though not more than he actually collects) and regardless of the length of absence from work, until the employee reaches retirement age. But the company may wish to put a dollar limit on its sick pay commitment.

---

[1] An additional and still more limited tax exemption is available for the first 30 days of absence from work, but the special conditions of this exemption render it impractical for executives.

Some companies may want to combine insured and self-insured arrangements. For example, the company may decide to continue an executive's salary during the first few weeks of absence out of regular payroll, but cover any further salary continuations under a disability policy (which may pay full salary or some lesser sum). Sick pay policy for executives may differ from that for rank-and-file employees.

Here, too, executives should be told exactly what coverage is provided, so they can better appraise the need to provide further disability insurance coverage on their own. If the arrangement pays less than full salary for some period during the absence, some executives may want to take out their own disability policy, to make up the difference. Any amount they collect on their own policy is exempt from income tax, even though they also collect from the company or its insurer. On the other hand, premiums they pay for this coverage are not medical expenses and are not deductible in any amount.

Special considerations when covering stockholder employees

A company's plan for providing medical expense reimbursement, health insurance or salary continuations may be limited to executives or other key employees as the company chooses. It need not be (though it may be) made available to rank-and-file employees. But there are two special factors to cope with where stockholder-employees will be covered:

1. The tax benefits under these plans are available only if the plan is one for employees. A plan for stockholders only would not qualify; the recipients of benefits would be taxable on company payments and the company should not expect to be allowed a tax deduction for them (though deduction was allowed in one unusual situation). Plans which are limited to stockholders who

are also employees can qualify as plans for employees, and have been treated as qualified in some actual situations. But such qualification often involves struggle and even lawsuits with the Revenue Service. The author instead advises having the plan include one or more employees who are not stockholders (or closely related to stockholders) where this is possible. Any non-stockholder-employees included in the plan should have the same rights as stockholder-employees. No persons who are stockholders and not employees should be covered.

2. A company can take tax deductions for health care payments only to the extent that these payments plus the salary and other benefits to the executive don't exceed reasonable compensation to the executive. In practice, the company's deduction goes unchallenged by the Revenue Service except where the corporate executive is also a stockholder or is closely related to a substantial stockholder. Even here, full deduction usually is allowed.

A complete analysis of reasonable compensation considerations appears in Chapters 2 and 3. In the author's opinion, the reasonableness test, when it involves health care payments, should apply the rule used for incentive compensation. That is, reasonableness should be judged on the basis of factors existing when the corporation agreed to cover the executive's health care costs, and not on the amount the corporation may happen to have to pay later under its commitment. For example, if the corporation's plan covers expenses which usually run up to $1,500 but which run on one occasion to $20,000 because of medical peculiarities in that case, the additional outlay would not necessarily tend to make unreasonable the total compensation to the executive involved.

This does not mean that the author believes the company should be allowed to deduct any and all expenses it bears for an executive's catastrophic illness, or that of a member of his family. It is seldom reasonable for a company to assume unlimited risk.

As a matter of business as well as tax protection, the author recommends that the company put a dollar ceiling on the amount of health care cost it will bear. Where coverage of catastrophic illness is required, this can be provided through insurance.

How to set up a health care plan

The executive enjoys the tax-favored benefits of medical reimbursement, health insurance and salary continuation payments only if these payments are made under a plan of his employer. A company has a plan only if it has a definite, predetermined commitment to do something specific when a covered employee falls ill. There is no plan if the company can decide on a case-by-case basis whether to extend benefits, and how much to pay, after illness occurs.

The plan need not be enforceable by the employee (need not be part of any employment contract, for example) and need not be in writing. However, the author recommends that the plan always be set down in writing and always be communicated to employees who will be covered. A plan of a corporation should be a formal act of the board of directors, recorded in the minutes of the directors' meeting and announced to covered employees, or written into the executive's employment contract. The company can have different plans for different employees or groups of employees, and can have one or more plans for some and none for others. A plan of a partnership or sole proprietorship could be expressed in an employment contract, or in another writing communicated to covered employees, but partners or proprietors can never themselves be covered by any plan.

The plan may provide for direct payment or reimbursement of expenses, for health insurance, for salary continuations, or for all of these. For example, it could provide for basic health insurance, plus supplemental reimbursement of expenses not covered by insurance, plus salary continuations during illness. Any or all of these payments could be limited as to dollar amounts, kind of expense, and period of coverage, as the company may think fit.

A sample medical payment plan appears on the following pages.

BOARD OF DIRECTORS RESOLUTION ESTABLISHING
MEDICAL PAYMENT PLAN

WHEREAS, - - - - - - - - - (name of company) desires to pay or reimburse, directly or indirectly, certain medical and dental expenses of the following employees of the company during their employment with the company

- - - - - - - - - (names of employees)

- - - - - - - - -

- - - - - - - - -

and of the spouse and dependents (as defined in Section 152 of the Internal Revenue Code) of each such employee,

AND WHEREAS, the medical and dental expenses to be so paid or reimbursed shall be those not compensated for by insurance or otherwise, which are treated as medical expenses under Section 213 of the Internal Revenue Code and Treasury Regulations thereunder, except that the amount of such expenses so paid or reimbursed to any employee shall not exceed $_____ (insert any dollar ceiling selected by the company) in any calendar year,

AND WHEREAS the company also desires to continue the salary of each of the above-named employees during a period in which they shall be disabled from performing their duties because of occupational or nonoccupational sickness or injury, for a period of not more than - - - - - - - - - consecutive - - - - - - - - - [and not more than a total of - - - - - - - - - in any - - - - - - - - -] (insert maximum period of absence selected by the company) [except that for absences extending beyond - - - - - - - - - days, the compensation for absence after that - - - - - - - - - th day shall be reduced to - - - - - - - - - percent of regular compensation],

NOW THEREFORE, be it resolved that the above plan for paying or reimbursing such medical and dental expenses and for continuations of salary be and hereby is adopted on behalf of the Company by its Board of Directors, to become effective as of _____ (use a present or future date; do not seek to make it retroactive),

AND BE IT FURTHER RESOLVED that the company at its discretion may directly pay any of the above medical and dental expenses instead of providing reimbursement therefore, and may require as a condition of reimbursement that any employee seeking reimbursement furnish to the company all bills for which reimbursement is sought,

AND BE IT FURTHER RESOLVED that a copy of this resolution be given by - - - - - - - - - - (any corporate officer) or his designee to each employee named above, which that employee is to read, sign, date and promptly return for retention in the personnel file of that employee,

AND BE IT FURTHER RESOLVED that the officers of the Company shall execute this resolution by all necessary and proper means.

chapter 12 Pension and profit-sharing plans designed for executives

A qualified pension or profit-sharing plan is by far the most important benefit a company can provide its executives, apart from the salaries it pays them.

Some practitioners and company officers, unfamiliar with pension or profit-sharing rules, tend to think of such plans as being for employees in general and not for executives. They have heard that qualified plans cannot discriminate in favor of executives, that they must be employee plans, not just *executive* plans.

It is true that a qualified plan cannot discriminate in favor of executives. Unlike the situation with group-term life insurance, qualified and nonstatutory stock options, financial counseling, interest-free loans, and other compensation benefits analyzed in this book, some rank-and-file employees must normally be entitled to pension or profit-sharing benefits if executives will receive such benefits.

But it is also true that such plans can be structured to benefit executives, and even specific executives, much more than they benefit other employees. The author knows of a profit-sharing plan which paid three executives over $1 million each. The plan had been designed to suit one of these executives, a major stockholder, though hundreds of rank-and-file employees also had some stake in the plan. He had introduced the plan with the knowledge, or at least the expectation, that through the plan he would retain more of the millions in company earnings put into the plan than if he had withdrawn his share of those earnings in the form of dividends and stock sale profits.

The benefits we will be analyzing here are those of qualified plans, that is, plans set up and operated to conform to the detailed requirements of the federal tax law. The tax rules are the keystone of any plan. Without them, the economic benefits, the distributions of hundreds of thousands of dollars to individual executives, would be out of the question. Pension plans which are not qualified, which do not conform to the tax rules, are therefore of little practical interest to executives.[1]

There are many types of qualified plan. Pension, profit-sharing, stock-bonus, and annuity plans are all expressly mentioned in the law. Thrift and savings plans are also recognized in practice.

Here we will examine pension and profit-sharing plans (including thrift and savings plans, which are types of profit-sharing plans). Annuity plans (a variant of a pension plan) and stock bonus plans (a variant of a profit-sharing plan) will be disregarded, but what is said here will be generally applicable to those plans.

The rest of this chapter will deal with the major opportunities for using pension and profit-sharing plans to build up executive wealth. It will concentrate on how plans can be designed to favor executives, and will also note the legal and practical limitations on such arrangements. But it should be stressed that the pension and profit-sharing area is extremely complicated—by far the most

---

[1] The author does not think of deferred compensation arrangements as (nonqualified) pension plans, though some practitioners do. In any case, deferred compensation plans *are* of practical interest to executives and are analyzed in Chapter 5.

complex subject discussed in this book. Here we will consider, in some detail, the major benefits and limitations. But no one should attempt to set up a qualified plan for his own firm, or modify an existing one, without extended consultation with a professional practitioner. Designing a plan which will take full advantage of opportunities available often involves the services of several professionals working as a team: lawyer, accountant and actuary.

How a qualified plan works

A qualified plan, in general, involves these three parties or groups: the employer, the employees who will be covered by the plan, and the trustee who will invest and administer the funds involved. The plan, a formal written document, sets forth the rules governing which employees will be entitled to benefits, when the benefits will become available, and how much they will be. The funds from which the benefits will be paid are amounts contributed by the employer (and sometimes by covered employees as well) and investment earnings on these funds.

The tax benefits of such a plan, which are what makes the plan important as a compensation device, are these:

1. The employer can deduct his contribution to the fund for the employees' benefit in the year the contribution is made. This is a departure from the usual rules in the compensation area, under which company deduction is postponed until the employee collects his share.

2. The employee is not taxable on company contributions to a fund for his benefit at the time the contribution is made, even though he has a nonforfeitable right to those contributions. This differs from the general rules for taxing deferred compensation.

3. Investment earnings on the amounts contributed to the fund are not taxable to anyone—employer, employee or trust—as long as they are held by the trust.

4. Amounts distributed to employees or their beneficiaries at retirement or other times can qualify for tax benefits, including capital gains treatment and exemption from estate tax. These benefits will be examined later in this chapter. The company and the trust have no tax liability on the distribution.

Example: Warfield is an executive covered by his company's profit-sharing plan. Company profit-sharing contributions are based on salary. Over the 20 years Warfield has been in the plan, company contributions for him amount to $7,500 a year. Assuming the profit-sharing trust earns a 7½ percent return from investing these contributions, Warfield's profit-sharing account would be worth $324,784.50 after 20 years, and could be much more if amounts forfeited by employees who leave are allocated to the accounts of those who remain. There has been no tax on contributions or earnings over the 20-year period. Warfield could withdraw his entire account in a lump sum, subject to favorable tax rules.

No discrimination

Qualified plans cannot discriminate in favor of executives, who are defined, for qualified plan purposes, as officers, stockholders, supervisory employees or highly-paid employees.

There can be no discrimination in their favor in coverage. This means a company generally cannot design a plan to cover only executives (or selected executives) and exclude others.

And there can be no discrimination in company contributions or employee benefits. That is, the company cannot set up a plan which covers all employees but gives only nominal amounts to the rank-and-file and massive amounts to the executives.

This ban on discrimination applies to the way the plan operates in practice, as well as to its technical terms. For example, a plan is allowed to exclude employees who have worked for the company less than some minimum period, without being considered discriminatory. But if the company fired all or practically all rank-and-file employees before they could attain that minimum period of employment, so that essentially only executives were covered, the plan would be discriminatory in practice and could not be qualified.

But despite these rules against discrimination, plans can be designed to favor executives. This will be shown in the material that follows.

Pension or profit-sharing plans

There are several significant differences between pension and profit-sharing plans, in advantages, restrictions, and practical operating considerations. A company can choose a pension or profit-sharing plan—or no plan—as it pleases. It may have both a pension and a profit-sharing plan, though, as will be shown later, this is not necessarily the way to maximize tax benefits.

The key differences between the two types of plans are these:

1. With a profit-sharing plan, no company contributions are made for covered employees unless there are profits. With a pension plan, company contributions are a fixed cost, like rent, whether or not it has profits. Thus, a company's economic risk is less with a profit-sharing plan. By the same token, benefits to employees may not be very substantial.

2. A pension plan must be a retirement plan. It must contemplate a distribution of benefits only when the covered employee retires (or dies or becomes disabled). A profit-sharing plan may be a retirement plan, but this is not required. The plan can be set up to distribute benefits during employment, as long as the employee normally must wait at least two years before he withdraws any particular company contribution.

3. If it is intended to provide executives with the maximum possible tax-favored benefit, a pension plan is preferable for older executives while a profit-sharing plan is preferable for younger executives. (The dividing line is said by some pension specialists to be about age 45.) This results from the rules governing deduction for company contributions to plans, to be discussed later in this chapter.

4. Some compensation planners believe that a liberal profit-sharing plan may stimulate employees to more productive work for the company, since they will share the benefits. On the other hand, pension plans may tie employees more securely to the company. Profit-sharing benefits usually vest and are distributed, at least in part, more rapidly than pension benefits. Thus, even if a pension plan and a profit-sharing plan are equally generous in terms of company contributions, an employee who leaves before retirement will have more to lose (and therefore will have a greater incentive to stay) under a pension plan.

Choosing a pension plan

Essentially, there are two types of pension plans: the fixed benefit plan and the money purchase plan.

The fixed or defined benefit plan is the more common type today. Under this plan, the covered employee will receive a specified benefit on retirement. This is usually an annuity of a specified percentage of his regular salary. The company's contribution is therefore on a basis designed to produce this benefit.[2] This is illustrated in *pension contributions* below.

Under the money purchase or defined contribution plan, the company makes a designated contribution for the employee each year. At retirement, the covered employee is to receive whatever

---

[2] Variable benefit plans are, in this sense, fixed benefit plans. They involve a determination to pay a specific benefit but with adjustment for changes in the cost of living, etc.

retirement benefits the contributed amounts (plus investment earnings in the interim) will buy.

Pension contributions

The pension benefits that any covered employee will receive are funded by employer contributions and investment earnings on those contributions. The typical pension plan contemplates providing specific benefits to covered employees. For example, the plan may promise to pay every covered employee 35 percent of his regular salary at his retirement at age 65, if he has worked for the company 25 years. It would determine (with the help of its professional advisers) the amount necessary to provide the promised amount at retirement, and would make annual contributions towards that amount.

Example: Genero Corporation, a newly-formed company, is setting up a pension plan for Baker, its president, and other employees. Baker's current base salary is $48,000 a year, and he is 45 years old. The company's plan promises a pension equaling 37½ percent of base salary, at retirement at age 65.

At current insurance company rates, it would cost $240,000 to buy an annuity paying $18,000 a year for the life expectancy of a man age 65. But of course this $240,000 will not be needed until Baker actually reaches age 65, 20 years hence. The company would therefore make annual contributions to Baker's pension fund in amounts which, with investment increments, will build up to $240,000 in 20 years. Assuming the company contributes the same amount each year, and assuming a 5 percent return on investment of these contributions, the company contributes $7,-248 a year towards Baker's pension.

When deciding upon the amount of benefit the company will provide, the planner will typically take into account the amount covered employees will receive under Social Security. Thus, if a company considers that retired employees in a particular group should not have to live on less than, say, $16,000 a year, in planning what it would provide it would reflect that the employee might in any case expect to get, say, $4,000 a year under Social Security. (The mere recognition of Social Security benefits in pension planning is not equivalent to *integration* with Social Security, discussed below.)

The reader will recall the rule that contributions or benefits cannot discriminate in favor of executives. This rule does not prevent providing greater benefits for executives than for rank and file employees. For example, suppose the pension benefit is to be 35 percent of base salary. This means that the pension for a $60,000-a-year corporate officer will be ten times that of a $6,000-a-year office clerk, yet this is not considered discrimination in favor of the officer. Also, company contributions to fund pensions may be many times larger for the older officers than for the younger employees, without being considered discriminatory. A plan is not discriminatory simply because its benefits bear a uniform relationship to compensation. Plans are commonly designed on this basis.

Gearing plans based on compensation in favor of company executives is aided by definitions of compensation which exclude items that rank and file employees receive but executives don't (for example, overtime pay and tips) and which include items executives are more likely to receive (such as bonuses).

How many employees must be included in the pension plan

Pension plan coverage may not discriminate in favor of executives. That is, in deciding which employees will get benefits under the plan, discrimination in favor of executives is barred.[3] But an

---

[3] Discrimination *against* executives is always permitted. A plan can be limited to rank and file employees.

acceptable, qualified plan can still exclude many employees, and these can in practice be rank and file employees, without being considered discriminatory.

There are two tests for deciding whether pension plan coverage is discriminatory: (1) the *percentage test* and (2) the *facts and circumstances test*. The plan is not discriminatory if either test is met.

1. *The percentage test* is an automatic numbers test. If a certain percentage of employees is covered, the plan's coverage automatically qualifies as nondiscriminatory.

In deciding who should be covered, the company may first exclude the following employees: (*a*) new employees, (*b*) part-time employees, that is, those whose regular work week is less than 20 hours and (*c*) seasonal employees—those who regularly work less than five months a year.

Usually, employees excluded under these tests are rank-and-file only. But occasionally, such a test would work to exclude a newly-hired executive. The plan would of course be discriminatory if it included him but barred other new employees.

Moreover, a plan is not discriminatory if 70 percent or more of the employees are eligible (disregarding any who are excluded under conditions (*a*), (*b*) or (*c*) above), and 80 percent or more of those eligible actually participate. This means that only 56 percent of those left after excluding new, part-time and seasonal employees need actually be covered.

Example: Wheeler Corporation has 135 employees. Of these, 105 (including all 6 executives) work in the main plant; the rest work in other locations. Wheeler adopts a benefit plan calling for matching contributions from employer and employee, which is not open to new, seasonal or part-time employees, or those working outside the main plant.

The excluded new, part-time and seasonal employees—assume

35 of these in all—are disregarded in the percentage computation. The company can also exclude up to 30 percent of other employees. Thus, it could properly exclude the off-plant employees—assume 30 of these. And 20 percent (here, 14) of eligibles that remain could be left out without disqualification, if they choose not to participate (as because they didn't want to join a plan in which they would have to contribute). Thus, a plan covering 56 employees, including all 6 executives, out of a work force of 135 is not discriminatory as to coverage.

2. *The facts and circumstances test* is used for many plans that fail the percentage test but can still be ruled nondiscriminatory, after considering all the circumstances. Thus, plans which exclude the following categories of employees can be qualified plans:

1. Employees below a certain age.
2. Employees who have worked for the company less than a certain number of years.
3. Employees who work in certain company departments.
4. Hourly or union employees. (This is probably, in practice, the most important excluded category; a number of plans are designed to exclude these and cover only salaried employees.)

A plan that excludes the above categories is not necessarily discriminatory but it may prove to be so in the particular circumstances of the case. The Revenue Service is the first judge of what is discriminatory, and there is no brief or simple way to describe the checkpoints the IRS consults in testing for discrimination.[4] Professional advisers would use their knowledge of what past IRS and court rulings have allowed, as a guide to what the company should provide. In borderline cases, the matter can be negotiated

---

[4] It has become harder in recent years to obtain Revenue Service approval for the exclusion of hourly employees.

and adjusted with the IRS as part of the process (discussed below) of obtaining IRS approval of the plan.

As an example of qualification under this test, one company had 109 employees of whom 11 were executives. Its plan covered salaried employees only, and therefore excluded 83 hourly employees. The IRS decided that the plan did not discriminate, even though it covered only 26 employees out of 109, of whom only 15 were rank and file.

Vested and forfeited benefits

Pension plans typically require a minimum period of coverage in the plan before the covered employee becomes absolutely entitled to pension benefits, that is, before any of his rights become vested. If his employment terminated before the expiration of that period, he would forfeit all contributions made on his behalf. This period for vesting is independent of any waiting period before the employee is first included in the plan.

In some older plans, no vesting is provided unless the employee works the full period required to qualify for his pension. Thus, some plans required, say, 30 years' service before any pension was due. Here, if the covered employee quit or was fired after working there 29 years and 11 months, no amount was vested—all contributions on his behalf were forfeited.

In the newer plans, vesting typically begins at some period short of full qualification. For example, a plan may call for full pension at age 65 after 25 years' service, but company contributions vest, wholly or in part, after 5 years. Here, if an employee worked less than 5 years before leaving, all company contributions would be forfeited. If he worked 5 years or more, company contributions made for the period he worked would vest. He would be entitled to pension benefits based on company contributions during the period he worked, plus investment earnings thereon. This would of course not equal a full pension, since he did not work the full qualifying period.

Moreover, an employee whose pension contributions have vested would not necessarily be entitled to collect the amount standing to his credit at the time he leaves the company. His vested pension benefit might not become collectible until he reaches the company's retirement age.

If a covered employee leaves before his pension share has fully vested, the contributions and earnings thereon (or the nonvested part) are forfeited. The forfeited amount is applied to reduce the amount the company will contribute in the future for those who remain in the plan.

For example, suppose a company contributes $120,000 annually to the pension plan for its covered employees. If a covered employee leaves and forfeits $15,000 of past contributions and investment earnings, this $15,000 is applied as part of the company's next contribution, reducing that to $105,000. Forfeited amounts generally may not be returned to the company and, in the case of a pension[5] plan, may not be allocated among the remaining covered employees.

There are essentially two reasons why pension plans contain forfeiture provisions:

1. To tie employees more closely to the company. Employee mobility is deterred if the employee will lose sizeable pension benefits by changing jobs.

2. To keep pension costs relatively low or—looked at another way—to maximize benefits for executives. The cost of covering employees who remain in the plan is borne in part by the covered employees who forfeit their shares. This is a major concern when

---

[5] This is an important difference between pension and profit-sharing plans, as will be seen in the profit-sharing analysis below.

designing a plan weighted to favor executives. Executives as a class are the group least likely to leave, least likely to forfeit their pension benefits. Thus, where a significant number of rank and file employees must also be covered, benefits for executives as a whole are larger (or the cost of the plan is lower) if vesting is long postponed. In short, even though many employees must initially be covered to avoid disqualification of the plan as discriminatory, postponed vesting means that the cost of the plan is only the cost of covering those who remain, and that diminished group will include all or most of the executives.

Contributions by employees

Some plans permit voluntary contributions by covered employees on their own behalf. And in some plans, an employee is covered only if he agrees to contribute to the plan.[6] These plans are called "contributory" plans.

A contribution by the employee would be invested, like the company's contribution. In a contributory pension plan, the employee's contribution and investment earnings thereon would go to provide retirement benefits in addition to those provided the the company.

The employee gets no tax deduction for his contributions to the plan. They are made with after-tax dollars. If his contribution is withheld and deducted from his pay, he is still taxable on that amount.

But there is a major tax advantage in contributory plans, especially to executives and other persons in high tax brackets. The investment earnings on amounts contributed to the plan are not taxable until they are withdrawn, years later. The invested funds grow faster by being free of tax burden during the invest-

---

6 It is, in fact, possible to set up a qualified plan to which only employees contribute.

ment period. They will be taxable when they are withdrawn, but then can be taxed at favored rates (discussed later in this chapter).

Example: Ward, an executive in the 50 percent bracket, is able to invest in either a corporate bond paying 6 percent or in his company's qualified plan whose investment yield is 6 percent. Assuming he invests $5,000 each year for 20 years, he would have $134,352 after taxes at the end of that period if he invested in corporate bonds, and $162,946[7] after taxes by investing in the qualified plan.

The plan would return the employee's own contributions to him (and maybe the investment earnings thereon as well) even if he forfeited company contributions and investment earnings thereon by leaving before these amounts vested.

Contributory plans are another means for favoring executives over rank-and-file employees. High-bracket persons are more likely to have funds to contribute (invest) than rank-and-file employees are. Thus, such plans are especially beneficial to executives. The higher a person's bracket, the more valuable is the tax exemption for investment earnings while they remain in the fund.

Still more favoritism for the executive arises if the plan requires the employee to contribute in order to qualify for a company contribution. Here, the company incurs costs only for employees who have investment funds available.

The Revenue Service has long recognized the potential which contributory plans have for discrimination in favor of executives. It therefore limits the amount which an employee can be required or allowed to contribute under a contributory plan. It says that an employee's voluntary contributions in any year can't exceed

---

[7] Assuming a 25 percent tax rate for the entire taxable gain on withdrawal. The actual rate could be lower or, more likely, somewhat higher.

10 percent of his compensation. If an employee *must* contribute in order to qualify for company contribution, this mandatory contribution can't exceed 6 percent of his compensation.[8]

The deduction rules

The key deduction rule for pension contributions is the same rule that applies to other company payments in the compensation area. The payment must be an ordinary and necessary business expense and must be reasonable compensation for services actually rendered. Reasonableness here, as elsewhere, is determined employee by employee.

But the determination of reasonableness takes into consideration all the current and past compensation paid the employee (in salary, pension contributions, and so forth), and the value of his services in the current year and all previous years. As IRS regulations put it, a contribution is deductible if it, together with other current compensation, "plus all compensation and contributions paid to or for such employee in prior years, represents a reasonable allowance for all services rendered by the employee by the end of the current year."

The first deduction hurdle—ordinary and necessary business expense—is easily surmounted. The Revenue Service is not disposed to question that there is a sound business reason for setting up a pension plan. And the reasonableness hurdle has not been a serious issue in tax litigation. This may be because pension plans usually are submitted to the Revenue Service for approval before they are put into effect (a matter discussed below). This process

---

[8] The Internal Revenue Service has ruled that voluntary contributions up to 10 percent and required contributions up to 6 percent are acceptable. It is the consensus among pension specialists that these 10 percent and 6 percent figures are maximums, and that plans with larger percentages would not qualify.

permits reasonableness questions to be raised and resolved in advance.[9]

Deduction is allowed only if the company's pension contribution is actually paid. The deduction is taken for the year payment occurs, with this exception: A company reporting on the accrual method takes the deduction for the year the contribution accrues if payment of the contribution is made by the due date (including extensions) of its tax return for that year.[10]

Deduction in the year of payment into the trust is actually a concession, a liberalization, granted to qualified plans. Under usual tax rules, deduction would not be allowed until the employee received (became taxable on) the company's payment.

Payment by promissory note does not count as payment qualifying for deduction, according to the Revenue Service. Federal circuit courts disagree; they allow deduction for payment by means of the company's promissory note if the company is solvent. Thus, companies willing to fight the matter in court would probably be allowed deductions for their payment by note, under current rules. (In other settings, including those involving compensation between related parties, the Revenue Service recognizes a good promissory note as payment, though in those cases the recipient is also currently reporting the note as income.)

Payment of a company's contribution in property is technically acceptable but is often unwise. The company's transfer of portfolio stock or other property to the pension trust as its contribution to the trust is considered a sale of the property for tax purposes. The transaction amounts to a satisfaction of the obliga-

---

[9] The approval process does not legally foreclose a later IRS challenge to reasonableness, and such challenges have actually been made. But such challenges have been rare, considering the amounts involved; the approval process may account for this.

[10] Deduction is postponed for the amount of pension contribution which exceeds the deduction ceilings noted below. These "excess" contributions are deducted as carryovers in later years.

tion to contribute to the trust (a sale). The company is considered for tax purposes as receiving an amount of cash equal to the fair market value of the property transferred. Thus, if the property is worth more than the company's basis for it, the company has a taxable gain—unless the company is transferring its own stock, which is tax-exempt. If the property is worth less than the company's basis for it, the company has a loss which it cannot deduct.

Despite the prospect of a taxable gain on the transfer of property, some companies that are short on cash might want to make such a transfer anyway. They should be able to establish the fair market value of the property involved, and where possible should select property whose value can easily be demonstrated. Property worth less than its basis to the company should not be contributed but should be sold (contributing the proceeds), so the loss can be recognized for tax purposes and deducted.

The amount deducted as a contribution to the pension plan is the property's fair market value (subject to the deduction limits). For example, if Whipple Corporation contributed shares of IBM stock worth $10,000 which it had bought for $6,000, it would have a $10,000 pension contribution deduction and a $4,-000 capital gain.

There are further deduction restrictions specially applicable to pension plans. These restrictions are complex and won't be analyzed here. Their purpose is to limit deductions where the company attempts to fund a large part of its pension obligation in a single year. For example, suppose a company sets up a plan to pay a pension at age 65 for employees with 20 years' service. And suppose the plan counts the period an employee worked for the company before the plan was adopted as part of his qualifying 20 years. (Most plans do.) For an employee who worked for 12 years before the plan was adopted, the company could in a single year pay in an amount attributable to those past 12 years as well as the current year. The deduction rules limit its deduction for such payment.

A further limitation: If a company has both a pension and a profit-sharing plan, its deduction for contributions to both in a year cannot exceed 25 percent of the other compensation paid covered employees for the year. This deduction ceiling can provide a reason not to add a profit-sharing to a pension plan, since there is no such ceiling on a pension plan alone. Thus, deductions equalling, say, 60 percent of compensation can be allowable if the company has only a pension plan, but only 25 percent is allowable if it has both a pension and a profit-sharing plan.

Contributions in excess of deduction limitations may be deducted in later years under deduction carryover rules. Companies tailor the amounts they pay into the fund so as to avoid postponement of deduction.

Distribution of pension plan benefits

Pension plans are retirement plans. An employee's share of the pension fund can be withdrawn before retirement only in case of death, disability, termination of employment or termination of the plan itself.

Pension plans contemplate payment of retirement benefits in the form of an annuity, usually for the life of the employee. However, pension plans may authorize the distribution of the employee's share in a lump sum, which he can invest in an annuity or in some other investment (or, of course, no investment). Where the plan gives the employee a choice between an annuity and a lump-sum payment, his choice may be influenced by the tax factors analyzed below.

Annuity.   An employee is taxed as follows on amounts he collects periodically, in the form of an annuity: If *he* did not contribute to the pension fund, everything he collects is fully taxable as ordinary income. Thus, if his pension is $600 a month, he reports the full amount as income and pays regular income tax on that amount.

If he contributed to the pension fund and the amount he contributed is less than he will collect as an annuity in the first three years of the annuity, he is exempt from tax on all annuity amounts until he recovers the full amount of his contribution. Thereafter, he is taxable on everything he collects. For example, if he contributed a total of $10,000 and draws a pension of $600 a month, he is exempt from tax on the first $10,000 of annuity payments (the first 16 months and $400 of the 17th month), and is taxable on all annuity payments thereafter.

If he contributed to the pension fund and the amount he contributed is more than he will collect as an annuity in the first three years, he is taxable on part and tax-exempt on part of each annuity payment received, for as long as the annuity is paid. The exempt portion or percentage is obtained by dividing the employee's contribution (his cost or "investment in the contract") by the amount he expects to collect under the annuity (which would be the amount he receives each year for his life expectancy, in the case of a life annuity). Thus, if an employee who has a 20-year life expectancy when he retires had contributed $30,000 and the life annuity will pay $600 a month, 21 percent ($30,000 ÷ $600 X 12 X 20) of each annuity payment is exempt.

The taxable part of a pension or annuity is retirement income, and so could qualify for the retirement income credit. Considering the fact that the credit is intended to benefit the ordinary retired taxpayer, computation of the credit is absurdly complicated. But the credit for any one individual can't exceed $228.60 a year. The credit is a direct reduction of tax liability; it is not a deduction.

Lump-sum withdrawal. Withdrawal in a lump sum is granted favored tax treatment, if the following two requirements are met:

1. The amount which represents the employee's share (or the balance of that share, if some amounts were withdrawn previously) is distributed within a single taxable year—which in almost all cases is within a single calendar year.
2. The distribution is on account of the employee's separation from employment.

If the employee contributed to the fund, he recovers his own contribution tax-free out of the lump-sum distribution. The balance is taxable. Part of the employee's receipts may be long-term capital gains; the rest is ordinary income subject to a special averaging provision (designed solely for qualified plans) whose effect is to reduce the tax below the amount that would be due at regular rates. In many cases, tax under the averaging provision is less than capital gains tax.

The newer the plan (or the more recent the employee's entry into the plan), the smaller the proportion of capital gain, and the larger the proportion of ordinary income subject to averaging.

Annuity or lump sum? Despite the tax favoritism for amounts withdrawn in a lump sum, it should not be assumed that the overall tax burden will be lower on a lump-sum withdrawal. The total tax take on a lump-sum withdrawal, as compared to tax on annuity collections, will depend on the amounts involved and on the taxpayer's other income and deductions in the years involved.

Whether to take down a lump sum or an annuity will depend on many nontax factors, such as the employee's health and competing investment opportunities. The practical effect of the lump-sum rules is that the tax burden need not be a major deterrent to lump-sum withdrawal. But each employee or beneficiary should decide on his own whether annuity or lump sum is preferable in his case. This is ordinarily a once-in-a-lifetime decision, and should be made with the help of a professional adviser.

After employee's death. These are the rules governing
pension plan distributions beginning after the employee's death:

For income tax purposes: An employee's heirs are entitled,
indirectly, to a $5,000 exemption ($5,000 for all together, not
$5,000 for each heir) on what they collect under a qualified
plan.[11] This tax exemption is achieved by treating the $5,000 as
a contribution by the employee to the fund, whether or not he
made other contributions. Thus, the first $5,000 (plus any actual
contributions he made) collected in annuity form is exempt from
income tax, and amounts collected thereafter are taxable, assuming $5,000 plus actual contributions do not exceed total annuity
payments in the first three years. If they do exceed total annuity
payments, the actual contributions plus the "exempt" $5,000 are
counted as employee contributions in computing the exempt
portion of each annuity payment.

If the employee's heirs make a lump-sum withdrawal, $5,000
is automatically treated as an employee contribution to the plan,
reducing to that extent the amount treated as capital gain (or as
ordinary income subject to averaging).

For estate tax purposes: There is a further tax benefit for
qualified plans. Amounts to be distributed to the heirs of a deceased employee out of his pension account are exempt from
estate tax to the extent they represent contributions by the employer. For example, suppose the value of the account was $400,-
000. The company had contributed $160,000, the employee had
contributed $40,000, and the balance represented earnings on
these contributions. Only $80,000 (20 percent of $400,000)
would be included in the estate as subject to estate tax, because
the employee's $40,000 contribution represents only 20 percent
of the amount contributed. For estate tax purposes, it makes no
difference whether the fund will be paid out as an annuity or in
a lump sum.

---

[11] The exemption is $5,000 or the amount of the total annuity or lump sum with-
drawal, whichever is less.

Chapter 15 considers ways to minimize the estate tax on executives covered by qualified plans.

Other withdrawals. Withdrawals which are not in the form of an annuity or a lump sum are covered in the analysis of profit-sharing plans.

Plans integrated with Social Security

Integration with Social Security is another way to design a plan to favor executives.

The integration concept starts with the fact that the company already bears part of the cost of a retirement plan for its employees, through its "contributions" or taxes under the Social Security system. It contributes an amount for each covered employee based on his compensation, up to the ceiling amount subject to Social Security tax, which is called the Social Security base. Under the Social Security system, a retired person's receipts or pension will depend on the amount of his covered salary (the Social Security base when he was working, or whatever lesser amount he actually received). Thus, the company could reason, employees are provided, through Social Security, with a pension based on their covered salary. But employees who earn more than the Social Security base are not in the same sense fully covered by Social Security. That is, while Social Security may provide a pension of, say, $3,600 (which represents 27 percent of a $13,200 Social Security base), for an employee who made $13,200 annually, it will provide no more than that for an executive made $48,000 annually. For the executive, Social Security provides a pension of only 7½ percent of salary.[12]

Hence the plan which "integrates" with Social Security. Though integration can be done in various ways, one acceptable

---

[12] The author is not suggesting, and does not believe, that this aspect of the Social Security system is unfair. Neither company nor executive has paid any Social Security tax (has made any "contribution") on compensation in excess of the Social Security base.

way is to design a plan in which the company contributes only for employees whose compensation exceeds the Social Security base amount (which we will assume is $13,200). This way, the company incurs pension costs only for employees who make more than $13,200, an arrangement which can exclude many or most rank-and-file employees but will cover all executives.

Under integration, combined Social Security and pension benefits for higher-paid employees are roughly the same percentage of compensation as Social Security benefits are for the lower-paid employees.

Integration is available for pension plans, and for profit-sharing plans which are retirement plans. Integration is optional. Most of today's plans are not integrated plans. But interest in such plans is growing, because of its opportunities to provide substantial benefits for higher-salaried employees at relatively low-overall cost to the company.

Insurance benefits

Pension plans are meant to provide retirement benefits. A plan can provide death benefits (life insurance) only if they are incidental to retirement benefits. Life insurance in a pension plan does not enjoy tax benefits. That is, a covered employee is taxed on the cost (determined under Revenue Service tables) of his current life insurance protection, and his beneficiaries are subject to income tax on the insurance proceeds they receive, up to the policy's cash surrender value just before his death.

Choosing a profit-sharing plan

The company may select a profit-sharing plan instead of a pension plan. Or, it may install both plans, at the same time or at different times. Each plan may cover the same or different employees, but the overall result may not discriminate in favor of executives.

Most of the rules governing pension plans also apply to profit-sharing plans. That is, the basic tax rules are the same, and the barrier against discrimination remains.

But there are significant differences between the plans, differences which can in particular situations make profit-sharing plans more attractive than pension plans.

Profit-sharing plans may be retirement plans. But unlike pension plans, they don't have to be retirement plans. Company contributions for the employee's benefit can be distributed to him before retirement (or death, disability, termination of employment or termination of the plan). It is only necessary that two years elapse between the time the company makes its contribution and the time the employee withdraws it.

Profit-sharing plans which are not retirement plans typically cover a larger percentage of employees than retirement plans do.

Profit-sharing contributions for employees

Profit-sharing plans, of course, contemplate company contributions out of company profits. The plan may define "profits" in any rational way. Profits need not be defined with reference to taxable income. A plan may provide for contributions out of past (accumulated) profits where current profits are lacking. And it may provide that contributions will be made only if profits exceed some particular figure. It may choose any percentage of profits, which in any year may vary with the amount of profit (5 percent of first $100,000, 6½ percent of next $100,000 for example).

No specific formula for computing the amount of profits to be contributed is necessary. The company may choose a different formula each year, after it sees what its profit picture for the year will be. However, the Revenue Service will not recognize it as a plan unless contributions are recurring and substantial. A plan which is set up to make a contribution in one year and never again would not qualify.

The author recommends that the company adopt a specific formula for computing the contributions it is to make to the fund. This is advisable to show that the plan is intended to be permanent, and also can help a bit to overcome IRS suspicions that the plan in question may be discriminatory. Furthermore, it will have more effect as a stimulus encouraging employees to produce profits if they know the company is definitely committed to contribute a certain portion of its profits. Also, a company using the accrual accounting method can deduct a delayed contribution (see page 179) if made under a specific formula.

The basic deduction limits already discussed in connection with pension plans apply to profit-sharing plans. That is, the contribution must be paid, it and other compensation must be reasonable, and so on. In addition, there is a specific percentage deduction ceiling for profit-sharing plans. The deduction can't exceed 15 percent of the compensation of covered employees. The deduction rules offer opportunities for carrying over and using in later years both contributions in excess of the 15 percent ceiling and credits arising from contributions below that ceiling. (Pension plans follow different principles, but their deduction rules are in essence more liberal.)

If a company has both a pension and a profit-sharing plan, the deduction for both can't exceed 25 percent of the other compensation of covered employees.

The amount a company contributes for covered employees typically is based on their compensation. A plan is not considered as discriminatory in favor of executives if company contributions bear a uniform relationship to the compensation of covered employers. Thus, a profit-sharing contribution for a $70,000 a year executive can be ten times the contribution for a $7,000 a year clerk without being discriminatory.

Company contributions could also be based on other factors, such as age or length of service.

A number of compensation planners have tried, without success, to design qualified profit-sharing plans based on both compensation and years of service. This would tend to favor executives by taking advantage of the fact that they are paid more and also that they are, as a class, likely to have worked longer for the company. Basing company contributions on either of these factors can be acceptable. Using both often (though not always) results in a discriminatory, nonqualified plan.

Vesting and forfeiture

The vesting and forfeiture provisions of a profit-sharing plan may resemble those of a pension plan, if the profit-sharing plan is designed as a retirement plan. In other situations, company contributions for covered employees are likely to begin to vest sooner than with pension plans. Thus, a plan might vest a percentage of a year's contribution after, say, three years, with an increasing percentage in later years. For example, 60 percent of a contribution might vest the third year of coverage, 80 percent the fourth year, and 100 percent the fifth year.

Contributions and earnings thereon that are forfeited by employees who leave before all contributions on their behalf are fully vested generally can not be returned to the company. The plan may provide that forfeitures go to reduce future contributions of the employer. This is mandatory for pension plans; it is one of two options in a profit-sharing plan. The alternative is to allocate the forfeitures among employees who remain. This is the preferred option where it is intended to have the profit-sharing plan favor executives, and is one factor which could incline a company to choose a profit-sharing over a pension plan.

There are three ways commonly used to allocate the forfeited amounts:

1. In the way company contributions to the plan are allocated. Thus, if contributions are allocated to each employee on the basis of length of service, forfeitures of contributions and earnings can be so allocated.

2. In proportion to the compensation of each covered employee. This is the same as (1) if the company's contributions are in proportion to the employee's compensation. Thus, if an employee forfeits $20,000 when he leaves, the account of a $70,000 executive gets $10 of this for every $1 that goes to the account of a $7,000 secretary.

3. In proportion to the size of the account of each covered employee. This in practice has proved most favorable to executives, and is now less likely to be accepted by the IRS as nondiscriminatory. The concept is this:

With a plan in which company contributions are proportionate to compensation, an executive's account in the plan will be leveraged upwards by these two factors: (*a*) contributions for him are larger in the first place, and (*b*) he is likely to have been in the plan longer, so that a larger number of contributions were made for him. Thus, the account of a $70,000 a year executive may be *30* times larger than that of a $7,000 a year secretary, and not just ten times larger, because the executive will have been covered longer. If an employee leaves and forfeits say, $12,000, the executive's account gets $30 of that forfeiture for every dollar allocated to the secretary's account.

The author knows of an IRS-approved plan containing such a favorable allocation formula (from the executive's standpoint), and a sample clause reflecting such a formula appears at the end of this chapter. But the Revenue Service has in recent years become more concerned that such a formula might amount to prohibited discrimination in favor of executives. It has therefore sharply narrowed the situations in which it will approve such plans. Apparently, only plans having a sizeable number of participants (several hundred or more) should seriously hope for IRS approval of an allocation formula based on the size of the accounts of employees who remain.

As with pension plans, company contributions (and employee contributions, if any) are invested by the trust. Unlike the rule with pension plans, a covered employee may be given the right to suggest the securities in which the funds are to be invested. This right has proved of more interest to executives than to other covered employees.

Distributions or withdrawals from profit-sharing plans

If a profit-sharing plan is designed as a retirement plan, distributions from the plan are treated in the same way as distributions from a pension plan. Thus, if the distributions are received periodically, in the form of an annuity, the rules covered in the pension analysis would apply: each annuity receipt is taxable in full unless the employee also contributed to the fund, in which case all receipts for a limited period, or a portion of the receipts for the duration of the annuity, are tax-exempt. If, instead, the employee withdraws his share in a lump sum, the rules previously analyzed for lump-sum withdrawals would apply: tax-exempt return of the employee's own contribution, with the balance taxable as ordinary income subject to a special averaging provision, and with possible capital gain benefits. (See pages 181–84.)

But profit-sharing plans need not be, and frequently are not, retirement plans. The employee will be allowed to withdraw all or some part of vested amounts periodically or otherwise, independently of retirement.

Amounts the employee has the option to withdraw could be considered made available to him for tax purposes. He would be considered to have constructively received those amounts. For example, suppose Brown has a profit-sharing account of $20,000, representing company contributions and earnings thereon, after five years in the plan. Assume that $12,000 of this account has vested and the plan permits employees to withdraw vested amounts after five years. Under constructive receipt principles, Brown could be taxable on $12,000 even though he makes no withdrawal, since $12,000 is made available to him.

To prevent subjecting Brown to a tax on funds not withdrawn, plans typically impose a penalty for withdrawing. For example, the plan might permit withdrawal of vested amounts except that the employee must forfeit 6 percent of the amount which he withdraws (which drops back in the fund for allocation as other forfeitures are allocated). Such a penalty or forfeiture prevents constructive receipt, since an amount is not considered made available if there is a substantial penalty or detriment for withdrawing it. Other, less common, ways to prevent constructive receipt would be to foreclose him from company contributions for a substantial period after withdrawal (which is a penalty in another form) or to require a committee approval of withdrawal, based on need, to pay for medical care or education, for example (here no amount is made available until committee approval is given).

Amounts actually withdrawn are fully taxable as ordinary income, without any annuity, averaging or capital gains tax benefits. The employee is taxed on the amount he receives, and is not taxed on forfeited amounts not collected.

For withdrawals of employee contributions and earnings thereon, see *thrift and savings plans,* below.

Some plans permit an employee to borrow part of his profit-sharing account. Borrowed amounts are not taxable income. Interest paid on borrowed funds is usually at a low rate, and is tax-deductible.

Withdrawing company stock. In some profit-sharing plans, an employee may have the opportunity to take some or all of his lump-sum distribution in the form of company stock. Here, there is a further opportunity for postponing tax on the employee.

Normally, an employee is taxed on the fair market value of property he receives, in the year he receives it. But where he receives stock in the company, he is taxed partly in the year he receives it and partly in the year he sells it. In the year he receives it, he is taxable on the amount the profit-sharing trust paid for the stock. Then, in the year he sells it, he is taxed on the selling price less the cost to the trust.

Example: When Grey retires, he receives a lump-sum profit-sharing distribution of 2,000 shares of stock in his employer. The profit-sharing trust's cost for these shares averaged $20 a share. When Grey received them, they were worth $50 a share.

Grey is taxed on $40,000 ($20 a share) in the year he receives them. If he sells all shares three years later at $52 a share, he is taxed on another $64,000, that is, $104,000 minus $40,000.

Distribution at death. Amounts distributed to an employee's heirs at his death would be taxed under the rules at page 184 governing after-death distributions from pension plans.

If a profit-sharing plan is not a retirement plan, there may not be any fixed time at which withdrawals must be made. Thus a plan may be designed to permit withdrawal of vested amounts after a certain time, but not require any withdrawals while the employee remains employed. This feature has also been used to favor executives by generating a saving in estate tax, a tax which often applies to estates of executives but seldom to those of rank and file employees.

The company may not have any mandatory retirement age for its executives. Thus, the executive may continue employed (at a diminished pace, if desired) beyond normal retirement age, and still be employed at his death. Profit-sharing distributions received by his heirs are exempt from estate tax, to the extent allocable to company contributions. There would be no such estate tax exemption had he received the distribution during his lifetime and held the funds at his death. The author knows of an instance in which such a profit-sharing arrangement saved several million dollars in estate tax for a single individual. For more on tax planning arrangements to save executives' estate taxes, see Chapter 15.

Thrift, savings and other contributory plans

The terms "thrift plan" and "savings plan" do not have a uniform meaning to all companies. As used here, both are contributory profit-sharing plans, that is, profit-sharing plans to which both company and employee contribute. The company's contribution comes from current or past profits, and the employee's from his own cash contributions or payroll deductions. (If the company's contributions were independent of profits, the arrangement would be, and would have to qualify as, a money purchase pension plan.) The term *savings plan* has been applied to a plan in which employee contributions are voluntary, that is, where the company will make contributions for each covered employee and the employee may make further contributions on his own behalf. The term *thrift plan* has been applied to a plan in which employee contributions are mandatory, that is, where an employer will make contributions on an employee's behalf only if the employee also contributes a certain minimum amount for himself.[13] (It should be understood that such contributions are

---

[13] Many practitioners use the term "thrift and savings plan" or "thrift plan" alone, without distinction between mandatory and voluntary plans.

mandatory only in the sense that the employee must contribute, on his own behalf, in order to obtain plan benefits. Contributions on his part are not a condition of his employment.) In such a plan, an employer might match employee contributions at the rate of 50 cents on the dollar, dollar for dollar, $1.50 on the dollar, and so on.

Employees get no tax deductions for their contributions to contributory plans. The tax attraction is the fact that investment earnings on such contributions are exempt from tax until withdrawn. So they grow faster and result in a larger after-tax fund when they are withdrawn, as is illustrated on page 177.

Voluntary plans cannot permit employee contributions in excess of 10 percent of their compensation.

Mandatory plans cannot require the employee to contribute more than 6 percent of his compensation.

Contributory plans, like other plans, will limit the times at which amounts can be withdrawn, for the convenience of plan administration. But contributory plans must also consider provision for withdrawal of the employee's contribution even though company contributions may not be withdrawable.

As a matter of employee relations, no company should construct a profit-sharing plan in which the employee would ever forfeit any of his own funds.[14] It would, however, be reasonable to restrict the time at which he may withdraw his own contributions, and restrict the amount he may withdraw and still remain in the plan.

The tax rules governing withdrawals of employee contributions as part of an annuity or lump sum have already been covered (pages 181–84). In other withdrawal situations, the return of the employee's own contribution is exempt from tax. Any excess over the amount he contributed is fully taxed ordinary income.

---

[14] Since these funds are invested, and investments sometimes drop in value, he may actually get back less than he puts in when he withdraws from the plan, but this would not be a forfeiture.

EIGHT WAYS PLANS CAN FAVOR EXECUTIVES

The following list highlights the ways in which pension or profit-sharing plans can be designed to favor executives:

1. In selecting the type of plan, pension or profit-sharing. A liberal pension plan is preferable to a liberal profit-sharing plan for persons over 45 or so. Thus, a pension plan can be selected, which will favor executives if they are significantly older than the average employees are.

2. In using the opportunity to exclude employees (chiefly rank and file) on the basis of age, length of service, hourly or union status, and so forth.

3. In using the opportunity to exclude rank-and-file employees based on their compensation below a certain amount, through integration with Social Security.

4. In using the opportunity for the covered employee to make voluntary contributions on his own behalf, since earnings on contributions are tax-exempt until withdrawn. This chiefly benefits executives, who may otherwise be taxed at high rates on their investment earnings, and who are more likely than other employees to have funds available for investment.

5. In using the opportunity to exclude employees (chiefly rank and file) who do not make contributions on their own behalf, in a mandatory contributory plan.

6. In using the opportunity to favor executives by basing company contributions or benefits on employee salary.

7. In using the opportunity in a profit-sharing plan to allocate the forfeitures of those who leave to benefit those who remain, including executives, on the basis of their salary or (in some cases) the size of their profit-sharing accounts.

8. In using the opportunity in a profit-sharing plan to obtain an estate tax exemption (which especially benefits executives) through remaining employed until death.

The rules set forth above apply to contributory profit-sharing plans generally, and not just to thrift and savings plans.

Other pension and profit-sharing considerations

IRS approval of the plan

A *qualified* pension or profit-sharing plan is one which meets the requirements of the law. An *approved* plan is something more. It is a plan which the IRS has ruled is a qualified plan. To tax practitioners and pension and profit-sharing specialists, the distinction is vital: A pension or profit-sharing plan involves a huge investment. The company makes substantial contributions each year, or at any rate, frequently. These contributions are invested by the trust for a long period—often decades—and can grow to enormous sums. Amounts distributed to employees frequently run to five and six figures.

The entire edifice is built on a foundation of tax benefits: immediate tax deduction for company contributions with current tax exemption for the employee; tax-exemption for investment earnings while held by the trust; and various tax benefits to the employee or his estate on withdrawal. The edifice topples if the plan is not qualified. The company's immediate deduction, or the employee's current tax-exemption, is lost; investment earnings become taxable as earned; and the tax benefits on withdrawal are forfeited.

With so much at stake, the company naturally seeks assurance that its plan will be treated as qualified. The Revenue Service is willing to provide such assurance. That is, it is willing after examining the plan and satisfying itself that the plan is qualified to issue a commitment (a determination letter, sometimes also called a ruling) that its Revenue Agents will treat the plan as qualified.

It will do this for existing plans and, more important, for contemplated plans before they go into effect. The commitment is effectively binding on the Revenue Service if the information given to the Revenue Service fairly and fully states the facts of the matter, and the plan is not deviated from thereafter.

Obtaining IRS approval is not a legal necessity. The plan must of course conform to the statutory conditions for qualification. Sometimes, however, taxpayers (and their tax advisers) disagree with the IRS on what these conditions actually require. A number of plans have been ruled qualified in court, over IRS objection. But seeking IRS approval is considered by practitioners to be a practical necessity in almost all cases. It is the author's own experience that the IRS is reasonable in granting approval.

Partnerships, proprietorships, and the self-employed retirement plan

All the rules and opportunities discussed earlier in this chapter apply to pension or profit-sharing plans established by partnerships or proprietorships, if the partners or proprietors are excluded.

The rules are substantially different if proprietors or partners are to be covered. Practically all devices for favoring executives in corporate plans are denied to plans covering proprietors or partners whose partnership interest is more than 10 percent.

Master or prototype plans

Some companies may choose to participate in a master or prototype plan. These are qualified and approved pension or profit-sharing plans sponsored by banks, insurance companies, mutual funds, trade associations and other entities. Joining such a plan is cheaper than setting up the company's own plan. On the other hand, the company's own plan can be tailored to its, and its executives', own situations, and can offer much more after-tax benefits than master plans do. Furthermore, front-end charges of an insurance company's master plan have been known to equal costs of a tailor-made plan.

SAMPLE PENSION OR PROFIT-SHARING PLAN CLAUSES

Eligibility

An employee shall be eligible to participate in the Plan as of December 31st following the date on which he shall have met the following requirements: (*a*) he has attained age _____, and (*b*) he has been continuously employed by the Company for a period of at least _____ full years; and (*c*) he receives a compensation in the form of salary, wages and bonuses (but not including overtime pay or tips) of at least $_____.

An employee shall not be considered as having been employed for purposes of (*b*) above for any year in which he worked for the Company less than _____ months, or for any year in which his regular work week averaged less than _____ hours.

Allocation of company profit-sharing contribution based on employee compensation

Amounts shall be allocated to the account of each participant in the proportion which his compensation bears to the total compensation of all participants for such years.

Contributory plans—employee contribution voluntary

Each participant may, but shall not be required to, contribute to the trust fund under the Plan in each calendar year in which he is a participant. If he elects to contribute, the amount he may contribute may not be less than 25 percent or more than 100 percent of the amount credited to his account under Section _____ hereof for the preceding calendar year, except that in no case may his contribution exceed _____ percent of his compensation for the year of contribution.

Contributory plan—employee contribution mandatory

Each participant shall contribute to the trust fund an amount equal to _____ percent of the total compensation paid him by the company for that year.

Allocation of forfeitures in proportion to compensation

Any amounts forfeited in accordance with Section _____ hereof shall be allocated to the accounts of remaining participants in the proportion that each participant's compensation during the calendar year preceding the allocation bears to the total compensation of participants for that year.

Allocation of forfeitures in proportion to account balances

Any amounts forfeited in accordance with Section _____ hereof shall be allocated to the accounts of remaining participants in the proportion that each participant's balance in his account on the date of allocation bears to the total balances in the accounts of all participants on that date.

Continued employment after "retirement age"

Retention of a participant in the Company's employ after the participant's normal retirement date shall be at the exclusive discretion of the Company, and shall be permitted only with the Company's written consent.

Changes in pension rules

As this chapter goes to press, Congress is considering a measure that would substantially change pension rules. Its importance to the U.S. economy is shown by the fact that House Speaker Carl Albert called it "the most important issue before Congress in 1974."

But only a small part of the pending legislation would significantly affect executives covered by qualified pension or profit-sharing plans. On this and the following pages, we examine the areas in which plans structured to benefit executives might be affected.

Coverage (participation). Under present rules,[17] a plan can automatically exclude employees with less than five years' ser-

---

[17] "Present rules" means rules in the law on January 1, 1974.

vice, without being considered as discriminating in favor of executives. Under the Senate's proposed rules, a plan cannot qualify if it postpones participation beyond one year's service or age 30, whichever is later.

Vesting and forfeiture. Present *law* does not require that any part of an employee's share in a corporate plan vest before he becomes entitled to withdraw his share (or the plan terminates). In practice, however, the IRS has required more liberal vesting, especially for profit-sharing plans. Long-postponed vesting favors executives, since as a class they are not likely to forfeit their shares by leaving before the shares become withdrawable.

Proposals pending in Congress would require vesting on a more liberal basis than the IRS has called for. In one version being considered (which has Senate approval) at least 25 percent of an employee's accrued benefit must vest after five years' service, with further vesting required in succeeding years.

Pension benefits. Under present rules, there is no dollar ceiling on the amount of benefits which a defined benefit pension plan may provide. Pending legislation would impose a ceiling. The Senate has voted that the company may not deduct the cost of pension benefits for any employee to the extent that benefit exceeds 75 percent of the average of the highest three years' compensation paid that employee, with a maximum benefit of $75,000 a year.

In a money purchase pension plan, the contribution is defined or prescribed but the benefit is not. Under present rules, the company can in some cases contribute up to 100 percent of the employee's compensation to such a pension, with deduction for the company and no tax to the employee. Under proposed legislation approved by the Senate, the employee would be taxed on any employer contribution on his behalf in excess of 20 percent of his compensation.

Benefits for stockholder-employees (*"proprietary employees"*). Under present law, the fact that a covered employee is also a stockholder ordinarily does not affect his right to benefits under a company plan, assuming the plan does not "discriminate."

The Senate's proposals to change these rules have been described as imposing a ceiling on the company's annual contribution for a stockholder-executive of 15 percent of compensation, but not more than $7,500. The proposal is actually more liberal than this, since benefits up to $75,000 a year—the ceiling discribed above for all covered employees—could be provided despite this limitation. A stockholder-executive subject to these provisions—called a "proprietary employee" in the Senate proposal—is an employee owning at least 2 percent of the stock who also, together with other proprietary employees, owns at least 25 percent of the total accrued pension benefit.

Under present law, an employee of a *Subchapter S* corporation (described in Chapter 4) who owns 5 percent or more of the stock is subject to tax on company contributions on his behalf, to the extent they exceed the lesser of $2,500 or 10 percent of his compensation. Under the Senate proposal, the ceiling on tax-free company contributions for a *Subchapter S* proprietary employee would be raised to the lesser of $7,500 or 15 percent of compensation. (The alternative $75,000 a year benefit ceiling would not be available.)

Alternative benefit ceilings   There are three different ways in which pending pension legislation might impose a ceiling on executive (or stockholder-executive) benefits. The *manner* of setting the ceiling is important, since some ways may not prove effective barriers to maximizing executive benefits.

1.   The legislation might treat a plan as disqualified if benefits (or contributions towards benefits) exceed a certain amount. This is the most severe course, since *all* pension advantages (with certain exceptions for company compensation deductions) are lost if ceilings are exceeded.
2.   The legislation might deny company deduction for contri-

butions in excess of ceilings. This might not be a serious limitation where executives control the corporation.

3. The legislation might tax the executive on contributions exceeding contribution or benefit ceilings. This might not be a serious limitation either. The arrangement would then resemble a contributory plan, under which the executive invests some of his salary in the plan. While the salary so invested is taxable when earned, investment earnings are tax-deferred.

Lump-sum distributions.   Under present rules, amounts withdrawn in a lump sum are taxed as long-term capital gains, except for amounts equal to the employee's own contribution (tax-exempt) and employer contributions after 1969 (ordinary income but with a special averaging provision reducing the tax impact). Under the Senate's proposed changes, the entire amount withdrawn is ordinary income subject to special averaging except for an amount equal to the employee's own contribution (tax-exempt) and the amount attributable to years before 1974 (long-term capital gain). The amount attributable to pre-1974 years is the total taxable lump sum distribution, *times* the number of pre-1974 years the employee was in the plan, *divided by* the total number of years he was in the plan.

Partnerships and proprietorships.   Under present rules, partnership or proprietorship contributions for a proprietor or more-than-10 percent partner cannot exceed the lesser of $2,500 or 10 percent of his earned income. Pending legislation would raise this ceiling to the lesser of $7,500 or 15 percent of his earned income.

chapter 13   The most valuable fringe benefits

No single definition for the term fringe benefits seems to satisfy everyone. What some companies and personnel specialists call fringes, others classify as necessities—pensions and vacations, for example.

The fringe benefits analyzed in this chapter should not be considered to include everything that might be made available to executives in the way of fringe benefits. Rather, the chapter covers those fringes (not discussed elsewhere in this book) which offer the most significant benefits to the executive, at relatively low cost to the company because of its right to deduct its fringe benefit outlays.

Financial counseling for executives

Financial counseling is one name given to an attractive fringe benefit offered by many of the nation's largest corporations. It is a package of financial advisory and planning services, performed by a team of professionals employed by firms engaged in the business of providing such services, for a fee, to company management. Some firms specialize in financial counseling exclusively; for others, financial counseling is a highly developed branch of their many activities. Well-known names in the field include: The Aims Group, Inc.; Donaldson, Lufkin and Jenrette, Inc.; and the U.S. Trust Co. An employer will engage a financial counseling firm to provide counseling services to selected executives at a fee per executive, to be paid by the employer or, occasionally, partly by employer and partly by executive.

The services provided vary somewhat from one counseling firm to another. Then, too, the employer hiring the consulting firm may ask for special services, or reject some services not considered appropriate to its own executives. But the services financial counselors typically provide executives deal with:

The executive's estate plan: The counselors determine the expected size of the executive's estate, assist him in planning how it should be disposed of at his death (including will-drafting advice), suggest suitable insurance arrangements and the proper balance between term insurance and other forms, advise on estate dispositions and will clauses that tend to minimize federal estate taxes, state inheritance taxes, and probate expenses, and provide guidance in assuring the estate's liquidity at the executive's death, to carry his widow and beneficiaries during the probate period and to cover outstanding debts.

The executive's tax returns: Attorneys or accountants on the counseling firm's staff may prepare the executive's federal, state and city income tax returns, and gift tax returns where applicable. The general review of the executive's financial affairs, which is the starting point of the financial consultant's analysis and recommendations, includes an examination of the executive's past income tax returns. Consultants have sometimes turned up reporting errors in the government's favor which have generated tax refunds. More often, however, the reporting defects uncovered have favored the executive. Prompt correction of these mistakes, as recommended by the consultant, has in some cases forestalled embarrassment or more serious difficulty with the Revenue Service.

The executive's compensation package: Many executives skilled in the most arcane aspects of corporate finance are embarrassingly unsophisticated about their own rights and profit opportunities under company plans. The counselor will outline the benefits, risks, and tax consequences of such common (but, to some executives, mysterious) company plans as stock options (Chapter 9), deferred compensation (Chapter 5), shadow stock (Chapter 5), split-dollar life insurance (Chapter 14), group-term life insurance (Chapter 14), thrift or savings plans (Chapter 12), and profit-sharing withdrawals (Chapter 12). Thus, one financial consultant reportedly saved an executive $67,000 in income taxes by recommending that a qualified stock option be exercised in installments over a period of years instead of all at once. (For more on this tax-saving move, see Chapter 9.)

The executive's investment portfolio: Advisers from the consulting firm will suggest suitable new investments or switches. One major element of their advice may be an investment in a tax shelter, such as a cattle breeding herd or a low-rent housing project.

The financial counseling firm's work is extremely detailed and complicated, calling for the services of attorneys, accountants, investment and insurance advisers, and on occasion professional estate planners and fiduciaries. It is, appropriately, expensive: Costs up to $3,500 per executive are common for the complete counseling program, and the executive's situation may thereafter be periodically reviewed (annually or semiannually) at an additional $1,000 or so for each review.

The selection of a counseling firm requires care. First, there should be complete assurance that each executive's confidences will be protected. There is the further need to be sure that the consulting firm is not promoting any interests of its own when it recommends any particular stock, tax shelter, insurance arrangement or other investment, or that any such interests are fully disclosed. Also, the executive must feel that he is getting advice in his own interests and independent of his company's preferences. Indeed, the employer which engages an outside consulting firm must accept the possibility that its executives may become less closely tied to the company economically and not more so. For one thing, advisers typically counsel executives to diversify their portfolios by getting rid of some of their company stock. Also, the consultant may criticize the company's present balance of cash compensation versus other benefits, and may urge changes which the company would prefer not to hear.

Financial counseling as it is presently practiced is considered by many to have been launched first by the Aims Group, in 1969. Its recent rapid growth has been traced to the wage controls that came in in 1971. Companies that found themselves limited in their power to increase salaries used financial counseling as an additional executive benefit.

Another factor contributing to the growth of financial counseling was the claim some counseling firms made that the services were tax-exempt to executives. These firms were aware that many companies have provided in-house legal and accounting services and investment advice for their executives for decades, without tax problems—that is, with no tax to the executive. Tax "exemption" here generally resulted because the services were performed by corporate employees whose salaries were included in the general "salaries and wages" line of the tax return. Little or no Revenue Service challenge arose because there was nothing to indicate that company accountants, lawyers or investment analysts were attending to executives' private affairs at company expense.

But financial counseling services are much more open to Revenue Service scrutiny, since the services are separately billed by an outside firm.

This feature has had a predictable result: a 1973 Revenue Service decision that the executive must report and pay taxes on the counseling services. Specifically, the Revenue Service considers that the amount the employer pays to the consulting firm is taxable as additional compensation to the executive on whose behalf the payment is made, and furthermore is subject to withholding tax.

However, a substantial measure of tax benefit and, in effect, tax exemption, is still available for financial counseling services, since the Revenue Service will allow the executive what can amount to sizeable deductions offsetting his income from services. Specifically:

1. Amounts paid for services directed to tax matters are deductible. Individuals are allowed to deduct costs of services in tax return preparation, tax disputes, tax advice, and tax planning. The amount allocable to tax matters could be a substantial portion of the bill, since the consultant, besides preparing tax returns, would give necessary tax advice connected with investments (especially tax shelters) and estate planning. It would therefore be appropriate for the consulting firm to expressly allocate a portion of its bill for each executive to tax advice, and could also be appropriate, in view of the sweeping importance of the tax treatment, to make the amount allocable to tax advice a sizable portion of the bill. Thus, the larger the portion properly allocable to tax advice, the smaller the amount which is actually taxable to the executive.

The request for allocation to tax advice should properly come from the company. The author knows of one prominent consulting firm which is willing to honor such a request.

2. Amounts allocable to investment advice would also in effect be exempt from tax to the executive, since he normally would be

allowed an offsetting deduction for the cost of such advice. The company should ask the consulting firm for a specific allocation to investment advisory services in each bill.

3. Costs allocable to explaining company stock option and other benefits to the executive would seem to be tax-exempt to him.[1] The consulting firm should allocate a part of its bill to such services. The executive would be taxed on the balance of the cost of his counseling, since he would not be allowed offsetting deductions for costs attributable to other services.

Example: Suppose the bill for consulting services to Walters, Apex Corporation's financial vice-president, is $3,500, of which $2,000 is for tax and investment services and therefore in effect exempt from tax. The company treats the $3,500 as additional compensation to Walters, and withholds an additional $1,260 from Walters' cash pay to cover the withholding liability on $3,500 in Walters' bracket. At the end of the year, it shows $3,500 as part of Walters' wages in the Form W-2 withholding statement given to Walters, and also includes the $1,260 in the amount withheld. On Apex's corporate income tax return, it would treat the $3,500 as salary to Walters (under "compensation of officers"), which is deductible to the extent that it, along with Walters' other compensation, is reasonable.

Walters would report the $3,500 along with his other salary income and claim a credit for the full amount withheld. He would also take a deduction (under "miscellaneous deductions") for the $2,000 allocable to tax and investment services, so that he is taxable only on the $1,500 balance. (The required withholding on the entire $3,500 may cause withholding to exceed the executive's tax liability. To prevent this, the executive could file a

---

[1] This is the author's opinion. The Revenue Service has not publicly discussed this.

revised Form W-4 with the employer to increase his withholding allowances and thereby reduce withholding on future salary payments. Otherwise, he could simply claim a refund of the excessive tax when he files his return.)

The after-tax cost of the $3,500 of consulting services for Walters is therefore $1,820 for Apex (assuming all Walters' compensation is reasonable) and $750 for Walters (assuming he is in the 50 percent bracket).

Any company offering such services to its executives should warn them of the Revenue Service rule treating the cost as taxable compensation (with some offsetting deduction).

This tax liability may deter some executives from accepting the offered services. Services refused would not be taxable income. But in most cases they should not refuse. Financial counseling gives the executive a systematic review of his affairs, which he has probably been neglecting for years, and helps him decide where he is and where he is going with his career and his estate. More important, it can produce actual, visible, immediate profits and tax savings for the executive far outweighing any tax cost, through the guidance provided on company plans, tax shelters, tax refunds, and other tax matters.

The company is free, from a tax standpoint, to give or withhold such services to executives or other employees as it chooses. Companies typically limit it to top executives, and sometimes to selected top executives. (Some companies furnishing executives with such services expected objections from stockholders. But there seems to be little vocal objection so far.)

No plan or other formality is required when setting up financial counseling for executives. But it is wise to include a waiver to be signed by executives who accept financial counseling. This waiver would represent the executive's agreement not to hold the employer liable for the consequences of following any advice furnished by the counseling firm.

Interest-free and low-interest loans to executives

Today, when mortgage interest rates reach 9½ percent, when rates on personal loans reach 12 percent, and rates on widely advertised executive loans made by companies in the midwest range between 18 and 24 percent, an interest-free or low-interest loan from the employer can be a fringe benefit of considerable value to executives.

For the executive who could use $50,000 or so to help buy a home or exercise some stock options, an interest-free loan from his company may be worth some $4,000–$5,000 in interest cost saved (though its after-tax worth is somewhat less, depending on his tax bracket, since his interest payments are deductible).

Interest-free and low-interest loans are also used as inducements on the hiring line. One well-known executive accepted a top position when the offer to sell him stock in the company substantially below its market value was sweetened by a low-interest loan for the stock's purchase price.

There is at present no official ruling from the courts or the Revenue Service on the tax treatment of interest-free loans to executives. But the tax profession is virtually unanimous that the employee who borrows from his employer is not taxable on the amount of interest the company does not charge (or, of course, on the principal amount). For example, if a company makes a $10,000 loan interest-free to an employee at a time when the rate on similar loans is 12 percent, it is clear to all (or almost all) tax practitioners that the $1,200 (12 percent of $10,000) a year value of that loan is not taxable income to the employee. If the employer were to charge, say, 4 percent, the $800 value of that bargain rate (12 percent of $10,000 less 4 percent of $10,000) would not be taxable. Of course, the employee could not tax-deduct any interest he does not pay.

These tax specialists also agree that the company should not be considered as receiving interest income with respect to interest not charged to employees (and could not treat that amount as a deduction).

Tax exemption for interest-free loans to executive borrowers is arrived at by analogy with the tax exemption for interest-free loans to stockholder borrowers. In 1955, a member of the duPont family and her husband took out an interest-free loan from a corporation they controlled. The Revenue Service sought to tax them on an amount equal to the then-current prime rate of interest on the money they had borrowed (about $2,000,000). They contested this, and the court ruled that an interest-free loan in this situation (corporation to stockholder) was tax-exempt. On the basis of this decision, tax specialists concluded that an interest-free loan from company to employee should likewise be tax-exempt. The Revenue Service and the courts have not since then upset this view. (There is, however, a possibility that the Revenue Service would undertake to tax the interest element in an interest-free loan from a corporation to an employee who also holds direct or indirect control of the corporation through stock ownership.)

It should be understood that the employee's tax exemption on the amount borrowed (the principal amount) is assured only if the transaction represents a true loan and is not disguised salary or bonus. While a $20,000 interest-free loan is tax exempt, $20,-000 which is actually salary is taxable income to the employee, and is deductible by the company to the extent it is reasonable for the services rendered.

If a loan is intended, it should be made in a businesslike way, with all, or at least most, of the formality appropriate to loans in business settings. It should be in writing and should have a fixed repayment date or installment payment schedule. It is reasonable to make it a secured loan, if the money is lent to provide funds to purchase a house (it could then be mortgage loan), or company stock (the stock itself might be security for the loan; for more on the problems here, see Chapter 7). If any interest will be charged, specify the amount and payment dates.

Including the above provisions does not guarantee that the payment will be treated as a loan. The Revenue Service is always free to seek to prove that it was really compensation. But observing all due formalities helps to incline the Revenue Service—and if necessary the courts—to treat it as a loan.

Many companies limit their interest-free or low-interest loans to certain specific employee purposes: to buy a home, company stock directly or through exercise of a stock option, a car or life insurance, or to pay family medical bills or school tuition. Even companies with no regular loan policies may make loans to executives who move to new job locations. Such loans are to help the executive buy a new home or, when made as a low-interest second mortgage loan on his old home, to help him carry it until it can be sold for a suitable price.

One elaborate transaction known within the tax profession involved a large company's purchase of a luxury home which it sold to its chief executive with no downpayment, no amortization of principal, low interest (4 percent), and principal due many years hence (apparently after the executive's planned retirement, when the house probably would have been sold). There is no public record that the executive was taxed on the low-interest element of this transaction or any other part.

Company considerations on interest-free loans

Though the company faces little danger of adverse tax treatment on an interest-free loan, there may be other unwelcome aspects worth considering before such a loan is made:

1. Some companies have had trouble obtaining repayment of funds they have lent. Their executives looked on the money as theirs, without strings. While this seems to be a problem that could be avoided by adequate communications before the loan is made, the strain and embarrassment at repayment time has soured some firms on making loans.

Some companies which make such loans provide for repayment by means of payroll deductions, while others expect separate repayment in installments. A requirement that the outstanding loan balance be paid in full on termination of employment is a common feature.

2. Corporate loans to executives who are officers may be subject to legal restrictions under state law. The rules vary widely. California law allows loans only with stockholder approval, while Delaware expressly allows the loans without such qualification, and New York allows them by strong implication.

Even where loans to officers are allowed, restraints may be imposed on loans to executives who are directors. It is important to check local law before lending to executives who are officers or directors.

Some companies which have decided against lending to their employees try to get outside lenders to make loan funds available. The likeliest source for such loans is, of course, the company's own bank. Leverage applied by the company can cause the bank to make loans to company executives on terms not available to the public at large. There is, of course, no element of compensation in such loans, and the executive would deduct the interest he pays. The executive can be expected to pay off a bank loan more readily than an employer loan, though some companies have still felt obliged to make good on bank loans on which their executives have defaulted (company payments here being considered taxable compensation to the executive, if he is still employed there).

Executive dining rooms

Lunches served in the executives' dining room are a tax-favored fringe benefit for the executive who receives them, and are fully deductible by the company. Employees, including executives, are not subject to tax on the value of meals furnished them free of charge on company premises if the meals are provided to meet the business convenience of the company. This business convenience test is satisfied with respect to the executives' dining room if the executives gathered there for lunch discuss business concerns during meals.

In most firms, business discussion in the executives' dining room can be taken for granted, and need not be structured by the company. (In any case, business discussion need not take place every day.) But it is wise for some personnel or other management officer to make occasional checks that business matters actually are raised at lunch, and to make an occasional record of matters discussed, in the event of a possible Revenue Service question.

The company's cost of the lunches would be deducted as a business expense. Though some companies provide lavish and elegant meals in luxurious surroundings, there seems to be no recorded instance of a Revenue Service challenge to the amount of the company's deduction for such magnificence.

Thus, a company could provide an executive with a lunch worth $6 some 200–250 times a year. Though he receives $1,200–$1,500 in value, he is completely exempt from tax, while his company deducts the cost of the meal and so bears only about 52 percent of the true cost.

Personnel planners and other management officers should recognize that there is another major reason for providing an executive's dining room: to keep executives' lunchtime alcoholic intake under strict control. Many, perhaps most, executives' dining rooms are liquor free. Limiting liquor consumption seems a sound business reason for providing an executives' dining room, entirely apart from any business discussions during meals. There is, however, no official decision on this point, and some firms (Wall Street brokerage and investment bankers come to mind) are known for the breadth and grandeur of their wine cellars, displayed and drawn upon at lunchtime.

Some companies use the executives' lunchtime as an opportunity to introduce new ideas. Guests from government, universities or other industries are invited, who may serve as catalysts for new thinking. For other firms, the executives' dining room serves to keep executives on the company premises and available in emergencies.

Sometimes, the executive is charged for his meal, usually a nominal amount, or in any case much less than its true value. If this is a flat charge which the executive must pay whether he takes the lunch or not, and deducted from his salary check, the amount he is charged is not part of his taxable income and the value of the meal is not taxable to him either (assuming business discussions take place during meals). If he is charged only for meals he eats, any amount deducted from his salary is income to him and he may not deduct the cost.

The Revenue Service technically requires that the meals be furnished on the company premises. This has in practice been stretched (by a court, over Revenue Service objection) to include a rented hotel suite, and could on the same theory be extended to a private room in a restaurant or club. But it seems advisable to follow the IRS requirement if possible: to use company premises if they are available, and if not, to avoid a public room in a restaurant.

No plan or formalities of any kind are required to establish an executive's dining room. But be prepared to show that business discussions typically take place during meals. Some companies have had unpleasant experiences with their company dining rooms. Employees who were not invited were sometimes demonstratively jealous of those who were. A few firms discontinued their dining rooms for this reason.

Covering executives' moving costs

Wise employee relations policy will completely relieve executives of any out-of-pocket expenses of moving to the area of a new job. Such moves, however welcome they may be when they represent a promotion or a more attractive or exciting location, still bring physical discomfort and family disruption. They should not also involve added expense to be paid with after-tax dollars.

Typical company-paid costs of moving executives from one job location to another are explored below. The analysis applies to the move of a single executive or a small group, and also to moves of the entire top management on a shift of corporate headquarters. A company can cover most moving costs with full deductibility for its outlays and full tax exemption for the executive. If a company limits its outlays to these tax-favored items, the actual cost of moving is limited, in effect, to about 52 percent of what it spends. For the company that wants to provide moving expense benefits or protection beyond the tax-favored items, suggestions are offered for restructuring the arrangement to qualify for tax benefits.

To illustrate the rules, we will take the case of Crawford, the company's regional sales manager located in Dallas, who is named national sales manager and transferred to company headquarters in New York City. Crawford has a wife and three children, and owns a home in Dallas which cost him $42,000 two years ago. All the company moving expense payments or reimbursements described below are deductible by the company and tax-exempt to Crawford (and to his family) except where otherwise expressly stated. Tax exemption for the executive is accomplished by treating company payments or reimbursements of expenses as compensation income to him but allowing him an offsetting deduction.

Travel fares for Crawford and all his family (but not servants) and including costs of meals and lodging en route: If the travel is done by auto, costs of gasoline, oil, tolls, etc. are included in the exempt amount. In any case, travel must be by the most direct route available and in the shortest time commonly required. Expenses of holiday stopovers, sidetrips, or detours are not covered.

Costs of transporting household goods and personal effects: This covers costs of packing and crating and also insurance and storage for up to 30 days after the goods are moved from the old homestead and before they are moved into the new.

Househunting costs: This covers costs of round-trip travel from the area of the old job to that of the new, to search for a new residence to buy or rent. The trip can be by the executive alone, or with his wife or others of his family, or by family members unaccompanied by the executive. Thus, Crawford and his wife could travel round-trip from Dallas to New York to look for a new home in the New York area, and either or both of them could make return trips as necessary for further searches or to negotiate or close deals. Furthermore, the costs are covered even though no new residence is taken because of the trip, but is only found after the move to the new location.

Temporary living costs: These are outlays for meals and lodging up to 30 days in the area of the new job location, following the move there but before moving into permanent quarters. For example, suppose Crawford arrived before the re-decorating work on his house was finished. He and his family lived in New York City hotels and ate in restaurants there for 11 days until the house was ready, at a cost of $75 a day. Company reimbursement of this $825 cost could be tax-exempt.

Home sale "losses": Many company payments connected

with the executive's sale of his old home or purchase of a new one, while deductible by the company, are taxable to the executive as additional compensation. These taxable payments usually result from company efforts to protect the executive from loss on "forced" sale of his home, the loss attributable to the fact that the executive must sell under a time pressure, without being able to wait for a fair price. The company may therefore pay him the difference between the fair market value of the property and what he actually collects on sale. (This was an IBM practice for a time.) The amount an executive receives from his company under this arrangement is taxable compensation income whether what he collects on sale is more or less than the house cost him.

For example, suppose Crawford sells his Dallas house for $39,-000 and his company pays him $3,000 to cover his loss on the sale. The $3,000 is taxable even though his total collections on sale ($39,000 plus $3,000) do not exceed his $42,000 cost of the house. The $3,000 loss he sustained on sale is not deductible, so it cannot offset the $3,000 of income.

Or suppose the company determined that the fair market of the Dallas home was $45,000, but Crawford got only $43,000 on sale, so his company made up the difference with a $2,000 check to cover this moving "loss." The $2,000 is taxable as additional compensation income. It cannot be treated as additional capital gain on sale, and cannot be exempted from tax (tax deferred), as capital gain would be, if he bought a new home at the same or a higher price.

Where it appears that the executive will not get full value on sale of his house, the company could rescue the executive by buying the house at a fair market value determined by independent appraisal (or an average of independent appraisals). This avoids any loss resulting from the "forced" aspect of the sale, though it would not protect the executive from loss attributable to any decline in value of the property below its cost. The executive's profit on sale to his company is capital gain, which can be tax-deferred if he buys a replacement residence; his loss on the sale is not deductible. Making the selling price equal the independent appraisal (or average of appraisals) tends to discourage the Revenue Service from claiming that the selling price was inflated to include some disguised compensation.

The company would face fewer time pressures than the executive in arranging the sale of the house, and therefore could hold out for a suitable price (and might rent it out meanwhile). It probably should treat profit or loss on the house as ordinary income or loss for tax purposes (though this is not entirely clear).

IBM has abandoned its previous practice of making taxable payments to reimburse executives for loss on sale of their homes and now follows the tax-favored course: buying the executive's home. But not all companies are willing to tie up funds in purchases of homes of moved executives. Some firms therefore have adopted these alternative approaches:

a. The company appraises the property and in effect guarantees that appraised value to the executive. The executive then seeks to sell it. If he sells for more than the appraised value, the company keeps the excess; if for less than the appraised value, the company makes up the difference, but the executive must accept any offer the company considers reasonable.

This plan, when used by a large insurance company, resulted in taxable income to the executive to the extent of the company's payment of the difference between the appraised value and the lower sales price. This was not considered the tax equivalent of a sale to the company, even though the company could have made a profit on the arrangement. The executive was still the owner of the house until it was sold, so the company's payment to him was taxable compensation.

b. The company arranges to have a real estate firm buy the home. A number of large firms have entered this field, and some small local firms may also be interested. Under the arrangement, a price for the executive's house is set by appraisal (maybe by the real estate firm, maybe by independent appraisal), and the executive can take this price or seek to sell it elsewhere. Assuming he sells to the real estate firm, the employer corporation thereafter may pay an amount to the firm as a commission, or may cover all or part of the firm's loss on sale of the executive's house if the firm should fail to sell it at a profit. There is as yet no published Revenue Service ruling on this arrangement, and its tax treatment is far from clear. The company would claim that amounts paid the real estate firm are for services performed for the company in lieu of costs the company would incur if it bought the homes directly. This would make the payments deductible business expenses of the company and nontaxable to executives. The opposing view would be to treat them as made for the benefit of the executives selling their homes, taxable to them as additional salary and deductible by the employer only as compensation, subject to reasonableness tests. The author inclines towards the latter view. For interest-free loans to executives in home sale and purchase situations, see page 212.

Home sale expenses: Company payment or reimbursement of certain kinds of costs connected with disposing of a former home or acquiring a new one qualify as tax-exempt to the executive. These are certain costs of buying or selling a home, or acquiring or breaking a lease. Specifically, items that can be covered tax-free include: brokerage commissions, attorney fees, title costs, appraisal fees, escrow fees, mortgage "points" paid for services (appraisal, processing, and so forth, but not "points" paid as interest), transfer taxes, payments to a landlord for release from a lease, and fees or commissions for obtaining a lease, a sublease, or an assignment of a lease.

Taxable amounts

The executive is tax-exempt on company payments or reimbursements of the above items if the amounts are reasonable. This reasonableness requirement does not preclude first-class travel or meals. There seems to be no recorded case where company payment of travel fares, meals and lodging was treated as partly taxable to the executive because it was extravagant and unreasonable.

But for some moving expense items there are additional limits. The exemption for househunting expenses, temporary lodging, and selling or leasing costs combined is limited to $2,500. Furthermore, the exemption for househunting and temporary living costs combined cannot exceed $1,000. Thus, if $2,100 were spent as selling costs and $600 on house-hunting (no temporary lodging costs), $2,500 would be exempt and $200 would be taxable. If $1,200 went to selling costs and another $1,300 to house-hunting and temporary lodging combined, $2,200 ($1,200 plus $1,000) would be exempt and $300 taxable.

No exemption is allowed unless the new place of work is at least 50 miles farther from the old home than the old place of work was. This in essence denies exemption for moves connected with job transfers between nearby towns or between the city and the suburbs. For example, if an executive commuted 12 miles to work at his old job, his new job would have to be more than 62 miles from his old home before his move to a new home would qualify for exemption. The length of his commute between his new home and his new job is irrelevant.

Also, in most cases exemption is barred unless the executive works full time, in the general area he moved to, for at least 39 weeks of the 12 month period following his arrival.

Moving for personal reasons is tax exempt. Executives sometimes pressure their companies to move them to a particular location which they happen to prefer for reasons of climate, recreation, and the like. This helps account for the corporate offices springing up on the California coast. Company payment or reimbursement of expenses of such moves made for the executive's own health, comfort, convenience or other personal reasons is still tax-exempt to him, since he can deduct these costs, assuming the regular exemption tests are met (chiefly, that he is employed full time 39 weeks of the year following his arrival).

In this situation, the company would treat its payment of moving expenses as additional compensation to the executive, rather than as an ordinary business expense. The company therefore could deduct this payment only if the amount paid, together with his other compensation, is reasonable.

Executives in the fringe benefit supermarket

Surveys show that nonsalary benefits to employees typically range from 30 to 35 percent of company payroll. Not every company falls within this range, of course. Fringes vary from one industry to another, and can include some items which executives may not count as anything extra in the way of benefits, such as the employer's Social Security contributions and vacation pay. Still, a company's outlay for noncash and fringe benefits is a sizeable expense item. Some companies therefore are undertaking, on a trial basis, to tailor these benefits exactly to each executive's needs and wishes.

"Supermarket" and "cafeteria" are names that personnel officers have given this new approach. Instead of giving an executive a cash amount in salary and bonus, plus certain predetermined noncash benefits, it lets the executive himself choose what he will take from a broad spectrum of benefits.

For example, suppose Gravesend Corporation pays Carey, its production manager, $50,000 salary plus another $20,000 in noncash benefits. Gravesend decides instead to offer Carey a flat

$70,000 which he can take any way he pleases (within certain limits): all cash now, or cash plus an extended vacation, or partly cash now and partly deferred cash, or partly cash, partly insurance and partly pension, and so on. This privilege to pick and choose among a number of benefits is what gives the names "supermarket" and "cafeteria" to the executive's rights under the plan.

Each executive will choose the mix of cash and benefits which he thinks best suits his financial needs and prestige. Many executives, especially the younger ones, will put heaviest emphasis on straight cash now. This is understandable, especially now that cash compensation bears a federal tax burden of not more than 50 percent (with some qualifications). But many companies will insist that the executive take minimum amounts of certain items such as vacation, salary continuation during illness, or life insurance. In addition, these factors should influence the executive's choice:

1. Tax-favored benefits provided by the company should be taken, or at least carefully considered, instead of taking an amount equivalent to their cost in cash. These benefits can increase the executive's current or future after-tax wealth, without the tax liability that would arise if the executive took cash and then sought to provide the benefits himself with after-tax dollars.

For example, company profit-sharing contributions, group-term life insurance contributions, health insurance premiums, and deferred compensation arrangements could all be provided for the executive without current tax to him. If he had sought to provide on his own for his life insurance, family medical bills, and income after retirement, his true cost of these items, in after-tax dollars, would be much higher. Thus, in the 55 percent bracket, an executive would save $5,500 (apart from a minor accident and health insurance deduction) by having his company provide these items at a $10,000 cost instead of taking an additional $10,000 of salary and providing them himself.

2. Some tax-favored benefits are also cost-favored if provided

by the employer. The employer typically can provide group-term life insurance, and accident and health insurance, at costs below what the executive would have to pay.

Companies adopting or experimenting with cafeteria plans should therefore explain the tax-favored options to executives.

It seems wise to require the executive to choose the particular elements of his meal before the start of the year. Thus, he should choose in 1974 for 1975. This is important for the company's own compensation program administration—for example, in determining the size of the group to be covered by group life or health insurance. It is also advisable for tax reasons, where a profit-sharing plan is involved. Here, it tends to prevent an IRS claim that an executive who chose a tax-exempt (tax-deferred) profit-sharing account over taxable current cash compensation should nevertheless be taxed now, under constructive receipt rules, as if he had received the profit-sharing contribution.

The company's deduction for compensation to executives generally would not depend on how much was paid in cash and how much in benefits. It could deduct the entire amount paid (subject to reasonableness limits) with this exception: For deferred compensation of the type discussed in Chapter 5, no tax deduction is allowed to the company until the executive receives the deferred pay.

Cafeteria arrangements so far have been limited to executives. No formalities are required of the company establishing such arrangements.

Making the executive's charitable donations

Helping to meet the executive's charitable obligations is a fringe benefit popular with a number of large companies.

Some firms agree to contribute to charities selected by their executives, up to specified dollar maximums. For others, the company may grant executives and other employees a kind of charitable allowance based on their performance on the job. Thus, one worker may be allowed to designate a charitable donee of $500 while another worker (an executive, for example) might be able to designate a charity to receive $5,000. Still another common charitable program has the company match charitable contributions of executives (or other employees) dollar for dollar up to a specified maximum.

Company contributions may be made in the name of executives or other employees, but they are by company check, payable to the charity. Amounts donated are not taxable to executives or other employees selecting the charitable donees, and they get no tax deduction for amounts contributed. All deductions are taken by the corporate employer, and are subject to its own deduction limit (generally 5 percent of its taxable income).

Supper money

Company-paid meal allowances to executives who work late at the office—"supper money"—have generally enjoyed a favored tax status. The company has deducted amounts it paid as general business expenses, while recipients have treated supper money as exempt from tax. Tax exemption for supper money accords with the present official Revenue Service position, though the IRS has not in fact recognized the exemption in all cases. (In the author's view, tax exemption is an act of uncritical generosity on Internal Revenue's part, which is not supported by statutory or judicial authority.)

There is no specific ceiling on the amount that can be paid as exempt supper money. In practice, employers usually pay $3 a meal. This seems to represent the figure which has been customary since the IRS granted tax exemption five decades ago. It obviously has not risen with the cost of living. This is probably because companies fear to risk Revenue Service reconsideration of the tax exemption, which might be triggered by a larger payment.

Supper money can be considered a fringe benefit for executives since rank-and-file employees normally must be paid overtime (taxable as ordinary income) when they work late. Though professional employees and certain other categories need not be paid overtime, there is no express objection to limiting supper money to executives if the company so chooses. Also, the company can set whatever length of after-hours work it pleases as a precondition to supper money (though 2–2½ hours is customary).

The exact value of supper money to any executive depends, of course, on the number of times he works late during the year. If he works late 60 times, supper money of $3 a night is worth $180 after taxes—equal to $360 before taxes in the 50 percent bracket.

Death benefits

Company payments to the widow or heirs of a deceased executive qualify for tax benefits.

The widow or other beneficiary is exempt from tax on up to $5,000 of death benefits, if the deceased employee would have had no right to receive the payments himself had he lived longer, or his right to receive them was subject to forfeiture.

The $5,000 exemption is a single exemption for all beneficiaries, not $5,000 for each. If company payments exceed $5,000, the $5,000 exemption is allocated among recipients in proportion to the death benefit they receive. Thus, if a widow receives $9,000 and a son $6,000, she is exempt on $3,000 and he on $2,000.

Besides this limited income tax exemption, voluntary or forfeitable amounts paid to the widow or other beneficiary are exempt from estate tax regardless of amount.

Since income and estate tax exemptions are available only for amounts which the company pays voluntarily, or which are forfeitable by the executive, executives sometimes seek contractual arrangements which make payments forfeitable. It is of course logically unwise for an executive with, say, a deferred compensation agreement to transmute a guaranteed payment under that agreement into a payment which he could forfeit by some future action or inaction. But it is in fact sometimes done, for the tax advantage, by executives who believe there is little danger that the amount will in fact be forfeited.

Amounts are made forfeitable by attaching conditions to them so that the executive loses the right to receive them if he resigns or is fired for cause. This might be done with a deferred bonus or other deferred compensation payable in installments; the executive would forfeit any unpaid balance when he leaves. Amounts which could become nonforfeitable in the future (through performance of services, lapse of time or some other event) are treated as forfeitable until nonforfeitability occurs.[2]

Nonforfeitable death benefits qualify for the $5,000 income tax exemption if they are paid under qualified pension or similar plans. This is explained in Chapter 12.

Amounts which the widow or beneficiary receives which exceed $5,000 can still be exempt from tax if they represent gifts by the company. The Revenue Service usually treats the excess as taxable income, either as compensation for the deceased executive's past services, or as dividends where the beneficiary is a stockholder (for example, where she has inherited the stock of a stockholder-executive). But courts often find the payments to be nontaxable gifts where they are made based on the beneficiary's need.

Death benefits paid as compensation for services are deductible

---

[2] The rules on forfeitability (substantial risk of forfeiture) in Chapter 8 do not apply here.

by the company. They can be compensation even though they are not required under a contract or other formal plan. The company's deduction is subject to the reasonable compensation ceilings (see Chapter 2), but deduction has been allowed for sizable sums. For example, deduction was allowed for $40,000 paid over a two-year period to the widow of a $40,000 a year president.

Companies occasionally treat payments in excess of $5,000 as gifts. Their motive here is to improve the chance that the widow or other recipient can treat receipts as a tax-free gift. Gift treatment by the company does not guarantee gift treatment for the widow. Also, deduction for the first $5,025 of such a gift payment, though not absolutely foreclosed by the Revenue Service, is doubtful. And in any case, deduction is barred for the excess over $5,025 of amounts treated as gifts.

To summarize, payments of not more than $5,000 under a voluntary or forfeitable arrangement as compensation enjoy full tax benefits: income tax exemption to the beneficiary, estate tax exemption for the estate, and deduction for the company. Departure from this arrangement risks loss of some benefits to someone.

Companies sometimes take out an insurance policy on an executive's life, naming the company itself as beneficiary. This is done so that the company will have the funds at the executive's death to cover any death benefit obligation. The company will not be allowed to deduct any of its premiums, but will not be taxable on the proceeds. When it uses the proceeds to pay death benefits, its payments and the beneficiaries' receipts will get the tax treatment described above.

Other fringe benefits valued by executives

Company payment of business or professional dues: A company's payment of dues for the executive's membership in a business association (such as the American Management Association, the American Bankers Association or the Sales Executives Club) or a professional association (a bar association or CPA society) is deductible by the company and tax-exempt to the executive. Thus, an executive who would maintain an association membership in any case can be relieved of the need to pay the cost of membership with his own after-tax dollars. Company payment for subscriptions to business or professional journals would get the same treatment.

Dues paid for membership in downtown luncheon clubs (such as New York's Banker's Club) are likewise deductible by the company and tax-exempt to the executive. Such clubs are considered to have a business purpose for the company, since business discussion and contacts of potential importance to the company take place there. (Deduction of the cost of meals is another matter, as is deduction of dues to a country club, yacht club or other social club. These matters are considered in Chapter 10.)

Company payment of officer liability insurance: An executive isn't subject to tax on, and his company may take a deduction for, company payment of the cost of insurance indemnifying its executives for expenses arising from their wrongful acts (or allegedly wrongful acts) committed in their official capacities, including: breach or neglect of duty, wrongful act or omission, error, misstatement or misleading statement, or "any matter claimed against them."

Lavish office furnishings: The Revenue Service does not seek to tax an executive on the value of office creature comforts furnished him, however splendid they might be. Also, company deductions for such grandeur generally are not questioned, except that it cannot take depreciation deductions on antiques and works of art which do not decline in value with the passage of time.

chapter 14   How to use life insurance

I N any survey of executive dissatisfaction with the federal tax structure, one of the most frequently heard complaints is that today's high taxes prevent an executive from building up a substantial estate to leave to his family. No single compensation arrangement can completely relieve this concern, but one kind of company-furnished benefit—life insurance—is uniquely suited to executives' needs. Life insurance proceeds are, of course, an element of the estate that the insured individual leaves his family, yet life insurance is more highly favored for tax purposes than other forms of investment for the executive, for several reasons.

First, insurance proceeds collected by his beneficiaries at his death are completely exempt from income tax. For example, if $30,000 was paid in premiums on a policy that paid $100,000 at death, there is a $70,000 profit on the insurance investment, all of which is exempt from income tax.

Second, insurance proceeds can also be exempt from federal estate tax and state inheritance tax. Unlike the income tax exemption for insurance proceeds, however, the estate and inheritance tax exemptions are not automatic; tax saving action is necessary, as shown later in this Chapter.

Third, the current premium cost of life insurance coverage can be provided to the executive in two tax-favored ways:

1. Group-term life insurance.
2. Split-dollar life insurance.

These tax benefits for insurance premium costs do not apply to premiums a company pays on other straight or term life insurance for the executive. Any employee, including an executive employee, must include in his taxable income any premiums the company pays on insurance covering his life if either (*a*) he names the beneficiaries of the life insurance or (*b*) the beneficiaries are named by the company but are those he would be likely to choose himself, such as his wife or children, or a trust for their benefit, or his estate or executor. The premiums are additional salary income to him, and are deductible as additional salary by the company (subject to reasonable compensation ceilings). This can still be an economic benefit for the executive (as shown in convertible term insurance below) but it is not a tax benefit.

Group-term life insurance

This is a way to provide substantial life insurance coverage for employees, without tax cost to them and with full deduction for the company. It is possible to limit coverage to executives, keeping down the overall cost to the company, or to cover executives for larger amounts than other employees.

For complete tax exemption, insurance must be term insurance, and the executive's coverage may not exceed $50,000. The actual cash value to the executive of getting term insurance coverage through his employer, instead of having to buy it himself with after-tax dollars, will depend on how much the insurance he would buy on his own would cost at his age; $50,000 of term insurance could reasonably cost between $350 and $1,250 in various age brackets.

Additional benefits are available for coverage in excess of $50,-000. Here, the executive continues to be exempt from tax on the cost of the first $50,000 but is taxable on the cost of each $1,000 of coverage in excess of $50,000. However, the amount he pays tax on is substantially less than the actual cost of such coverage, because the taxable amount is dictated by a table provided in Revenue Service regulations.[1] The amounts in the table are less than the company actually pays. Yet the company can still deduct its actual cost, and not the lesser amount its executive is taxed on.

Example: Caldwell, in his fifties, is a $35,000-a-year vice president at Dunmow Corporation. He has $100,000 of coverage under Dunmow's group-term plan. The insurance costs Dunmow $15 per $1,000 of coverage, or $1,500.

Caldwell is exempt from tax on $50,000 of insurance coverage, but is taxable on the cost of any excess (assuming he pays nothing for his coverage), so he is taxable on the cost of $50,000. But cost is figured under Revenue Service tables which tax Caldwell at the rate of $8.16 per $1,000, or $408. Thus, Caldwell gets value of $1,500 and pays tax on $408. In Caldwell's probable tax bracket (after itemized deductions, and so forth), his actual cost of this $100,000 of coverage, the tax cost, is about $147.

Dunmow would still deduct its $1,500 cost (subject to reasonable compensation limits). Its deductible cost is not limited to the $8.16 per $1,000 used to figure Caldwell's tax.

If the executive pays part of the cost of coverage in excess of $50,000, the amount he pays reduces dollar for dollar the amount he is taxable on.

---

[1] See page 250 for this table and how it is used to compute an executive's tax.

Example: Assume that in the above example Caldwell got $100,000 of coverage but had to pay for $20,000 of it, while his company paid for the $80,000 balance. Since Caldwell pays $300 ($15 per $1,000, for $20,000), he is taxed on only $108 ($408 minus $300).

Having the executive pay for part of his own coverage is, of course, less attractive to him than if the company covers the entire $100,000, since the executive must pay out $339 ($300 plus $39, the tax cost of $108 of taxable income), instead of $147. Still, it has advantages where the company is willing to pay only part of the cost of coverage over $50,000, or where the company will pay the entire cost of a specific amount but the executive wants more. This route, therefore, is preferable to providing the extra $20,000 of term insurance on his own, and outside the plan. Thus, if he got $80,000 under the plan and $20,000 elsewhere, at a cost of about $440 (figured at $22 per $1,000 since he could not get the benefit of group rates), his cost would be $530, that is, the $90 tax on $249 (the taxable income from the $30,000 of group insurance in excess of the exempt $50,000), plus $440 paid for the extra $20,000 of insurance.

Other group-term insurance benefits

The executive's spouse and dependents can be given tax-free life insurance coverage up to $2,000 each. If coverage for any such person exceeds $2,000, the executive is taxable on the cost of the entire coverage of that person.

Retired executives—that is, executives who no longer work for the company and who have reached retirement age—are tax-exempt on all their coverage, even if it exceeds $50,000.

While permanent insurance is not tax-exempt, a policy provision allowing the executive to convert his policy from term to permanent when he leaves the company will not make his coverage (up to $50,000) taxable to him. Some companies do not welcome this convertible feature, thinking it provides something of an incentive to change jobs.

Group-term insurance for executives only: There is no express provision in the tax law which prevents companies from granting group-term life insurance to executives only, and excluding all other employees. But Revenue Service regulations somewhat inhibit company efforts to make such insurance "executives only."

First, there must be a group. To the Revenue Service, this means that the company cannot individually select those to be covered. Rather, those covered must be a class or classes of employees (or, of course, all employees). This, however, does not prohibit the company from limiting coverage to, say, all officers, or all department heads, or all employees making over $25,000, or all employees over age 50 with more than 15 years' service, or some other reasonable classification which may cover only those intended to be benefited. Also, it is not necessary that they be covered by a single master policy; a group of individual policies for each covered individual is also acceptable.

Second, the group covered must not be limited to *stockholder-employees.*

Third, in most cases the group must consist of ten or more persons. This rule admits of a few exceptions. The Revenue Service accepts groups of less than ten, where there are fewer than ten full-time employees and all full-timers are covered. (There is, by the way, sometimes a practical difficulty with small groups. Some insurance companies are reluctant to write sizable group policies for groups of fewer than ten members.)

To summarize the effect of these rules, a company can, as an economy measure or for other company policy reasons, exclude rank-and-file employees from group-term coverage if (*a*) it covers a group of employees, selected on the basis of position (officers, department heads, managers, etc.), salary, age, length of service, and so on, (*b*) the group is not limited to stockholders, *and* (*c*) there are at least ten in the group.

For example, suppose a company has 110 full-time employees, including six officers (of which four are stockholders) and five department heads. Limiting group-term coverage to the six officers is not allowed under the above rules (since the group is less than ten), but limiting coverage to all officers and department heads would be allowed.

However, a company could provide group-term coverage for all employees, or one or more classes of employees, and still favor executives by giving them greater coverage. Thus, the company could adopt a plan which provides group-term coverage which is a percentage of salary (assuming that percentage applies uniformly to all covered employees). For example, the company could provide $2 of coverage for every $1 of salary (a uniform 200 percent), so that the $8,000-a-year employee gets $16,000 and the $50,000-a-year executive gets $100,000.

Or, instead, coverage could be provided based on salary brackets if the brackets are set by the insurance company rather than the employer. These brackets allow considerable flexibility. For example, employees in a $10,000–$20,000 bracket could be given $20,000 of coverage while those in the $20,000–$30,000 could be given $50,000.

The company could not individually select the amount of coverage for particular employees, but must use the uniform percentage system, the bracket system, or some other formula. A sample plan of group-term insurance appears at page 248.

Split-dollar insurance

This is another form of tax-favored insurance for the executive. It is a way whereby the company and the executive split the costs and the benefits of the insurance. It is permanent, not term, insurance and is used especially for the younger executive or manager who is unable to afford a large insurance commitment on his own. Under a split-dollar arrangement, the company and the executive each are obliged to pay part of the premium cost of insurance on the executive's life, but after the early years of the policy the executive normally no longer has to pay anything.

The company pays that part of the annual premium which equals the increase in the policy's cash surrender value for the year. For this payment, the company becomes entitled to receive at the executive's death that part of the insurance proceeds which equals the policy's cash value (which in the policy's later years may exceed the company's actual investment in the policy).

The executive pays the balance of the premium due, that is, the total premium less the portion paid by the company (and disregarding for the moment dividends on the policy, which are considered below). This means, in practice, that the executive pays a substantial part of the premium cost in the first three or four years, and little or nothing thereafter. (See below for company loans to help pay these premiums.) At his death, the executive's beneficiaries will collect the entire proceeds of the policy except for the cash surrender value which is paid to the employer.

The amount to be collected by the executive's beneficiaries at his death declines each year as the cash surrender value mounts. This is why split-dollar insurance is so often designed specifically for the younger executive. The split-dollar arrangement gives him maximum protection while his children are young, which drops as they get older and the amount needed for their support until they can become self-supporting declines. (The same sort of thinking lies behind recommendations of some insurance advisers and salesman that executives should carry large amounts of term insurance while their children are young, which can be terminated as the children get older. Decreasing term insurance is sold on this basis.)

The policy may technically be owned by either the company or the executive. The author generally advises that the executive own the policy, but with adequate protection for the company's investment. (Thus, the policy may be assigned to the company, as shown in the sample split-dollar arrangement at page 249.)

Like other life insurance proceeds, the proceeds of split-dollar life insurance come to the beneficiaries (including the company as beneficiary of the cash surrender value) free of income tax. Moreover, the insurance proceeds can be made exempt from estate tax in the executive's estate, see below. But there is a tax liability, and there are several tax and business planning opportunities, connected with payment of the insurance premiums.

The executive is subject to tax on part of the premium cost of split-dollar coverage. The Revenue Service considers that, to a degree, a split-dollar insurance arrangement uses the employer's payments for the executive's benefit. This makes the payments compensation, in part. Specifically, the executive is taxable on an amount equal to the cost of one-year term insurance for the amount of his coverage in that year, reduced by the amount of premiums he actually pays.

Example: A $100,000 policy is taken out for Davis, on which his share of the first premium is about $600. His share of the $100,000 is reduced by the cash surrender value of the policy (which goes to his employer), so his coverage is about $93,000. He is taxable on the cost of $93,000 of term insurance for one year, at his present age, but this taxable amount is reduced by the $600 premium he pays. In practice, he would therefore have little or no taxable income this year.

But two years later, he pays only about $200 of premium cost, and his share of the policy is now about $80,000 (since the cash surrender value is now about $20,000). He is taxable on the cost of $80,000 of term insurance at the age he is two years hence, reduced by the $200 he paid as premium. Now he is taxable on about $400. So for this year his split-dollar insurance costs him $356 in the 39 percent bracket, that is, $200 plus the $156 tax on $400.

The cost of term insurance, used to determine the amount taxable to the executive, is prescribed by a Revenue Service table. (The table, which is not the same as that used for group term life insurance, appears at the end of this chapter.) In general, the table reflects a cost of term insurance which is less than the actual cost of such insurance. This means that though the executive is taxed on his split-dollar insurance benefit, he is taxed on less than the true value of what he gets, and thereby makes a tax saving on the premium cost as well as on the proceeds.

The Revenue Service recognizes the possibility that the cost figures in its table may sometimes be higher than some insurance companies actually charge. Therefore it permits the tax to be computed by using the rates actually charged by the insurance company involved, where these are lower than those in the Revenue Service table.

Policy dividends: The rules described above assume that any dividends on the policy are paid to the employer, or go to reduce its premiums. Such dividends are not taxable to the employer. If policy dividends are paid to the executive, they normally are taxable income to him. (They would be exempt from tax to the extent that the premium he paid that year exceeded the value of his term insurance coverage for that year.) Dividends payable to the executive are sometimes used to buy additional insurance for him. Some executives do this because they want to offset, in part, the drop in insurance coverage that occurs automatically as the cash surrender value, payable to the employer, increases. Dividends so used normally are also taxable income to the executive.

Employer's tax treatment; financed life insurance: The employer is not allowed any tax deduction for its split-dollar insurance premium. It will collect the cash surrender value completely free of income tax, but it gets no current deduction for the premiums paid to create that cash surrender value.

Though the company will get back the amount it put into the policy when the executive dies (and sometimes a bit more), some companies are reluctant to tie up their funds that long. They therefore may want to take care of some of their premium cost by borrowing against the cash surrender value.

This practice of borrowing against the cash surrender value to pay a premium—called "financed life insurance"—minimizes the company's cash commitment in split-dollar arrangements. It does not affect the tax treatment of the premiums or the proceeds. But there are limitations on a company's tax deduction for interest it pays on funds borrowed to buy or carry financed life insurance. In general, the company cannot deduct interest on financed life insurance, whether the loan comes from the insurance company or another source, unless at least four years' premiums out of the first seven years' premiums are paid without borrowing. Also, in the years in which the premiums are paid with borrowed funds, the amount borrowed against the cash surrender value cannot exceed one year's premium. Thus, the company could pay premiums from its own cash funds the first two years, and then in the third year borrow the amount of that year's premium, deduct any interest on that borrowing for that year, borrow again in the fourth year the amount of that year's premium (and deduct interest), pay the premium in the fifth year without borrowing (but deduct the interest on the two previous loans still outstanding), and so on.

After the seventh year, the company can borrow the balance of the cash surrender value, if it wishes. It then is not limited to borrowing only a single year's premium.

There are several other exceptions (besides the four-out-of-seven-year exception) to the rule barring the company's interest deduction, but they are of little practical value. Interest on financed insurance may be deducted if the insurance is connected with the company's business, but the Revenue Service doesn't consider split-dollar insurance business-connected. Interest on financed insurance is also deductible (even if no other exception is met) if it is less than $100 a year. But this $100 ceiling is quickly passed if there is a sizeable premium, or more than one year's premium, or several executives are covered.

Company insurance loans to the executive: The executive covered by split-dollar insurance must make a sizeable premium payment in the first year, and further premiums in the following year or two. He therefore might welcome a company loan of the amount needed for these premiums. This loan may be made interest-free, without tax consequences to either lender or borrower. (See the analysis of the interest-free loan as a fringe benefit in Chapter 13.) If the company will charge interest, the executive can deduct this for tax purposes. It is not subject to the financed insurance limitations above.

Split-dollar for executives only: The company may limit split-dollar coverage to executives, or to selected executives, or to any other employees as it chooses. No plan is required and no formalities of any kind are prescribed. Terms of a sample split-dollar arrangement, involving a policy owned by the executive, appear on pages 248 and 249.

How one split-dollar plan worked: The table on page 243 shows the economic and tax results of an actual split-dollar arrangement examined by the Revenue Service. The arrangement involved an executive, aged 45 when the policy was taken out, who was covered by a 10-payment life policy with a face amount of $100,000, on which policy dividends are credited to the employer. Column 9 shows the amount taxable to the executive for the policy year indicated. Note that in this case he is taxable (after

(1)	(2)	(3)	(4)	(5)	(6)	(7)	(8)	(9)
Policy year	Cash value per $100,000	Gross premiums	Amount provided by employer, Y	Amount paid by employee, B	Proceeds payable to employee B's beneficiary	Cost of insurance per $1,000	Value of insurance to employee, B (6) × (7)*	Value provided by employer, Y (8) − (5)
1	$ 7,291.00	$7,899.50	$7,291.00	$608.50	$92,709.00	$ 6.30	$584.07	$ –0–
2	14,775.00	7,899.50	7,484.00	415.50	85,225.00	6.78	577.83	162.33
3	22,465.00	7,899.50	7,690.00	209.50	77,535.00	7.32	567.56	358.06
4	30,375.00	7,899.50	7,899.50	–0–	69,625.00	7.89	549.34	549.34
5	35,791.00	5,268.50	5,268.50	–0–	64,209.00	8.53	547.70	547.70
6	41,356.00	5,268.50	5,268.50	–0–	58,644.00	9.22	540.70	540.70
7	47,080.00	5,268.50	5,268.50	–0–	52,920.00	9.97	527.61	527.61
8	52,977.00	5,268.50	5,268.50	–0–	47,023.00	10.79	507.38	507.38
9	59,062.00	5,268.50	5,268.50	–0–	40,938.00	11.69	478.57	478.57
10	65,356.00	5,268.50	5,268.50	–0–	34,644.00	12.67	438.94	438.94
11	66,385.00	–0–	–0–	–0–	33,615.00	13.74	461.87	461.87
15	70,462.00	–0–	–0–	–0–	29,538.00	20.73	612.32	612.32
20	75,373.00	–0–	–0–	–0–	24,627.00	31.51	776.00	776.00

*The figures in column (8) represent the figures in column (6) multiplied by the corresponding figures in column (7) and divided by $1,000.

the 10th year) even though no premiums are paid in those years. He is enjoying insurance coverage attributable to company payments in previous years.

Convertible term insurance

The young executive with a growing family may feel the need for a sizeable amount of insurance and yet be unable to afford much in the way of straight life coverage. For this situation, some companies have decided to join their young executives in arranging for convertible term insurance.

A substantial amount of convertible term insurance, say $60,-000, is taken out for the executive, and the cost is paid by the company. In later years, when the executive's salary has risen enough for him to be able to afford $60,000 of straight life coverage, he converts the policy to straight life and thereafter pays the premium cost himself.

This arrangement offers economic benefits to the executive, but no special tax benefits. The insurance here is not group-term insurance. He therefore is subject to tax on the actual cost of the term insurance paid by the company; the company can deduct its payments as additional compensation. The economic benefit lies in the fact that instead of paying the cost of the term insurance with after-tax dollars, he pays only the tax on an amount of income equal to that cost.

Example: Youngblood, age 32, is furnished $60,000 of convertible term insurance by his employer. Five-year convertible term insurance at age 32 costs $5.19 per thousand, or $311. Assuming Youngblood is in the 36 percent bracket (taxable income between $24,000 and $28,000 on a joint return), his cost, the tax cost, of this company-paid insurance is $112, instead of the $311 cost if he had provided it out of his own pocket.

Saving estate tax on life insurance

Proceeds of insurance on a deceased executive's life generally are included in his estate for estate tax purposes and therefore may be subjected to estate tax. But estate tax can be avoided by taking these two steps:

1. the executive should not make his estate, or his executor, the beneficiary. He should name as beneficiary his spouse, child or other individual he seeks to benefit, or a trust for such beneficiary,

2. he should give away all his rights in the policy (in most cases, these are given to the beneficiary) or have the beneficiary take out the policy initially.

Some executives will understandably consider this second step a drastic one. The author agrees. Insurance can be valuable property, which should not be surrendered lightly, even to the beneficiary. But it is essential for the insured executive to give up all his rights to the policy if he means to keep insurance proceeds out of his estate for estate tax purposes. Giving up all rights means parting with the right to surrender the policy for cash, the right to borrow against it, the right to change the beneficiary, and other rights.

In the case of a transfer of a straight life policy (including an endowment policy or accelerated payment life policy) which has been in existence for a substantial period of time, the executive's transfer of the policy to avoid estate tax can occasionally subject him to federal gift tax. Employers today rarely provide such policies, so gift tax planning for this situation need not be considered here (but the tax saving techniques explored in Chapter 15, on planning the executive's estate, are applicable).

To avoid estate tax on group-term life insurance, both the policy and state law must permit the insured executive to make an irrevocable assignment of all his rights under the policy (including the right, if any, to convert the policy to permanent insurance) and the executive must actually make such an assignment. The tax profession is not unanimous that estate tax can ever be avoided on group-term life insurance (on the theory that each year's premium payment by the employer is a gift in contemplation of death by the executive, so that the entire proceeds are included in his estate at death). The author does not share the view that the estate tax cannot be avoided here, and in any case, transferring all rights to group-term insurance does no tax harm. Gift tax is seldom a factor since the value of term insurance is relatively small.

Saving state inheritance tax on insurance

While the rules vary from one state to another, state inheritance tax on life insurance is normally at least as easy to avoid as federal estate tax. In many states, inheritance tax is avoided simply by naming as beneficiary the insured person's spouse or child. In others, there is no inheritance tax on insurance if there is no federal estate tax on it.

Insurance for the company

The personnel planner must distinguish the insurance arrangements discussed above, which benefit the executive, from those designed to benefit or protect the company. Thus, so-called key man insurance covers the company against loss of a valued executive by providing a cash fund to the company at his death; the executive is not directly affected by this transaction. Or, the company may arrange insurance to fund its obligation to executives or their beneficiaries under deferred compensation contracts or death benefit arrangements. Here, too, while the insurance proceeds may eventually be spent on the executive's behalf, he is not directly affected by the insurance aspect. His tax treatment, and that of his beneficiaries, is governed by the nature of the underlying transaction (e.g., death benefit rules), and not by life insurance rules.

SAMPLE GROUP-TERM LIFE INSURANCE ARRANGEMENT

No formal plan of group-term life insurance is required. A group-term arrangement limited to executives could be adopted by a board of directors resolution, as follows:

Upon motion duly made, seconded and carried it was

RESOLVED that the corporation provide and pay the costs of term insurance, for a group of employees consisting of . . . [all officers and heads of department]* [all employees whose annual salary, including commission and bonus, shall exceed $ . . .] [all employees over age . . . who shall have been continuously employed by the corporation for not less than . . . years] in an amount for each employee within the group which shall equal [$ . . .] [. . . % of the annual salary of the employee].

SAMPLE SPLIT-DOLLAR INSURANCE ARRANGEMENT

The letter below reflects a split-dollar arrangement in which the policy is owned by the executive:

Mr. [Executive]   [Date]
[Home Address]
Dear Mr. . . . ,

This letter, when signed by you and returned to us, will constitute our mutual agreement with respect to a policy of life insurance in the amount of $100,000 which it is understood will be issued to you by . . . Life Insurance Company:

1. You will apply for the policy and become the sole owner thereof, with the entire right, except as hereinafter set forth, to designate the beneficiary or beneficiaries of the policy and the manner in which the proceeds of the policy will be distributed.

2. The premiums on the policy will be paid as follows: For convenience, a check covering the entire annual premium will be drawn by us

---

* The group selected under any of these formulas, or any other suitable formula, should include at least 10 persons, at least one of whom is not a stockholder.

and forwarded to the insurance company. However, you will pay us the amount of the premium for the first year, reduced by the cash value of the policy on its first anniversary. For all succeeding policy years, we will pay an amount which, when added to all previous payments made by us, will equal the cash value of the policy at the end of that policy year, and you will pay, not later than the due date of the premium for that year, the amount which equals the balance due of the net premium (gross premium less policy dividends) for that year.

3. The entire amount of our payments under this policy shall constitute an indebtedness, without interest, from you to us. As security for the repayment of this indebtedness, you will deliver to us physical possession of the policy and will execute and deliver to us a collateral assignment of the policy in accordance with the manner of assignment approved by the insurance company.

You or we may cancel this agreement upon . . . days written notice to the other.† Within that . . .-day period, you may satisfy the indebtedness, in which case we will cancel the indebtedness and collateral assignment and return to you physical possession of the policy. If you should not satisfy the indebtedness within that period, we shall have the right to surrender the policy for its cash value, recover therefrom the amount of your indebtedness to us, and turn over to you any amount in excess thereof which we shall have received.

4. At your death while this agreement is in force, the indebtedness shall be satisfied out of the proceeds of the policy, and the balance of the proceeds shall be distributed to or for the benefit of your beneficiaries as you shall have designated.

Very truly yours,

_____

[Employer]

Accepted: by _____

_____   President

[Executive]

---

† Provision covering termination of employment.

IRS TABLE OF TAXABLE GROUP-TERM INSURANCE COSTS

The table below shows the figures used to compute the cost of group-term insurance taxable to executives. The table is used where the executive has insurance coverage in excess of $50,000. (A 1-month period is shown in the table since he is taxable on a monthly basis if he is covered for varying amounts during the year.) The rate is the same whether the executive is male or female.

The taxable amount for a full year (assuming he has the same coverage throughout the year) is the cost per $1,000 in the executive's age bracket, times 12 (months), times the amount in thousands of his coverage in excess of $50,000.

Thus, if Brown is age 37 and is covered for $70,000, the taxable cost for a year is $33.60, that is, $.14 (the rate for 35 to 39) × 12 × 20 (70 [thousand] less 50 [thousand]).

	Cost per $1,000 of protection for 1-month period
Under 30	8 cents
30 to 34	10 cents
35 to 39	14 cents
40 to 44	23 cents
45 to 49	40 cents
50 to 54	68 cents
55 to 59	$1.10
60 to 64	$1.63

IRS TABLE FOR COMPUTING SPLIT-DOLLAR INSURANCE COSTS

The table below shows the figures used to compute the cost of one-year term insurance for purposes of taxing the executive covered by split-dollar life insurance.

The taxable amount is the premium cost figure shown opposite the executive's age times the amount in thousands of his interest in the policy in that year, minus the amount he paid during the year towards the premium.

Thus, if Harris is age 34, the policy's face amount is $100,000, the cash surrender value (payable to his employer) is $15,000, policy dividends go to the employer, and Harris paid a premium of $150, Harris is taxable on $106.70, that is, $3.02 (the rate per $1,000 at age 34) times 85 (100 [thousand] less 15 [thousand]) or $256.70, minus $150, the premium Harris paid.

Uniform one year term premiums for $1,000 life insurance protection

Age	Premium	Age	Premium	Age	Premium
15	$1.27	36	$ 3.41	56	$14.91
16	1.38	37	3.63	57	16.18
17	1.48	38	3.87	58	17.56
18	1.52	39	4.14	59	19.08
19	1.56	40	4.42	60	20.73
20	1.61	41	4.73	61	22.53
21	1.67	42	5.07	62	24.50
22	1.73	43	5.44	63	26.63
23	1.79	44	5.85	64	28.98
24	1.86	45	6.30	65	31.51
25	1.93	46	6.78	66	34.28
26	2.02	47	7.32	67	37.31
27	2.11	48	7.89	68	40.59
28	2.20	49	8.53	69	44.17
29	2.31	50	9.22	70	48.06
30	2.43	51	9.97	71	52.29
31	2.57	52	10.79	72	56.89
32	2.70	53	11.69	73	61.89
33	2.86	54	12.67	74	67.33
34	3.02	55	13.74	75	73.23
35	3.21				

chapter 15 Planning the executive's estate

Put simply, an estate plan is a program, adopted during a person's lifetime, for the distribution of his property at his death. The estate plan must make adequate provision for his family, and may need to include arrangements for maintenance of the family while awaiting probate of the will and satisfaction of bequests. It will involve the selection of a reliable executor to carry out the deceased person's intentions. It will try to insure liquidity of the estate, so that current liabilities of the deceased and his estate can be satisfied without forced selling. It will attempt to minimize the taxes imposed on the estate, so that the heirs can enjoy a larger share of the property left behind. And so on.

Estate planning is a vastly complex operation on which many scholarly treatises have been written. The complexity arises partly because the rules of property ownership, probate, estate administration, and state inheritance taxation vary from one state to another. It is also comes about partly because of the many differing ways individuals decide to divide up their property at death.

Here we will be concerned with a key aspect of estate planning which all executives can be assumed to hold in common: the wish to minimize the government's tax collections from their bequests.

It is well known by now that the Federal government, through the instrument of the estate tax, is the largest single "beneficiary" in many estates. Few individuals who possess substantial wealth can completely avoid the imposition of this tax on their estate.[1] But there are many ways to reduce this tax. We will explore those most useful for executives.

We will be considering practical, proven arrangements for tax saving. Nonetheless, this word of caution should be given: Tax saving is only one element in an estate plan. There will be other financial concerns. Moreover, family considerations, not economic considerations, should control.

A successful estate plan is often the work of a team of skilled professionals: attorney, accountant, insurance and investment advisors and, occasionally, a corporate fiduciary. Companies that wish to help their executives in the design of a satisfactory plan often engage a firm of financial counselors who are especially skilled in estate planning for executives. (See Chapter 13 on this.)

Planning for executive benefits

An essential element in any estate plan is a determination of the assets that the individual can be expected to own at his death, and an assessment of their probable value. The individual and his estate planner will therefore begin by making a list of what he owns. Estate taxes are often unnecessarily high, and distribution to beneficiaries unnecessarily skimpy, because the estate plan

---

[1] Briefly, the Federal estate tax is a tax on the net value of a person's assets in excess of $60,000. Net value would be assets less liabilities, as further reduced by the amount he leaves his spouse (up to half his net assets), the amount left to charity, and certain other deductions. The estate tax is imposed on the amount of the estate, considered as a separate entity, rather than the amount left to any particular individual.

failed to take account of some valuable property items not brought to the planner's attention.

All too often, this failing arises in planning an executive's estate. The plan is designed without reflecting all of his benefits as an executive. The estate plan should therefore give full recognition to the following important items of executive compensation and executive wealth.

Life insurance proceeds: These include the proceeds of company-sponsored life insurance, such as group-term or split-dollar insurance, along with any insurance the executive provides on his own. Tax planning considerations to eliminate estate and inheritance taxes are noted below.

Pension, profit-sharing benefits: These include the amount standing to the executive's credit in his company's pension, profit-sharing, thrift or other qualified plan. Tax planning considerations to minimize estate taxes are discussed below.

Death benefits: Some companies provide tax-favored death benefits (apart from insurance, pensions, and so forth.) Such benefits may be a flat sum, or the continuation of the executive's salary to his widow or heirs for a period after his death. (See Chapter 13.)

Deferred compensation: If an executive with a deferred compensation arrangement dies before collecting all deferred amounts, the arrangement generally requires that the unpaid balance be paid to his estate or heirs. (See Chapter 5.)

Company stock: The executive should take account of all company stock he owns, whether it was received as direct payment for services (whether or not it is "restricted" stock), or bought under a bargain purchase arrangement, an installment purchase, or a stock option. (See Chapters 6, 7, and 8.)

Stock options: Unexercised stock options may have value and should be brought into the estate plan if they can be exercised by the executive's estate or heirs. (See Chapter 9.)

Social Security death and survivorship benefits: These are available to the families of executives as well as others.

Company loans: These may fall due at or shortly after the executive's death. The estate plan should arrange funds to cover any repayment liability. (See Chapter 13.)

Life insurance

Life insurance, provided by the company, is one of the most common of all executive benefits. Thousands of executives are covered by company-sponsored, tax-favored, group-term life insurance or split-dollar life insurance, or both. Some executives also are given convertible term policies or other policies which provide welcome insurance protection though they offer no income tax benefits.

Every estate plan must take account of all the executive's life insurance coverage, whether provided by the company, by the executive himself or, as in the case of split-dollar insurance and some group-term insurance, partly by each. The executive must be advised that his family's insurance benefits may be sharply cut down by federal estate taxes and state death taxes unless protective action is taken during his lifetime.

Briefly, Federal estate tax on an executive's life insurance is avoided if he assigns (gives away) all his rights in the policy, normally to his spouse, some other beneficiary (but *not his estate*) or a trustee. This action is considered in Chapter 14.

In many states, the state inheritance tax on life insurance is avoided simply by naming as beneficiary the insured person's spouse or child or, sometimes, trusts for them. In states with stricter rules, state inheritance tax is still avoided if there is no Federal estate tax on the insurance (because it was assigned away).

The executive can consult his own insurance agent for the

mechanics of assigning his life insurance policy.[2] But in connection with company-sponsored life insurance—and especially group-term life insurance—many companies voluntarily point out to their executives the tax saving aspects of policy assignments and, with help from their insurance companies, make insurance assignments easy to accomplish.

Pension, profit-sharing accounts

If the executive participated in a qualified pension or profit-sharing plan, his estate or heirs will be entitled to receive the balance in his account at his death. The entire amount is included in his estate for estate tax purposes if the estate is named the beneficiary of his interest. But only the amount in the account which is attributable to his own contributions to the plan (if any) is subject to estate tax if some beneficiary other than the estate is named.

For example, suppose the company made total contributions of $300,000 as Brown's share of a profit-sharing fund to which Brown contributed nothing. And suppose Brown's share in the fund is worth $600,000 at his death. If Brown had named his estate as beneficiary, this $600,000 would be included in his estate. If he had named, say, his son Gerald as his beneficiary, it would be exempt from estate tax. If the $600,000 represented the entire taxable estate, naming Gerald (rather than the estate) saves $180,700 in estate tax.

If the company and the executive both contribute to the pension or profit-sharing fund, the amount attributable to the executive's own contribution is included in his estate in any case. Here, if the executive had contributed $150,000, then $200,000

---

[2] The executive should of course have first discussed the wisdom of such an assignment with his attorney or other estate planning adviser.

($150,000/$450,000 [$150,000 from Brown + $300,000 from the company] × $600,000) is included in his estate for estate tax purposes even if he designates a beneficiary other than his estate. In this case, assuming $600,000 is the entire taxable estate, naming Gerald as his beneficiary saves $130,000 of estate tax.

This estate tax benefit is available only for amounts not withdrawn by the executive from his pension or profit-sharing fund during his lifetime. Amounts in his possession are subject to estate tax. Thus, some executives favor profit-sharing plans and employment policies which together will enable them to work on beyond what is ordinarily thought to be retirement age. They seek to die in harness, with their profit-sharing account intact in the profit-sharing trust, so that their beneficiaries will enjoy the estate tax saving. A sample profit-sharing plan provision which reflects this arrangement appears in Chapter 12.

Planning bequests that save estate taxes

Here we will consider ways in which the executive can leave his wealth to his family at the lowest cost in estate tax.

Bequests to spouse (marital deduction). Amounts a person leaves to his spouse are exempt from estate tax up to half the value of his estate. This exemption is accomplished by means of the estate tax marital deduction. The marital deduction equals the amount the spouse gets at the decedent's death, or half the value of the decedent's estate, whichever is less.[3]

The marital deduction is a major element in any program for saving estate taxes. But the executive must be aware that it is allowed only for property which his spouse, upon his death, will take as absolute or effective owner. The property should be left

---

[3] The marital deduction is not allowed for community property—the system in Arizona, California, Idaho, Louisiana, Nevada, New Mexico, Texas, and Washington—but community property laws produce a similar estate tax result.

to her outright, without qualifications or, failing that, should meet *both* these conditions:

a.   She has full rights to current income from the property.
b.   She has the right to dispose of the property itself during her lifetime or at her death.

Bequests which satisfy both these tests would include a legal life estate to the wife with the remainder to her estate, or income to her in trust for life with the trust corpus payable to her estate. If she is given only a life estate, the marital deduction would not be allowed.

The marital deduction is based on the size of the entire estate (technically, the *adjusted gross estate*), and not just the assets covered by the will. Such items as insurance proceeds and jointly-owned property may be part of the adjusted gross estate, increasing the allowable marital deduction.

Property left to the wife outright, or under conditions satisfying the above tests, will be subject to estate tax in her estate if she owns it at her death. Yet only half the husband's estate can qualify for marital deduction. Anything left to her in excess of that amount is taxable in her husband's estate and in hers as well, if held by her at death. Where the husband wants to give her a larger-than-50 percent share of his estate, while still avoiding the second estate tax (on the wife's estate), he could (1) leave her half his estate, either outright or by a bequest satisfying both tests and, (2) leave her a life estate or life income interest in other property.

This way, during her lifetime she will enjoy more than half the income from the husband's property, and will be able to dispose of the half left to her. But her estate will not be subject to estate tax on property in which she had only a life interest.

The husband's will can arrange that his widow's life interest will, at her death, be followed by a life estate to their children. This is one aspect of generation-skipping, discussed below.

Bequests to grandchildren, etc.: generation skipping: Suppose Bowers, an executive, has a son Ralph, and a grandson Tom. Bowers dies, leaving his property to Ralph, which is reduced by the estate tax on Bowers' estate. Some years later Ralph dies leaving his property (including what he inherited from his father) to Tom, which is reduced by a second estate tax on Ralph's estate.

Generation skipping is the device which tax practitioners and other estate planners have worked out to avoid this second estate tax. Instead of leaving his property outright to Ralph, Bowers leaves Ralph a life estate or life income interest, with the remainder or principal payable to Tom at Ralph's death. This form of bequest does not reduce Bowers' estate tax. But it eliminates any estate tax on Ralph, with respect to interests acquired from Bowers. Ralph has only a life interest, one which terminates at his death, which is not subject to estate tax.

Generation skipping is sometimes accomplished by leaving the property first to the executive's widow for life (marital deduction is not allowed for such a bequest), then to his son for life, and then to his grandson. The only estate tax here (apart from any estate tax when the grandson dies) is on the executive's own estate.

Assigning the estate tax burden

It is appropriate for the executive to specify in his will exactly which of his bequests should bear the burden of Federal estate taxes and state death taxes, and which should be exempt from such taxes. This is essentially a matter of state law; ordinarily, state law accepts and applies such directives.

Thus, if Philips leaves half his estate to his son and half to his nephew, with the Federal estate tax to be borne solely out of the nephew's share, this directive will normally be honored, assuming the nephew's share is adequate to cover the estate tax. The son would get half the estate, and the nephew would get the balance, less estate tax on the entire estate.

Such a directive, properly applied, can also operate to reduce estate tax. The marital deduction (or the charitable deduction) is larger if the surviving spouse's share (or the charity's share) is exempted from having to bear part of the estate tax. The increased deduction reduces the taxable amount.

Lifetime gifts that save estate tax

Estate planning is not limited to designing clauses in wills or other documents which will become effective only upon the executive's death. Many executives should consider adopting a program of making sizeable gifts within the family during their lifetime.

Federal estate tax applies to the amount a person owned at his death. Amounts he gave away during his lifetime, instead of upon his death, ordinarily are not subject to estate tax. This is true even though the gifts are made to his wife, children, or other family members who would share in his estate under his will, or if he left no will. A program of lifetime gifts is currently a widely-used method of avoiding estate tax, and should also be explored as a means of avoiding state death taxes and reducing probate costs.

One common tax-saving gift is the family home. A house owned by the executive at his death would be part of his estate and potentially subject to estate tax. But if he gave it to his wife during his lifetime, free of restrictions on her ownership, it usually would be exempt from estate tax in his estate if he dies before her, even if he continued to live in the house with her after making the gift.

One type of gift which is not an effective tax-saving device is the taking of property in joint ownership. Suppose an executive buys property in his and his wife's names as joint tenants or tenants by the entirety, or transfers property which was his alone to himself and his wife as joint tenants or tenants by the entirety. This form of co-ownership[4] has the attraction that at the death of one of them, the entire property will pass to the other without the cost or delay of probate.

But it has no attraction for estate tax purposes. On the death of one joint owner, the value of the entire jointly owned property is included in the estate of the deceased co-owner, except to the extent the surviving co-owner contributed towards the cost of the property, or where it was acquired by a gift or bequest from another. In the usual case, where the executive acquires the property entirely with his own funds, takes title jointly with his wife, and dies before her, the value of the entire property is included in his estate at his death, even though she owned half of it before he died and all of it thereafter.

To avoid this result, he could have given her the entire property before his death. No estate tax here, in most cases. Or, he could have given her a half share as a tenant in common. Here she would not automatically get his half on his death; that would depend on his will or state inheritance laws. But there would normally be no estate tax on her half.

A program of lifetime gifts to minimize estate taxes is likely to emphasize gifts to the executive's children. Gifts of securities or cash to children typically are made under the simplified procedures of the Uniform Gifts to Minors Act. This law is generally applicable throughout the United States. Once such a gift is made under this law, the income from the donated property ordinarily is taxable to the child and not to the donor. But the person obligated to support the child (usually, the child's father who also

---

[4] It is not community property.

usually is the donor) is taxable on the income if it is used for the child's support.

If the donor (again, usually the father) names himself as the custodian of the gift to the child, and dies while the child is still a minor, the value of the amount held as custodian is likely to be subjected to estate tax in the custodian's estate.[5]

When deciding what kind of property to give to a child or other donee, consider favoring gifts of income-producing property such as securities, rather than valuable but non-income property such as land held for investment. Income earned on the property after the gift is not taxable to the donor. If the income is received by the donor's child, taxes due on this income will be less (because of the child's low bracket) than if it were received by the executive donor. Also, the income paid to the donee would not be part of the donor's estate, and therefore would not be subjected to estate tax in his estate.

Avoiding gift taxes

Lifetime gifts have this potential tax drawback: If they are to save estate tax, they may instead be subject to the Federal gift tax. However, this tax is not a major deterrent to the practice of making lifetime gifts to avoid the Federal estate tax, for these reasons:

1. There are several ways to cast gifts to avoid or reduce gift tax. (See below.)

2. Gift tax rates are 25 percent less than estate tax rates, so that an overall 25 percent tax saving may be accomplished by making a taxable gift. (But remember that a gift tax is due before, often long before, an estate tax would become due, and that the

---

[5] The author understands that the late Senator Robert Kennedy was custodian for gifts to his children at the time of his death.

donor would be giving up the income that would be earned by any sums paid out as gift taxes.)

3. Estate tax and gift tax are each imposed at separate, graduated tax rates. It can therefore be preferable to pay some gift tax and some estate tax, rather than all of either. For example, gift tax on $40,000 and estate tax on $20,000 is cheaper than either gift or estate tax on $60,000.

One type of lifetime gift which is not exempt from estate tax is the "gift in contemplation of death." Yet estate planners point out a tax saving potential even in such gifts.

Suppose a person dies within three years after making a substantial gift. Tax law allows the Revenue Service to include the gift in the donor's estate even though he didn't own it at his death, if he made the gift in contemplation of his death, that is, as an advance distribution of his estate. Thus, the gift is brought back into his estate (for tax purposes) and can be made to bear an estate tax.

This estate tax potential is sometimes raised to discourage aged persons from making lifetime gifts intended to reduce their estates. This advice usually overlooks a tax saving opportunity. If the lifetime gift is subject to gift tax, the gift tax paid is credited against any estate tax, reducing that tax dollar for dollar. Moreover, the gift tax itself, though credited against estate tax, is not included in the taxable estate. The combined tax credit and exclusion for gift tax means that in a $200,000 estate, which includes a $20,000 gift in contemplation of death on which a $4,200 tax was paid, an estate tax saving of $1,260 is achieved. A saving of several million dollars reportedly occurred on a multimillion dollar gift in contemplation of death by a member of the duPont family.

If a person's gifts during his lifetime total $30,000 or less, he is never subject to gift tax. Thus, thanks to this lifetime exemption, most taxpayers are exempt from gift tax.

Also, there is no gift tax unless the donor's gifts to any one person during the year total more than $3,000. This rule, called the *annual exclusion,* makes it possible for an executive to avoid gift tax on gifts he makes to save estate tax by keeping annual gifts to $3,000 or less (per recipient).

Tax saving techniques

1. Instead of making a $5,000 gift this year, which would trigger a gift tax if the lifetime exemption has been exhausted, one can avoid gift tax by giving $3,000 this year and $2,000 next year. If he is giving property worth $5,000 instead of cash, he could give a 3/5ths interest this year and the balance next year.

2. Another way to save gift tax is to spread the gifts among the members of the family the executive intends to benefit. For example, instead of making a gift of $12,000 to his son, which could incur a gift tax, he could give $3,000 each to his son, his son's wife, and their two children, thereby avoiding gift tax.

3. The husband-wife split gift is a third gift tax saver.[6] A gift by husband and wife together is treated as made half by each, if they wish, even though only one of them owns the property being donated. For example, if Charles owns property worth $6,000 which he gives to his son, Phil, it is treated as a gift of $3,000 by each spouse if Charles's wife Maude joins in the gift. Assuming they make no other gifts to Phil that year, the split gift device, coupled with the annual exclusion, completely avoids gift tax on the gift.

4. A marital deduction is allowed on a gift to a spouse.[7] That is, half the value of the gift is ignored for tax purposes; only the

---

[6] Technically unavailable for gifts of community property, but the tax result is the same for joint gifts of such property.

[7] Except for a gift of community property, but the tax result of such a gift is about the same.

balance is subjected to gift tax. Moreover, the $3,000 annual gift tax exemption is available on the half of the gift taken into account for tax purposes. For example, if a husband gives his wife $5,000 in a lump sum this year, half would be ignored under the marital deduction and the balance would escape tax under the annual exclusion, since it is less than $3,000.

chapter **16**   **Government controls on executive compensation**

MOST companies with 60 or fewer employees are exempt from government pay controls.[1] Executives and compensation planners for these firms therefore need not be concerned with the pay control rules in this chapter.

For the remaining firms, government economic controls represent a significant limitation on a company's power to design a fully satisfactory compensation package for its executives. This chapter will show where the limitations fall, and when and how some pay ceilings can legally be avoided.

Pay control ceilings on cash pay

As the basic rule, executive salaries may not increase for a year by more than 5.5 percent. Thus, if 1973 salaries were $500,000, 1974 salaries can not be more than $527,500.[2]

---

[1] Companies with 60 or fewer employees are exempt from pay controls unless they are engaged in construction or providing health care, or have annual sales or revenues of over $50 million, or fall within a few other limited categories.

[2] The rules on salary, perquisites, incentive compensation, and nonstatutory stock options apply to executives of all firms which are not exempt from government controls.

The allowable amount of increase is not determined executive-by-executive. Instead, the *executive control group* is used. The executive control group includes all officers of the firm, regardless of aggregate direct remuneration, and also all employee directors of the firm whose aggregate direct remuneration exceeds $30,000 each during the firm's fiscal year. Officers include the president, vice president, secretary, treasurer, comptroller, or any other employee of an incorporated or unincorporated firm performing services corresponding to those performed by these officers. Assistant vice presidents and second vice presidents usually are not officers, nor are other "officers" whose duties are limited to serving specific customers or accounts. *Aggregate direct remuneration* includes salary, fees, perquisites, per diem reimbursements, and other forms of remuneration.

Total salaries within the executive control group may not rise more than 5.5 percent over the amount of salaries on the base date (the day before the firm's current fiscal year began). This 5.5 percent ceiling can not be increased through promotions or permanent or prolonged vacancies. For example, if a $35,000 a year manager (employee director) were promoted to a $55,000 a year vice president, the $20,000 increase would be counted as an increase applicable the group as a whole. Also, if a $60,000 a year vice presidency is eliminated, the total base salary would be reduced by $60,000. But the 5.5 percent ceiling could reflect newly-created positions within the executive control group.

Exception: Companies may elect a somewhat more liberal rule than the one described above. The 5.5 percent ceiling still applies, but the computation of the amounts may vary. Under the exception, the executive control group could exclude promotions from the computation. That is, salary increases resulting

---

The rules on other forms of compensation are those for firms subject to mandatory controls, such as firms in the health industry. Firms not subject to mandatory controls can be made subject to the mandatory rules if they do not comply voluntarily with the salary controls.

from promotions, involving materially changed duties and responsibilities, would be exempt from pay controls, Also, computation of the 5.5 percent ceiling would be based on salary plus company contributions to fringe benefits.

The exception is achieved technically by allowing the company to elect to have the executive control group treated as an *appropriate employee unit.* The appropriate employee unit concept is applicable to rank-and-file employees as well as to executives, in the sense that there may be different appropriate employee units for different categories of employees, and one such category could be executive employees.

An appropriate employee unit is all employees in a bargaining unit or recognized employee category. The bargaining unit may exist in a plant or department, or the entire company. The composition of the unit is determined by "contractual or historical wage and salary relationships."

As the rules are applied to executives, an appropriate employee unit apparently could be a single individual, if he has a separate employment contract. But normally the unit is some larger group which, depending on circumstances, would include all executives in a department, plant or area, or entire company. Also, appropriate employee units which include both executives and nonexecutive personnel have been recognized. The appropriate employee unit has relatively little significance for executives with respect to pay controls on salary and job perquisites, but is important in other contexts, discussed later. Apart from the computation rules discussed above, all rules discussed in this chapter apply whether or not the company has elected to treat the executive control group as the appropriate employee unit.

Salary distribution not affected: The 5.5 percent ceiling does not limit raises to any particular executive employee. As long as pay within the executive control group as a whole does not rise more than 5.5 percent, the company can pay each executive within the group what it pleases. Thus, with ten executives paid $50,000 each the previous year, the company could give nine executives a 2 percent raise (to $51,000) and one executive a 37 percent raise (to $68,500).

Computing the salary increase: To find the percentage of increase, compare the average salary within the group at the base date with the average salary at the end of the year. Salary is taken into account in the year the services to earn it are performed, not the year payment is made. Thus, pay controls would be violated if pay in an executive control group was raised from $500,000 one year to $525,000 the next year (a 5 percent present increase) but with a further deferred $75,000 (15 percent) to be paid three years hence. This would be true even if the executives in the group had to continue in the company's employ for that three-year period in order to collect the deferred amount.

Note that this system of measuring pay increases takes into account the rate of pay at year's end, rather than the amount of pay during the year. For example, if executive Wheeler (assumed for simplicity to be an executive control group) of a company using the calendar year should have an $80,000 salary on January 1, 1974 and an $84,400 salary on December 31, 1974, his pay would not violate pay controls. It would not matter, for purposes of the controls, whether he got his raise, say, February 1, 1974, or December 1, 1974. But Wheeler would get $3,667 more for the year with the February raise. Thus, companies that want to pay the maximum allowable amount should make raises early in the fiscal year.

Material later in this chapter will consider ways in which the 5.5 percent ceiling can be exceeded or stretched, through exceptions to pay controls, incentive compensation, and noncash compensation.

Job perquisites

The 5.5 percent government ceiling described above for base salary also applies to job perquisites. That is, the dollar value of job perquisites for the appropriate employee unit in one year can not be more than 105.5 percent of what it was the year before.

Job perquisites are defined to include company-furnished cars or housing, company-paid country club fees and dues, financial counseling furnished by the company (see Chapter 13), and other such similar items. Though no reference to tax laws is made, these prequisites would in fact be taxable to the executive, and subject to tax withholding by the company. The amount of the perquisite, for pay control purposes, would be the company's current cost for the item, except that reasonable cost is used where there is a cost, such as depreciation on company cars, beyond *current* cost.

How pay ceilings may be exceeded

Existing contracts

The 5.5 percent ceiling on pay increases does not apply to increases called for by a contract—an instrument written and signed by employer and employee—which was in effect on November 13, 1971. Thus, if an executive's employment contract, in existence on November 13, 1971, gave him a 15 percent salary raise for each of six years, the raise is allowed despite the 5.5 percent ceiling. Compensation increases in the contract may also be based on profits, sales, or other variables.

Executives holding such contracts are excluded from the executive control group, and their salaries are excluded from the group's total salary. Thus, their pay increases do not hurt other executives.

Sales or production incentives

A plan or practice in effect on November 13, 1971 which grants awards directly based on an employee's own performance in sales or production, is exempt from pay controls. Thus, sales commissions to a sales executive could be exempt.

This kind of plan or practice generally is not subject to the rules set forth below for incentive compensation. But new (post-November 13, 1971) sales or production incentive plans and practices, and plans and practices of new organizations, are subject to the rules described below for new (or new organization) incentive compensation plans or practices.

Hardship relief

If the government pay controls cause "extreme hardship or severe inequity," relief may be granted upon application to the Office of Wage Stabilization, P.O. Box 983, Washington, D.C. 20044.

Incentive compensation

Though increases in executive salary and job perquisites are subject to the 5.5 percent limits described above, further increases in compensation are allowed under incentive compensation plans or practices. There are some differences in rules for plans or practices in effect on November 13, 1971 (sometimes called "existing" plans or practices) and plans or practices set up thereafter, when pay controls were in effect ("new" plans or practices).

An incentive plan or practice qualifying for treatment as an existing plan must meet all of the following tests:

a. For a plan, a payment or award under the plan must have been made during at least one of the last three plan years ending before November 14, 1971. For a practice, the payment or award must have been made in at least two out of the last three practice years (one year if the practice was in existence less than two practice years). The "year" is the year of the company for which the plan or practice applies—normally, the company's fiscal year.

A *plan* is a written instrument which is not signed by the executive.

A *practice* is an unwritten arrangement resulting from custom or practice.

b. The total maximum amount payable under a plan is determined by a definite method or clear formula. A definite method or clear formula is not required for a practice, but there then is a special limitation on the amount that may be paid without violating pay controls.

c. The plan or practice is administered in accordance with its terms (for a plan) or custom and habit (for a practice), and in the customary manner, with no deviation designed to circumvent the pay controls.

The maximum amount (allowable amount) that can be paid under a plan or practice is based upon a payment made before November 14, 1971. Specifically:

For the first plan or practice year ending after November 13, 1971, the amount was 105.5 percent of the largest amount paid under the plan or practice in any of the last three plan or practice years ending before that date.

For each plan or practice year thereafter, it would be the amount allowed in that first post-November 13, 1971 year multiplied by 105.5 percent for each succeeding year the plan was in operation. (There is also a mathematical adjustment for increases or decreases in the number of employees in the plan.)

Example: Suppose a company using a September 30 fiscal year has a plan for paying incentive compensation of 5 percent of consolidated net profits. Net profits and allowable awards as of September 30 for 1969–74 are as follows:

Year	Profits	Allowable award
1969	$ 400,000	$20,000
1970	1,000,000	50,000
1971	900,000	45,000
1972	1,200,000	52,750
1973	1,000,000	50,000
1974	1,500,000	58,712.07

The $52,750 award (105.5 percent of $50,000) in 1972 is the maximum allowed without violating pay controls even though the plan itself calls for a payment of $60,000 (5 percent of $1,-200,000). Under the plan itself, no more than $50,000 (5 percent of $1,000,000) may be paid for 1973. For 1974, the maximum allowable award is $58,712.07 (105.5 percent of 105.5 percent of $52,750).

This example ignores the mathematical adjustment made where the number of employees differs from the number in the preceding year, and the special limitation in the case of an incentive practice which does not have a definite method or clear formula.

Excessive payments: A payment in excess of the ceiling described above does not necessarily violate pay controls. The excess is considered additional salary to the covered employees. It is added to the other salaries paid in the appropriate employee unit. For example, suppose base salaries in the appropriate employee unit covering executives totaled $1,000,000 in 1973 and $1,-050,000 in 1974. And suppose incentive compensation for these executives in 1974 exceeded the allowable amount by $4,000.

This $4,000 would not in itself be considered to violate the pay controls, but would be added to the $1,050,000. Here, the total increase over 1973 ($54,000) would not exceed 5.5 percent, and so would be within pay control ceilings.

Two limitations on incentive compensation awards arise if the plan or practice covers members of the executive control group and also other employees:

1. The proportion of the total incentive compensation award which goes to the executive control group in the current year can not exceed the proportion which went to that group in a selected prior year (the base year), with appropriate adjustments for changes in total executive salary between the base year and the current year. This rule therefore prevents increasing the incentive compensation of executives by dropping non-executives from the plan.

2. If those in the plan or practice are not identical with those in any appropriate employee unit, a payment in excess of the 105.5 percent ceiling described above would violate pay controls, and therefore may not be made without prior CLC approval.

Incentive plans or practices include those which pay in stock or other property as well as those paying in cash. They therefore cover performance share plans and other plans paying compensation in stock or other property (see Chapters 6, 7, and 8), phantom stock plans (Chapter 5), cash bonuses (Chapter 3), *nonstatutory* options in stock or other property (Chapter 9) and profit-sharing plans which are not qualified plans under the rules given in Chapter 12.

The amount of a payment in property is the property's fair market value when the property is awarded (disregarding any conditions or restrictions) less any amount paid by the executive. A nonstatutory option is considered incentive compensation when it is granted and again when it is exercized. The fair market value when granted is 25 percent of the stock's fair market value at grant plus any amount by which that value exceeds the option price. The fair market value when exercized is the fair market value at that time less 125 percent of the fair market value when granted. In making these valuations, any restrictions on the option, or on the shares under option, are disregarded. (These values are not used for tax purposes.)

New plans or practices: Most incentive plans or practices adopted after November 13, 1971 require governmental approval (presently, approval of the Cost of Living Council), if they include any member of an executive control group. (Governmental approval was not required for some plans adopted between January 10, 1973 and August 29, 1973.) During the first 12-month period of operation of such an approved plan, the amount of incentive compensation to employees in the plan unit may not exceed the amount established by the Cost of Living Council (or, for earlier plans, by the Pay Board). Thereafter, the incentive compensation may not exceed that amount multiplied by 105.5 percent for every year of plan operation thereafter. Amounts paid in excess of these allowable amounts are treated as described in the section on *excessive payments,* above. CLC approval is not required when replacing a plan or practice which has expired with another one, if the old plan or practice was in effect on November 13, 1971, was operated in accordance with pay controls, and the replacement plan or practice operates in accordance with those controls and does not increase the compensation available under the old one. Also, CLC approval is not required for a modification of an existing plan or practice which does not increase the incentive compensation available before modification.

New organizations: These can set up incentive compensation plans or practices. But if a member of the executive control group is covered, the organization must file a detailed report on each plan or practice with the Cost of Living Council. The report must show among other things that the incentive compensation plan or practice is not intended to circumvent salary controls, and that the plan or practice is reasonably consistent with the Economic Stabilization Program. If the plan meets these requirements, the company can in the plan's first year of operation pay employees in the plan unit the amount dictated by the plan if that amount is reasonably consistent with the Economic Stabilization Program. In later years, the allowable amount is the amount in the first year, multiplied by 105.5 percent for each subsequent year of operation. Amounts paid in excess of this ceiling are treated as described in the section on *excessive payments,* above.

A new organization is a sole proprietorship, partnership, corporation or other entity formed after November 13, 1971 which is not a successor to any other entity, with this exception: a corporation succeeding a proprietorship or partnership is treated as a new organization.

Stock options

Stock options may be subject to pay controls. The rules depend on the type of option (qualified or nonstatutory), and when the option plan was adopted (before November 14, 1971, or on or after that date). Rules for qualified options apply only to the relatively few firms subject to the mandatory economic stabilization controls.

The rules for options granted under a plan adopted before November 14, 1971 are as follows:

1. If the option was granted in writing before December 17, 1971, the option is not subject to pay controls regardless of when it is exercised.

2. For options granted after December 16, 1971, options may be granted and exercised if all these tests are met:

a. Stockholders approve the plan within 12 months of its adoption.

b. The plan states the maximum number of shares available for options.

c. The option price is not less than the stock's fair market value when the option is granted.

d. The plan is administered in the customary manner.

Normally, a qualified stock option plan for executives (see Chapter 9) would meet these tests.

The number of shares which may be made available under such a plan without violating pay controls is determined under a complex formula. Briefly, it may not exceed the average number granted under the plan during all its years of operation. Shares in excess of this average number may not be granted without prior CLC approval.

This sets the limit for the number of shares made available (without violating pay controls) to all the employees in a plan unit. It does not affect the employer's power to allocate options within that unit.

Option plan adopted after November 13, 1971

New plans: A company may adopt a new option plan only with governmental approval (presently, CLC approval). A plan is new if such a plan did not exist in the company before November 14, 1971. The new plan must meet the tests above for pre-November 14, 1971 plans, apart from the dates involved.

For the first year of the option plan, the company may issue shares up to the number of shares authorized by the CLC (or for earlier plans, by the Pay Board). For later plan years, the limit is the same, except for adjustments reflecting changes in the number of employees in the plan unit.

Options of new organizations: A stock option may be adopted by a new organization which files a detailed report with the CLC. (See the section on *new organizations* in *incentive compensation,* above.) The plan must meet the tests above for pre-November 14, 1971 plans, apart from the dates involved. For the plan's first year, the company may issue shares up to the number reported to the CLC, if the grants are not to circumvent the salary stabilization program and are reasonably consistent with the Economic Stabilization Program. In later plan years, the company can normally grant up to 25 percent of the total number of shares authorized under the plan.

Other stock options

The rules described above apply to options of the qualified stock option type, described in Chapter 9. Other stock options, that is, the various types of nonstatutory option analyzed in Chapter 9, are subject to the rules given above governing incentive compensation.

Qualified benefits

Certain benefits, sometimes described as fringe benefits but called "qualified benefits" in the pay control rules, may be increased or even introduced without being subject to the 5.5 percent ceiling. These are company contributions under pension, profit-sharing and savings plans (Chapter 12), health plans (Chapter 11), and group insurance plans (Chapter 14). Note that company payments under such plans are normally tax-exempt to covered employees.

Increased contributions, or contributions under new plans, are subject to the ceiling of the "qualified benefit standard." This permits increased (or new plan) contributions under either of the following formulas, whichever is larger:

a. Contributions do not exceed 0.7 percent of the base salary plus a catch-up percentage which may be as much as 1.5 percent of base salary.

b. Contributions up to 5 percent of the base compensation, if the total cost of qualified benefits does not exceed 10 percent of the base compensation rate.

Companies can increase their executives' pay by adopting plans providing these benefits, or by increasing benefits currently provided, without violating pay controls, if they stay within the limits set forth above. This would be especially welcome to executives, since these benefits are normally exempt from tax as well.

Suppose a plan currently in effect calls for the executive to make contributions on his own behalf. The company could increase his compensation by making all or part of *his* contribution. This increased company payment, though the equivalent of salary, is treated instead under the qualified benefit standard.

If an increased or new contribution exceeds the qualified benefit standard, the excess is considered salary for purposes of the 5.5 percent ceiling.

Penalties

There is a civil penalty of up to $2,500 for violating pay controls, and a criminal penalty of up to $5,000 for each *willful* violation. Companies can not take tax deductions for payments subject to criminal penalties. Also, executives receiving excessive amounts can be required to repay them to the company.

It is not a violation of pay controls to bargain for excessive amounts, only to pay or receive them.

Index